DRYDEN'S AENEID

A Selection with Commentary
Edited by
Robin Sowerby
Lecturer in English, University of Stirling

Published by Bristol Classical Press
English Editors: David Hopkins & Tom Mason
General Editor: John H. Betts

Cover illustration: Virgil — an imaginary portrait reproduced from an engraving by P. Fourdrinier for Dryden's *The Works of Virgil* (7th edition, 1748); Dryden — reproduced from an engraving by P. Fourdrinier for the same edition.

Printed in Great Britain

First published (1986) by

BRISTOL CLASSICAL PRESS
Wills Memorial Building
Queens Road
BRISTOL BS8 1RJ

British Library Cataloguing in Publication Data

Virgil
   Dryden's Aeneid : a selection with commentary.
   I. Title II. Dryden, John *1631–1700*
   III. Sowerby, Robin IV. Aeneid, *English.*
   Selections
   873'.01   PA6807.A5D7

ISBN 0–86292–228–3
ISBN 0–86292–082–5 Pbk

© Robin Sowerby, 1986

Contents

Introduction	1
The Selection, the Text and the Notes	45
Names and Persons	47
Checklist of Passages	53
Dryden's Aeneid	54

Introduction

> Works of imagination excel by their allurement and delight; by their power of attracting and detaining the attention. That book is good in vain which the reader throws away. He only is the master, who keeps the mind in pleasing captivity, whose pages are perused with eagerness, and in the hope of new pleasure are perused again; and whose conclusion is perceived with an eye of sorrow, such as the traveller casts upon departing day. By his proportion of this predomination I will consent that Dryden should be tried.
>
> <div align="right">(<i>Life of Dryden</i>)</div>

Samuel Johnson here recommends Dryden's *Aeneid* in the expectation that some degree of pleasure can be derived from it, and it is in the belief that it holds more delight for the modern reader than any other version that it has been chosen for this selection.

Dryden undertook the main task of the Virgil translation late in life (it was begun in 1694 and published in 1697) when he was no longer writing satires and political poems after losing the laureateship in the revolution of 1688. But he was already well practised in the art of translation before it came to be the occupation of his enforced retirement, having published translations from Ovid in 1680 and a selection from Horace, Theocritus, Lucretius and Virgil in the *Sylvae* of 1685. Dryden wrote extensively about translation, but the main thrust of the attitude that shaped his practice is contained in the following passage in the preface to the *Sylvae*:

> ... a translator is to make his author appear as charming as possibly he can, provided he maintains his character, and makes him not unlike himself. Translation is a kind of drawing after the life; where everyone will acknowledge there is a double sort of likeness, a good one and a bad. 'Tis one thing to draw the outlines true, the features like, the proportions exact, the colouring itself perhaps tolerable; and another

thing to make all these graceful, by the posture, the shadowings, and, chiefly, by the spirit which animates the whole. I cannot, without some indignation, look on an ill copy of an excellent original; much less can I behold with patience Virgil, Homer, and some others, whose beauties I have been endeavouring all my life to imitate, so abused, as I may say, to their faces, by a botching interpreter. What English readers, unacquainted with Greek or Latin, will believe me or any other man, when we commend those authors, and confess we derive all that is pardonable in us from their fountains, if they take those to be the same poets whom our Oglebys have translated? But I dare assure them, that a good poet is no more like himself in a dull translation, than his carcase would be to his living body.

(p. 391)[1]

It will be inferred from this that Dryden allows himself much poetic licence when translating. He is not concerned to be faithful to the letter of his original. At the same time Dryden used the liberty he took with an overriding sense of responsibility to the original, and what he feels responsible to most of all is the spirit that animates the whole and the poetic excellence that will be betrayed if the translation is dull.

Dryden had long been a careful student of Virgil and above all of Virgilian expression and Virgilian metrical practice. In the 'Dedication of the *Aeneis*' he wrote:

Long before I undertook this work, I was no stranger to the original. I had also studied Virgil's design, his disposition of it, his manners, his judicious management of the figures, the sober retrenchments of his sense, which always leaves somewhat to gratify our imagination, on which it may enlarge at pleasure; but, above all, the elegance of his expressions, and the harmony of his numbers.

('Dedication of the *Aeneis*', p. 1051)

His study of Virgil must have begun at Westminster school, to be continued at Cambridge when Virgil was doubtless presented to him as a model of elegant Latin for imitation in Latin verse. As a model of elegant Latin Virgil has been uniquely venerated in Western culture. For Dante, Virgil is not only the most virtuous of the pagans and the prophet of Christianity (in his fourth 'Messianic' eclogue) but also the author of 'lo bello stile' (*Inferno* Canto I, 87). In the Renaissance Petrarch aspired to restore Virgilian Latin to the world, and Vida's *Art of Poetry*, the first of many in modern Europe, was very largely the art of poetry that the early humanists discovered and venerated in Virgil's poems. As Cicero was, for the humanists, the model for Classical Latin prose, so Virgil's poems in their refinement of expression and perfection of form represented Latin verse in its 'golden age' in the time of Augustus. Dryden inherited the 'Maronolatry' of the humanists calling himself a 'religious admirer'[2] of Virgil, and applied the classical standard to dismiss modern Latin:

> It is little wonder that rolling down through so many barbarous ages from the spring of Virgil, it bears along with it the filth and ordures of the Goths and Vandals.
> ('The Dedication of the *Pastorals*', p. 871)

Because of his uniqueness as a model of elegant Latinity no other ancient poet had quite the significance for Dryden, even though it is evident from his prose comments and from the translations themselves that he felt a greater affinity for aspects of Horace, Lucretius, Ovid, Juvenal and later Homer. Virgil's elegant Latin posed for Dryden the question: could there be an equivalent in English?

In translating Virgil, Dryden sought both to satisfy the demands of his age for Roman majesty,[3] and to bring to a triumphant conclusion the drive towards elegant refinement that he had begun when he rejected the metaphysical mode in his youth and that he had only fitfully realised in his laureate poems. In a 'Postscript to the Reader' appended to his Virgil translation, he modestly claims to have given to English poetry what above all he had keenly studied in Virgil's Latin:

> For what I have done, imperfect as it is for want of health and leisure to correct it, will be judged in after ages, and possibly in the present, to be no dishonour to my native country,

> whose language and poetry would be more esteemed abroad, if they were better understood. Somewhat (give me leave to say) I have added to both of them in the choice of words, and harmony of numbers, which were wanting (especially the last) in all our poets, even in those who, being endued with genius, yet have not cultivated their mother tongue with sufficient care; or, relying on the beauty of their thoughts, have judged the ornament of words, and sweetness of sound, unnecessary. One is for raking in Chaucer (our English Ennius) for antiquated words, which are never to be revived but when sound or significancy is wanting in the present language. . . . Others have no ear for verse, nor choice of words, nor distinction of thoughts; but mingle farthings with their gold, to make up the sum.
>
> (p. 1424)

This claim, if true, would give his Virgil a pre-eminent place in his own career, and a prominent place in the history of English poetry.

The truth of it cannot be tested properly in the confines of this introduction, but the following speech in which Jupiter prophecies the Roman dominion and the Augustan peace illustrates Dryden's great strengths as a translator of Virgil:

> Then Romulus his grandsire's throne shall gain,
> Of martial towers the founder shall become,
> The people Romans call, the city Rome.
> To them no bounds of empire I assign,
> Nor term of years to their immortal line. . . .
>   An age is ripening in revolving fate
> When Troy shall overturn the Grecian state,
> And sweet revenge her conquering sons shall call,
> To crush the people that conspired her fall.
> Then Caesar from the Julian stock shall rise,
> Whose empire ocean, and whose fame the skies
> Alone shall bound; whom, fraught with eastern spoils,
> Our heaven, the just reward of human toils,
> Securely shall repay with rites divine;
> And incense shall ascend before his sacred shrine.
> Then dire debate, and impious war shall cease,
> And the stern age be softened into peace:
>
> (I, 375–79, 386–97)

Here is what Dryden describes as 'the clearness, the purity, the easiness and the magnificence' of Virgil's style ('Dedication', p. 1055). It is particularly in the combination of magnificence and ease that Dryden's achievement lies. This is a rare balance giving grandeur without pomposity, and elegance without loss of strength. For Dryden's Jupiter is dignified, eloquent and emphatic. His fluent language strikes a truly imperial note, worthy of the deity who presided over Roman rule.

> Now thy Forum roars no longer
>   fallen every purple Caesar's dome—
> Tho' thine ocean-roll of rhythm
>   sound for ever of Imperial Rome—[4]

Virgil's Latin has always been admired as the classic expression of the 'imperium Romanum' that impressed itself upon the world, and of his translators only Dryden's language comes anywhere near the sovereign power of the Latin evinced in its rigorous clarity of syntax, in its polished elegance and emphatic gravity of expression, and in its rhythmic assurance and majesty of cadence. We may recall here Dr. Johnson's verdict on Dryden's contribution to English poets:

> What was said of Rome adorned by Augustus may be applied by easy metaphor to English poetry embellished by Dryden ... He found it brick and left it marble.
>
> (*Life of Dryden*)

Some idea of the elegant refinement which Dryden admired in Virgil and to which he aspired himself can be suggested by comparing Virgil with his rude predecessor in epic Quintus Ennius (239–169 BC). Culture came late to the Roman state which had existed in happy ignorance of the civilised arts for several centuries until the Roman rise to power in Italy brought them into contact with Greek cultural centres in southern Italy and Sicily. Here began the gradual civilisation of the Romans by their Greek educators and the slow metamorphosis of the Roman into the Graeco-Roman. Refined culture did not come to Rome until the late Republic and the Augustan age. The achievement of Virgil and

Horace is all the more remarkable because it went against the natural grain of the Roman character, as Virgil recognises when he admits Roman inferiority to the Greeks in all but the ruling arts (VI, 847–53; Dryden, 1168–77). Ennius, half Greek himself, was a noble pioneer in the arduous process whereby culture was gradually translated from Greece to Rome; in his epic poem the *Annales*, he adopted the dactylic hexameter, Homer's metre, abandoning the native Saturnian which was never again used for serious purposes. Fragments of the *Annales* survive which show his ability to exploit the monumental brevity of Latin in grandly resounding single lines:

> moribus antiquis res stat Romana virisque
>
> on men and morals of established worth stands firm the
> > Roman state

In the opening of the poem the spirit of Homer appears to Ennius in a dream in which he tells Ennius that he is Homer's reincarnation. In the surviving fragments are several imitations of passages in Homer that have also been adapted by Virgil. In one such, when Ennius wanted to describe preparations for a funeral he thought of the preparations made by the Trojans for the funeral of Patroclus (*Iliad* XXIII, 114–122):

> *Incedunt arbusta per alta, securibus caedunt.*
> *Percellunt magnas quercus,* exciditur ilex,
> fraxinus frangitur atque abies consternitur alta,
> *pinus proceras pervortunt*; omne sonabat
> arbustum fremitu silvai frondosai.

> Then strode they through tall timber-trees and hewed
> With hatchets; mighty oaks they overset;
> Down crashed the holm and shivered ash outhacked;
> Felled was the lofty fir; they wrenched right down
> Tall towering pines; and every woody tree
> In frondent forest rang and roared and rustled.[5]

There is a certain rugged strength here in Ennius. His Romans march into the woods and deal with the trees in no uncertain manner, as we might expect the early Romans to deal with any obstacle natural or human standing in their way. The emphatic verbs, eight in all, with insistent figurative associations of conquest and overthrow, tell their own story. Here is a blunt assertion of Roman power, and Ennius's verse is, comparatively speaking, a blunt instrument. Judged by later Augustan practice his verse is irregular in its scansion, and the poet is clumsy in his use of the caesura. Even an unpractised ear can detect the roughness of the lines which are made up of a series of weighty blocks united by strong alliteration, strong assonance, and marked by a predominance of long syllables (italicised). These units are not at all smoothly connected. The syntax and rhythm are abrupt.

Here is Virgil's refinement:

Itur in antiquam silvam stabula alta ferarum.
Procumbunt piceae, sonat icta securibus ilex
fraxineaeque trabes cuneis, et fissile robur
scinditur; advolvunt ingentes montibus ornos.
(*Aeneid* VI, 179–82)

They go into an ancient forest, the deep dens of wild
beasts. Down fall the pitch pines, the holm oak rings
struck with axe blows, ashen timbers are made with wedges
and the oaks that are split are divided up; they roll
mighty rowans down the mountains.

Virgil's refinement is first and most obviously a matter of metrics. Virgil 'is everywhere elegant, sweet and flowing in his hexameters', remarked Dryden ('Dedication', p. 1045). The rhythmical pattern of his lines is much more subtle. This is partly a result of the greater lightness of touch given by the use of words with short syllables to make up dactyls. Virgil has thirteen dactyls in four lines to Ennius's ten in five. In so far as it is a mechanical matter, it is also a result of smoother connection between units of sense within and between lines. The abruptness of syntax and rhythm, and consequently of sense has been eliminated.

But Virgil's lines are also much more expressive. How much more sense and meaning Virgil has managed to concentrate in four lines than Ennius has in five. Virgil gives us a moving picture from entry into the wood, to the cutting of the trees with axes and wedges, to the rolling down of the trees from the mountains, well suggested in the rolling rhythm of the final clause. Ennius, on the other hand, emphasises his one ruling idea by insistent repetition as one tree after another is brought low in a grand assault that is magnified in the noise of the final line. Whereas Ennius builds up to a climax of sound signalled by the change of tense in 'sonabat' and culminating in the chiming rhyme of 'silvae frondosai' (an archaic genitive), sound in Virgil is incorporated into the moving picture (his 'sonat' comes early in the second line) and his sound effects are subordinate and subtler. So too is his syntax. This can be illustrated by looking at Virgil's combination and apposition of nouns and adjectives. Whereas in Ennius most of the adjectives refer to the might and height of the trees being hewn down and there is nothing subtle about their placing, in Virgil's first line, in the neat balance of clauses there is a play whereby 'alta' suggests both the height of the trees and the depth of the forest. 'stabula' (from which stables) with its domestic associations acts subtly against 'silvam' with which it is in apposition and 'ferarum' which is dependent upon it to evoke the mysterious wildness and antiquity of the forest just entered. 'Ashen timbers' is not just a poetical periphrasis for the straightforward 'ash' of Ennius because mention of timbers takes the process of wood cutting a stage further. The process is further extended in the adjective 'fissile' in which we see the timbers being broken up, so that they may be rolled down the mountain. In Virgil the action progresses not only in the verbs but through the careful choice of noun and adjective. Ennius in what is a simple list of trees uses 'quercus' for oak, while Virgil uses the word 'robur' which besides meaning oak has the figurative significance of strength or hardness. The phrase 'fissile robur' is a cunning conjunction, a fine poetical beauty which suggests the climax of effort in the cutting process as the hardest wood finally yields up its strength (helped by the emphatic placing of 'scinditur'). There is care too in the choice and order of trees. The soft pine woods (by far the most useful for the purpose in hand because of the pitch they contain) come down first while the harder woods need repeated blows of the axe and the application of wedges. Apart from the realistic moving picture of the whole process of wood cutting, there is also in Virgil, in contrast to the indiscriminate felling in Ennius, an impression of concentrated application and well directed effort. Native Roman strength is controlled and directed, so that while there is indubitable power in old Latin, there is certainly much more poetic energy in Virgil's refinement of it.

The refinement of Latin whereby the language became what it is not in Ennius, a medium of subtle and controlled strength, reflects deep changes in Roman sensibility brought about in large part by the experience of empire. The *Annales* was written in the wake of the Roman rise to Mediterranean power; Ennius celebrates the assertive power of Rome in the victories of the Scipios over the Carthaginians in the Punic Wars. One hundred and fifty years later when Virgil wrote the *Aeneid* in the first decade of the rule of Augustus, Roman power had been extended by the conquests of Julius Caesar and consolidated under the Augustan imperial settlement. Virgil's Jupiter celebrates not only the conquering power of Rome but also the 'pax Augusta'. In the first place this is the restoration of the rule of law at home after the upheavals of civil war in the late Republic. Similarly when Jupiter sends Mercury to impose his will upon Aeneas lingering at Carthage, it is not simply Roman power that is to be asserted through Aeneas but the rule of law:

> Not so fair Venus hoped, when twice she won
> Thy life with prayers, nor promised such a son.
> Her's was a hero, destined to command
> A martial race, and rule the Latian land;
> Who should his ancient line from Teucer draw;
> And on the conquered world impose the law.
>   (IV, 334–39)

Gradually in the course of the poem Rome's civilising mission is more clearly revealed: it is the imposition of Roman order and the moral exercise of Roman power throughout the world:

> Let others better mould the running mass
> Of metals, and inform the breathing brass,
> And soften into flesh a marble face;
> Plead better at the bar; describe the skies,
> And when the stars descend, and when they rise.
> But, Rome! 'tis thine alone, with awful sway,

To rule mankind, and make the world obey:
Disposing peace and war thy own majestic way.
To tame the proud, the fettered slave to free,
These are imperial arts, and worthy thee.[6]

(VI, 1168–77)

Nowhere is this order and power more apparent than in the Latin language itself. Virgil's Latin in its disciplined clarity, its controlled assurance and its dignified elegance expresses this power and order in its most civilised and refined form.

Virgil's lines on the felling of the trees bear out all that Dryden has to say about Virgil's distinguishing poetic character:

> I looked on Virgil as a succinct and grave majestic writer, one who weighed not only every thought, but every word and syllable: who was still aiming to crowd his sense into as narrow a compass as possibly he could; for which reason he is so very figurative, that he requires (I may almost say) a grammar apart to construe him.
>
> ('Preface to *Sylvae*', p. 392)

Here is Dryden's version of the passage discussed:

> An ancient wood, fit for the work designed
> (The shady covert of the savage kind),
> The Trojans found: the sounding axe is plied:
> Firs, pines, and pitch-trees, and the towering pride
> Of forest ashes, feel the fatal stroke;
> And piercing wedges cleave the stubborn oak.
> Huge trunks of trees, felled from the steepy crown
> Of the bare mountains, roll with ruin down.
>
> (VI, 261–68)

Coming straight from Virgil to Dryden, a first reaction may well be one of disappointment that in Dryden's eight lines the concentration has altogether gone. This is deliberate choice on Dryden's part:

But having before observed that Virgil endeavours to be short, and at the same time elegant, I pursue the excellence and forsake the brevity.

('Dedication of the *Aeneis*', p. 1054)

It is equally evident that Dryden's imagination has warmed to the activity in the Latin and it is perhaps surprising to find that he is more morally imperious than Virgil with something of the figurative emphasis of Ennius. Dryden's Trojans are not like Ennius's early Romans; the trees are not conquered, but their towering pride does suffer a mighty ruin (hence the figure of the 'steepy crown' of the mountain now bare of trees). This figurative emphasis is a source of grandeur in the lines. At the same time there is great energy in Dryden; he is careful to retain Virgil's progressively moving picture: the axe is plied, the trees feel the stroke, wedges cleave the oak and the felled trees are rolled down. The most striking beauty in the Latin, the climactic phrase 'fissile robur', for which there are no words that could give a literal equivalent in English, is rendered in the finely balanced line

And piercing wedges cleave the stubborn oak

in which the figurative meaning of 'piercing' extends the feeling of the previous line. This is a strong 'full resounding' line that in its pattern and movement emphasises the climactic action in which the hard wood finally yields. The overall rhythmical pattern and movement (varied with enjambement and breaks and pauses at different points in the lines) is carefully responsive to the movement of meaning most obviously in the rise to a climax in the cutting of the oaks and in the final couplet where the interrupting clause and the enjambement suspend the sense which is simply and satisfyingly resolved in the roll of the last four words.

The distinction and quality of Dryden's version become more apparent in comparison with versions of other translators. The earliest is Gavin Douglas:

Ontil ane ancyent forest socht thai then	*sought they*
Entrand in mony dern wild bestis den;	*secret*
Ful of roset down bet is the fyr tre,	*resin; beaten*

Smyte with the ax dyd rayr the akis hie,   *did roar the oaks*
Gret eschin stokkis tumlys to the grond,   *ashen trunks*
With weggeis schydit gan the byrkis sound,   *shattered; birches*
The felloun elmys weltis down the hillys.   *fallen; rolled*
                          (written 1513, published 1553)

Douglas confessed that he had not the resources in Scots to render Virgilian eloquence, and contented himself with the more modest aim of doing justice to Virgil's sense. This he does in a consistent narrative style that moves well and conveys something of the energy of the original. Once the initial linguistic difficulties have been overcome (and they are less formidable than might first appear to be the case) Douglas's version is one of the few translations that can be read with pleasure over a long stretch. This could not be said of the version of Thomas Phaer:

Into a forest old they gon and hauntes of beastes unmilde
Down tombling crake ye tres, upriseth sound of axes strokes
Both holmes and beeches broad and beames of ash and sides
    of okes
With wedges great they clyve, and mountain elmes with
    leavers roll.
                                                    (1573)

There are three crude couplet versions of this passage in the seventeenth century before Dryden:

            To an old wood they go
Where fierce wild beasts did lurk. There down they throw
Fir trees, and beech resounding hatchets blow;
As trees and oaks they cut and cleave with wedges,
And from the hills huge elms they roll on sledges.
                                            (Vicars, 1632)

They cut down ancient woods, wild beasts' abodes;
Elms ring with axes, fir trees fall in loads;
Ash and hard oak they cleave, and from the tall
Mountains, whole woods of stately cedars fall.
                              (Ogilby, second edition, 1654)

They haste to thickets of an ancient wood,
Which long for cruel beasts a covert stood;
Where by the force of oft repeated strokes
They pitch trees fell, with ash and sturdy oaks;
From rocky mountains greatest pines they throw,
Whose lofty tops fill all the vales below.
(The Earl of Lauderdale, written in the 1680s, published 1709)

All these translators exaggerate grossly; Ogilby and Lauderdale use ridiculous hyperboles and so fall into bombast in their attempt to write in an elevated style. Dryden by contrast elevates not by exaggerating physical action but by bringing out its figurative significance. It hardly needs saying that his greater artistic refinement is the expression of a more refined sensibility. Dryden sometimes uses more daring hyperboles than are to be found in Virgil and the couplet form offered temptations to wordplay and witticism that detract from the purity of his style. But these are mere blemishes; overall Dryden is remarkably faithful to his description of Virgil's poetic character:

> He is everywhere above the conceits of epigrammatic wit and gross hyperboles; he maintains majesty in the midst of plainness; he shines but glares not, and is stately without ambition.
> ('Preface to the *Sylvae*', p. 393)

The first complete Virgil after Dryden is that of Joseph Trapp. His version in blank verse has been praised for its faithfulness in rendering Virgil's sense.

Into an ancient wood the deep recess
Of beasts they go: down fall the pitchy pines;
With blows of axes, oaks and ashen trunks,
And splitting timber, cleft with wedges, sound;
And from the hills the lofty beeches roll.
(1731)

Striking after Dryden is the lack of clarity in the overall picture. Although all the elements of Virgil seem to be there, Trapp has not managed to render the energetic moving picture with its climax in the splitting of the hard wood. His climax is in the sound at the end of the fourth line, not in the successful effort as in Virgil and Dryden. Even on the narrow criterion of 'accuracy', Trapp fails. The notes that he appended to his translation (some of which are included in this selection) show that Trapp had a keen eye for poetical beauties in Virgil. But seeing and successfully translating are two quite separate abilities. His version is inelegant (his syntax and word order are often perplexed) and no more 'accurate' than Dryden's.

The Virgil of Christopher Pitt to some extent displaced Dryden's in popularity in the eighteenth century. Like Trapp's, it has been thought to be more faithful to its original than Dryden.

> And to the lofty forest bend their way . . .
> Then fled the savage from his dark abode;
> The well plied axes echo through the wood.
> The piercing wedges cleave the crackling oak;
> Loud groan the trees and sink at every stroke.
> The tall ash tumbles from the mountain's crown;
> Th'aerial elms come crashing headlong down.
>
> (1753)

An oddity here is the addition in the second line. Even on the assumption that 'savage' is animal rather than human, Pitt's sentiment violates the feeling of mystery with which Virgil has invested the ancient forest. Pitt's is a polite Virgil of the drawing room. It is apparent here that Pitt like Dryden takes liberties with his original but without Dryden's habitual insight and sound judgement. Dryden enunciated a clear principle to which he is surprisingly faithful:

> The additions I also hope are easily deduced from Virgil's sense. They will seem (at least I have the vanity to think so) not stuck into him, but growing out of him.
>
> ('Dedication of the *Aeneis*', p. 1054)

In this passage his idea of the towering pride suffering a mighty ruin could be said to originate in 'procumbunt' which, besides the literal meaning of falling forward has the figurative significance of being beaten down or lying prostrate. In a famous passage Virgil uses the word of Priam's fifty chambers decorated in gold brought low by the Greeks on Troy's last night. Dryden's addition here, unlike that of Pitt, does not take us away from the spirit of the original. Pitt has not only borrowed from Dryden but has also drawn upon Pope's rendering of the funeral preparations in the *Iliad* upon which Virgil's passage is ultimately based:

> Loud sounds the axe, redoubling strokes on strokes;
> On all sides round the forest hurls her oaks
> Headlong. Deep-echoing groan the thickets brown,
> Then rustling, crackling, crashing, thunder down.
> (Pope's *Iliad* XXIII, 146–49)

Pitt is an accomplished versifier, but all his lines have a similarly smooth rhythmical pattern. Rhythm is not as in Dryden and Pope responsive to sense but is mechanically imposed to suit the requirements of a ready made style. Pitt's version is enervated Virgil with superficial elegance achieved at the expense of sense and meaning. This superficiality is apparent in the telling change he has made to Dryden's one smooth and 'full resounding' line. In replacing 'stubborn' with 'crackling' (taken from Pope for its alliterative effect), Pitt has moved the emphasis from effort to sound and in so doing weakens Dryden and Virgil, for in 'crackling oaks' there is more sound than sense. Of sound and sense in Virgil, Dryden wrote:

> His verse is everywhere sounding the very thing in your ears whose sense it bears, yet the numbers are perpetually varied to increase the delight of the reader; so that the same sounds are never repeated twice together ... though he is smooth where smoothness is required, yet he is so far from affecting it that he seems rather to disdain it. He frequently makes use of synalaephas [elisions] and concludes his sense in the middle of the verse.
> ('Preface to the *Sylvae*', p. 393)

Dryden's Virgil is not smooth like Pitt's. The passage under discussion exemplifies Dryden's metrical variety and shows how effectively the practising poet was able to translate his study of Virgil into successful poetry. A comparison of Dryden with Pitt brings to life Pope's praise of Dryden's versification:

> Wit grew polite and numbers learned to flow:
> Waller was smooth; but Dryden taught to join
> The varying verse, the full resounding line,
> The long majestic march and energy divine.
> ('Epistle to Augustus', 266–69)

William Morris's version (in the metre of Phaer) makes Virgil remote, and the modern reader will be struck by the quaintness of his language and style:

> Then to the ancient wood they fare, high dwelling of wild
>   things;
> They fell the pine, and 'neath the axe the smitten holm oak
>   rings;
> With wedges they cleave the ashen logs, and knotted oaken
>   bole,
> Full fain to split; and mighty elms down from the mountains
>   roll.
> (1876)

How much more affected by the vice of 'poetic diction' is Morris than Dryden, whose language by contrast has immediacy and directness. It was living English when Dryden wrote it and is still living today. Here Morris fails to render the climax of effort in 'fissile robur'. His version is difficult to read at any length because of its heavy dragging rhythms. If the comparison with Pitt serves to bring out Dryden's subtle strength, then in comparison with Morris we can appreciate the graceful turns of Dryden's verse, his lightness of touch and his fluent narrative speed.

A characteristic vice of C. Day Lewis in his translation is an injudicious mixture of colloquial and formal patterns of speech. Here he has borrowed from Morris:

> Into the age-old forest, where only wild things lurk,
> They go: spruces are felled, the holm oak rings with axe
>   blows,

Wedges are used to split ash logs and the cleavable wood
Of oaks, immense rowans are rolled down from the heights.
(1952)

Gone is the Victorian poeticality. But compared with Lewis, Morris's style is at least self consistent, and in Morris's second and fourth lines there are effects of rhythm and sound that are responsive to the sense. How slack, flat and inharmonious Lewis is in comparison. All the translators manage some sound effect in the second line, but Lewis merely weakens the ringing sound of Morris. Lewis's third line begins in a straightforwardly prosaic fashion but ends with the strange infelicity of 'cleavable wood/Of oaks', reminiscent of the most awkward schoolboy tendency to translationese. Needless to say he fails to find an equivalent in modern English of the concentrated energy of Virgil. It is difficult to see any consistent tendency in this inelegant version; it has the virtues neither of poetry nor of prose.

Finally here is the version of Robert Fitzgerald:

Into the virgin forest,
Thicket of wild things, went the men, and down
The pitch pines came, the bitten ilex rang
With axe blows, ash and oak were split with wedges,
Mighty rowans were trundled down the slopes.
(1981)

But Fitzgerald only manages to report what happened. He is no more successful than Lewis in conveying the concentrated effort and energy of the original. It is unlikely that a twentieth century poet could ever give the world the imperial splendour of Virgil's golden Latin artistry, but we may surely hope for rather more poetic energy than this.

This extract from Dryden is not an obvious purple passage in his *Aeneid*. Since very little of Ennius survives beyond single lines, only one or two passages of Ennius and Virgil can be juxtaposed for comparison. This has dictated the choice of this particular extract for discussion. Yet Dryden's translation here is touched by genuine poetic fire. Other supposedly more accurate versions do not in fact render the energetic movement and activity of Virgil's lines.

Although Dryden's handling of language in his *Aeneid* does not always show the restraint and discrimination that he recognised as characteristic of his original, Dryden alone of Virgil's translators has a measure of success in meeting the challenge of Virgil's Latin, and in finding an English style that is answerable to the artistic refinement of Virgil's golden Latin. If his success as a translator of Virgil is limited in ways that the remainder of this introduction will seek to clarify, the limitations have to be set against the fact of an overriding poetic achievement.

Dryden renders excellently those parts of the *Aeneid*, such as the speech of Jupiter, that could be said to celebrate the Roman achievement. But of course Rome is in the future in the *Aeneid*, the present action is all to do with difficulties and obstacles lying in the way of the Roman destiny, so that after announcing his subject Virgil immediately moves on to the anger of Juno who has pursued the Trojans across land and sea for seven years:

> Such time, such toil required the Roman name,
> Such length of labour for so vast a frame!
>
> (I, 48—49)

So Dryden translates Virgil's monumental line that more than any other points to the subject of his epic:

> Tantae molis erat Romanam condere gentem.
>
> (I, 33)

Dryden's emphasis here grew naturally from the larger interpretation which is apparent in the translation as a whole. The Latin word 'moles' is literally a shapeless huge heavy mass or bulk of matter; figuratively it is difficulty or trouble. With 'condere' meaning to found or to build there is a building metaphor here which Dryden has rendered with an equivalent metaphor in 'so vast a frame'. His emphasis is once again on Roman grandeur: time, toil and labour were necessary for the building of such a mighty edifice. With the emphasis falling upon the figurative meaning of 'moles', however, a slightly different version might result. Lewis and Short, the nineteenth century Latin lexicographers,

INTRODUCTION

transmit a common Victorian reading of the poem which emphasises the sacrifice necessary for empire when they offer as a translation of 'tantae molis' 'such was the cost'. Something similar was in the mind of Douglas:

> Lo quhou gret cure, quhat travell, pane
>   and dowt   *how great care what*
> Was to begyn the worthy Romanys blude!

Gone is the building metaphor and with it the grandeur of Rome. Here Douglas has internalised the labour; it is 'care, travail, pain and doubt'. This is an earlier reading of Virgil that saw in the travail and journey of Aeneas an allegorical representation of man's earthly pilgrimage through this vale of tears. Virgil's line, it seems fair to say, definitely contains all that is in Dryden, but it also offers the secondary possibility of Lewis and Short and of Douglas, a possibility which is more remote from Dryden's translation than from the original. Now it would be quite wrong to let too much depend on the translation of one line, however telling that might be, but it is a criticism of Dryden's translation that he has ironed out basic ambiguities that are present not merely as nuances in particular passages (in a particular passage the translator may have to choose which of number of possibilities he can best render) but in the larger meaning of the whole poem. This is particularly true of Dryden's version of the Dido episode in book four.

Readers of Virgil have generally judged book four to be the most intense and poetically successful part of the poem. Yet its place in the overall structure has always occasioned debate. In the Middle Ages, in loving and then leaving Dido, Aeneas is one of the great deserters and traitors; such is he for Chaucer. Even the most partisan admirers of Virgil's hero are uneasy about his behaviour at Carthage. If Aeneas is to be the pious hero whose actions we are to admire, why did Virgil construct the Dido episode in the particular way he did? He might have made Dido like Calypso in Homer's *Odyssey*, a figure who constrains the hero against his real will; or he might have made her like Medea in Apollonius Rhodius, an enchantress who uses potions and spells to ensnare her man. Dido does indeed resort to magic, but this of course is a disguise under the cover of which she plans suicide when all is lost and Aeneas has sailed away. More remarkably, though every Roman reader must have thought of the recent history of Antony and Cleopatra when reading the Dido episode and seen in Aeneas a figure who unlike Antony does the Roman thing and leaves, Dido is not like the Cleopatra of common repute, a figure of irresistible sensuality.

Dido has beauty and dignity; in book one Virgil likens her to Diana as he likens Aeneas to Apollo in book four. Virgil's presentation of the two figures serves to suggest what they have in common. They share a godlike beauty and grace. Both are leaders of exiled peoples who have lost their home, and their misfortunes have made them compassionate. Nor is Carthage like the sensual Egypt of Shakespeare's *Antony and Cleopatra*. Dido comes from a civilisation comparable in its wealth and art to Troy and she is building a city that is all that Aeneas could wish his own to be. There is much greater contrast between Troy and Carthage on the one hand, and the austere simplicity of Laurentum and Pallanteum on the other. In Italy, where the inhabitants mock Trojan dress and find the civilised enjoyments of the Trojans unmanly, Aeneas is much more of a stranger than ever he is in Dido's city. Nothing could be more human than the love that Dido feels for Aeneas growing as it does naturally from common sympathies and experience. Though we see things very much from Dido's viewpoint, for Virgil has shielded Aeneas and we are not allowed much insight into his feelings, the love affair is not one sided, even though they disagree whether it constituted a marriage. Neither is it the squalid affair that Rumour makes of it later. Aeneas is not directly blamed for staying at Carthage; at most he loses his epithet 'pius'. As far as he is concerned, we are in suspense until the command of Jupiter which makes him dumb with fear and requires him to sail. At this point we feel the sacrifice that his mission entails encapsulated in the famous half line 'Italiam non sponte sequor': 'I do not seek Italy of my own free-will'. He is here the reluctant Roman. As for Dido, at this moment she is immediately lost and becomes the victim of the Roman destiny. Her death is brought about by the collapse of her self esteem when she feels she has betrayed her first love and her moral principles to no avail. Virgil has therefore presented the affair so as to impress us with the cost to both of the protagonists:

Tantae molis erat Romanam condere gentem.

Although Dryden valued this episode highly, there is little to suggest in his prose comments that he thought that the Dido episode was really integral to the poem's theme. He refers to it as an 'ornament' ('Dedication', p. 1031), but feels that Virgil in allowing his hero to fall from grace had made a mistake of judgement;

> Upon the whole matter, and humanly speaking, I doubt there was a fault somewhere; and Jupiter is better able to bear the blame than either Virgil or Aeneas.
> ('Dedication of the *Aeneis*', p. 1027)

Jupiter's command that Aeneas must leave Carthage for the sake of the Roman future is indeed the decisive moment for both Aeneas and Dido, and Dryden's handling of Aeneas's response is characteristic:

> At vero Aeneas aspectu obmutuit amens,
> arrectaeque horrore comae et vox faucibus haesit.
> ardet abire fuga dulcisque relinquere terras,
> attonitus tanto monitu imperioque deorum.
> heu! quid agat? quo nunc reginam ambire furentem
> audeat adfatu? quae prima exordia sumat?
> atque animum nunc huc celerem, nunc dividit illuc
> in partisque rapit varias perque omnia versat.
> haec alternanti potior sententia visa est:
> (IV, 279-87)

> The pious prince was seized with sudden fear;
> Mute was his tongue, and upright stood his hair.
> Revolving in his mind the stern command,
> He longs to fly, and loathes the charming land.
> What should he say, or how should he begin?
> What course, alas! remains, to steer between
> The offended lover and the powerful queen?
> This way, and that, he turns his anxious mind;
> And all expedients tries, and none can find.
> Fixed on the deed, but doubtful of the means;
> After long thought, to this advice he leans:
> (IV, 404-14)

Dryden's version appears bland in comparison with that of Douglas here:

Bot than Ene half mad and dum stude als,	*only then; dumb was also*
Upstart his hair, the voce stak in his hals.	*stuck in his throat*
Sayr he langis to fle and to depart;	*sore he longed*
And that sweit cuntre, on the tother part,	*sweet country*
To leif ful laith wes hym, or go at large.	*loath was*
Astonyst he wes to syt sa hie a charge—	*endure*
Or dysobey the gret godis beheste	
(Allace! quhat suld he do? oneth he wist);	*what should; scarcely*
Or with quhat wordis suld he now assay	*make trial of*
The amorus queyn forto requir and pray;	*queen to ask*
Or on quhat wyss hys taill he mycht begyn;	*what way his tale*
Baith to and fra compasyng, hys breist within,	*both; from considering*
Feill purpossys for every part about.	*many*
And, at the last, thus as he stude in dout,	
Thys resson hym semyt fynaly the best:	

Douglas has brought out the 'care, travail, pain and doubt' in this moment. On the one hand, Aeneas longs to depart, yet he is loath to go. Should he disobey the god? How was he to approach the queen? There is considerable emotional turmoil here. Looking at the original, it is apparent that Douglas has intensified the turmoil, in the sense that in his version Aeneas actually wonders whether to disobey the god. There is nothing so explicit in Virgil. The most that could be said is that in 'heu quid agat?', many possibilities might be flashing through Aeneas's mind. Dryden has moderated Aeneas's reaction and has a different idea of the dilemma he faced. His Aeneas is not thunder-struck and the astonishment has been suppressed (Virgil's line 282). The implied antithesis between longing to stay and loathing to go which Douglas makes the central dilemma is condensed into one line by Dryden:

He longs to fly and loathes the charming land.

The longing and loathing greatly outweigh what is 'charming' to Aeneas. The ambiguity of 'heu quid agat?' (Aeneas is still in indecision) is diminished as Dryden's Aeneas is now firmly resolved. It is merely a question of what he is to *say*, for he is a stage further ahead of Aeneas in Douglas and for that matter in Virgil. Where Douglas gives us emotional turmoil, Dryden has a swift analytical clarity. His Aeneas is already debating 'how to steer between/The offended lover and the powerful queen'. He is already thinking of what Mercury will warn him in his second coming as Dryden's prose comment confirms:

> Yet the deity was forced to come twice on the same errand; and the second time, hero though he was, he frighted him. It seems he feared not Jupiter so much as Dido ... she was injured: she was revengeful; she was powerful. The poet had likewise before hinted that her people were naturally perfidious; for he gives their character in their queen, and makes a proverb *Punica Fides* many ages before it was invented.
> ('Dedication of the *Aeneis*', p. 1029–30)

When the vision came to Dryden's Aeneas, the demands of piety are met with instant compliance and without the least hint of a struggle so that Dryden here restores to Aeneas what he has been denied hitherto in the fourth book, the epithet 'pious'. Virgil, with more propriety, waited until Aeneas's resolution had been put to the test, until after he had faced Dido and told her that he was going. Dryden's haste is indecent, and Douglas's version is not only more sensitive but seems more in the spirit of the original if we are to read between the lines. Yet Dryden does have some right on his side. Essentially at the crucial juncture Aeneas does not have any doubt that the demands of piety are to be met, and Dryden's translation arised from a considered and deliberate judgement of what is at issue in the poem.

The central value of the *Aeneid* is of course piety (the Latin word is 'pietas'). Aeneas was already famous for his piety in Greek legend, and the image of Aeneas departing from Troy bearing his aged father on his shoulders is found on vases as early as the sixth and fifth centuries in Greece and Etruria. His piety and virtuous reputation were therefore rooted in his dutiful conduct towards his father. Virgil inherited this image, extended it and made it central to his poem in a particularly Roman way. On Troy's last night, Aeneas departs through the flames not only with Anchises on his back but with his son Ascanius in his hand. Anchises carries with him the images of Troy's gods, the 'Penates'. Here concentrated in a single image is the partriarchal ideal of Roman society: the gods, the fatherland, the grandfather and father, the father and son, and the son and grandson each bound together in the closest relation thereby ensuring the survival and continuous life of the family and the city. The ultimate sanction of this is of course. Jupiter himself, 'pater Romanus' in the heavenly sphere, who ratifies the decision to leave Troy and sends an omen in the form of a shooting star to guide them on their way.

In the first half of the poem Aeneas is uncertain of himself and reluctant; Anchises is the decisive figure, having faith in the Italian future, interpreting omens, dreams and prophecies during their wanderings and after his death influencing Aeneas through the medium of dreams at Carthage and in Sicily. The climax of the first half of the *Aeneid* is the visit to the father in the underworld which Aeneas makes at the prompting of Anchises. Here is the final consummation of the filial bond and the revelation of the Roman future and of Rome's imperial mission to Aeneas. In the descent into the underworld may be seen that reverence for the ancestors which was a dominant feature of the traditional Roman religion, and here also is an acknowledgement of the power of the father, 'patria potestas', which in early Rome had been absolute. After this communion with his father, Aeneas is more confident in his interpretation of omens and signs, and there are no more backward glances towards Troy. Where on Troy's last night Aeneas had taken upon himself the burden of the past as he carried

Anchises on his shoulders through the flames, at Pallanteum as he prepares to do battle he takes upon his shoulder the great shield engraved with the fame and fortune of his Roman descendants. He holds this shield as he makes vows before the final combat where he is described as 'father' and 'source of the Roman race' (XII, 166). His son Ascanius 'the other hope of Rome' (XII, 168) is at his side. To Ascanius he sets himself up as an example to be followed. The dutiful Aeneas, who has learnt the lessons of piety and is steadfastly carrying them out, now himself imparts them. Aeneas might here be said to be a Roman archetype, or perhaps it might better be said that the poem illustrates what must go into the making of a true Roman father. In prophesying that his poem will be immortal 'as long as the house of Aeneas dwells on the Capitol and the Roman father shall have power' (IX, 448–49), Virgil reveals the true Roman in himself.

Granted his role in the poem as the chosen instrument of the gods and the part he must play in the grand patriarchal design, it is not altogether surprising that Aeneas emerges as a shadowy figure, little more than a symbol, passively acquiescent in the will of the gods or of his father. But what is perhaps surprising is that Aeneas nowhere shows any relish or enthusiasm for the great enterprise in which he is engaged nor does he himself show much enterprise or positive will in carrying out his task. In this he is sharply to be distinguished from those stern examples of Roman gravity afforded by the heroes of early Rome so much admired by Macaulay on which Virgil might have chosen to model him. Nor is his progress triumphant like that of the efficient and fortunate Caesars; he comes through but at every stage there is loss and misfortune. How different in spirit too is Virgil's Aeneas from the resourceful and quick-witted Odysseus of Homer. When Anchises shows him the spirits destined to be reincarnated, he exclaims 'what is their dread desire for the light?' (VI, 721). His is a melancholy spirit and his tearfulness has been much commented upon. 'They make Aeneas little better than a kind of a St. Swithen hero, always raining' ('Dedication' p. 1023) complained Dryden of his seventeenth century critics. Admittedly most of the criticisms refer to his reactions in the first part of the poem when he is learning his task, but it is true to say that the effort involved in being faithful to his destined role manifests itself characteristically in tearfulness until the war in Italy when tears are compounded with anger. After the death of Pallas, Aeneas commits acts of savagery alien to his better self beginning with the sacrifice of captives to the spirit of Pallas in the manner of Achilles who had similarly sacrificed captives to the spirit of Patroclus. Unlike the Homeric Achilles, however, Aeneas is not a natural warrior who finds the battlefield a stage upon which he can excel and achieve fame and glory. As he formally bids farewell to Pallas on his last journey back to Evander, Aeneas sees war as a grim manifestation of destiny involving sorrow and misery. And this is the note, compounded with anger, upon which the poem ends. It took a most untypical Roman to present his Roman hero in this way.

Aeneas, therefore, finds that the Roman destiny entails continual hardship and the cost of it all is most intensely dramatised in the Dido episode. All Virgil's presentation of character and circumstance here suggests that Aeneas is naturally at home in Carthage. But Jupiter decrees that he must sail. Aeneas tells Dido that he does not go willingly to Italy. Thereupon his own individual will and all his vital instincts are subdued in the service of the patriarchal ideal. Thereafter there is no possibility of any spontaneity for Aeneas—'Italiam non sponte sequor'; he remains the creature of his ruling gods. Consequently the ritual burning of the portrait and belongings of Aeneas upon Dido's pyre together with their marriage bed is an act of most potent symbolism, since in it is contained not only Dido's love turned to hatred but also the self-immolation and sacrifice of Aeneas at Carthage. In leaving Dido Aeneas could be said to be losing part of himself, though he is never fully aware of this and sails away in ignorance of what has happened to Sicily where he invokes the spirit of his father and thence to the underworld where he consummates the sacrifice. There Anchises hails his son for finally coming the hard way of piety ('vicit iter durum pietas' (VI, 688)) and says that he much feared for him at Carthage. Aeneas replies that it was his father's image often coming to him that had compelled him to make the journey.

The most obvious victim of the hard way of 'pietas' is Dido who is ruthlessly sacrificed to the Roman destiny. For Dido Aeneas's desertion of her shows his essential nature whatever others may say of the man who saved his country's gods from Troy with his father on his shoulders. She wishes she had torn him limb from limb, or served up Ascanius for him to feast upon and so extinguished the whole race with father and son. Finally she curses Aeneas, wishing him every misfortune and hoping that he will be torn from Ascanius and meet an early death. It is a most powerful feminine protest against piety and the grand patriarchal design. The protest also occurs in minor episodes such as the burning of the ships by the Trojan women and in the lament of the mother of Euryalus. In the Dido episode, however, the protest at the sacrifice demanded by the hard way of 'pietas' is the heart of Virgil's most intense poetic effort. That Virgil's creative powers should have been most fully released here must prompt thought about the nature and value of 'pietas' in the poem as a whole.

At the beginning, Virgil demands of his muse that she tell him why a man so famous for his piety ('insignem pietate virum' (I, 10)) was so persecuted by the queen of heaven:

Tantaene animis caelestibus irae?

(I, 11)

Can such rage in heavenly bosoms dwell?

Juno's anger underlies the poem and sets it in motion. She has none of Jupiter's devotion to the Roman destiny and opposes all the effort which goes into the founding of the Roman patriarchal state. She plots to keep him at Carthage, induces the Trojan women to burn the ships and raises a Fury from Hades to cause the war in Latium. In this endeavour is her most potent line:

Flectere si superos nequeo Acheronta movebo.

(VII, 312)

If I cannot move the gods above I will move hell.

That Freud should have used this line as an epigraph for *The Interpretation of Dreams* because he believed that it was 'intended to picture the efforts of the repressed instinctual impulses' might confirm the thought that Virgil has struck deep truths in his dramatisation of the myth of Aeneas, and that his muse in answering the question posed at the poem's opening knew all about civilisation and its discontents. Aeneas experiences to his cost the harshness of the demands of piety to which the claims of love and his individual will have to be subordinated at Carthage. All that happens subsequently leading up to the anger and pain of the final moment in a symbolic sense is the fulfilment of Dido's curse. What seems clear is that if the *Aeneid* is an object lesson in the piety that constituted 'disciplina Romana', then it is in the cost as much as in the gain that the lesson lies.

But for Dryden piety is an uncomplicated virtue, Aeneas is the pattern of a virtuous man, and the Dido episode is an error of judgement on Virgil's part. Individual parts of book four are well translated, but the drama of Dido and Aeneas did not fully engage Dryden's imagination. When Aeneas says laconically to Dido 'Italiam non sponte sequor', we feel the suppression of feeling in Aeneas and the half line expresses the burden of sacrifice entailed in the Italian mission. The issue is muted and suppressed in Dryden's translation, almost as if he could not allow Aeneas openly to express the unRoman thought that he did not go to Italy willingly:

Forced by my fate I leave your happy land.

(IV, 517)

In his prose comment Dryden interprets the intervention of Jupiter not as a sudden Roman thought that painfully cuts across his love for Dido but as one that comes to replace it now that he has taken his physical pleasure. At this point Dryden believed that Aeneas was already 'cooling' towards Dido; he was coming to his senses and falling out of love. The prose comment is symptomatic of a tendency of Dryden in the actual translation itself to be almost more Roman than Virgil himself.

Crucial to the effect of book four is the extent to which Virgil's protagonists are complementary figures, like the deities to which they are likened, Apollo and Diana, the twin children of Leto. There is an underlying identity of spirit, though Dido's is expressed passionately and Aeneas's is subject to control. Dido is an independent character of course (it often used to be said that Dido is the only genuine 'character' in Roman literature) but she also represents that part of himself which Aeneas denies in putting the claims of piety before those of love. Herein lies the peculiar concentration and intensity of feeling in book four. But Dryden makes the episode more human in the wrong way by undermining the identity of spirit and emphasising trivial sexual differences which diminish the representative characters of Dido and Aeneas. At the same time he diminishes the human element by making the conflict seem more like one between duty and sensual pleasure. Dryden's Jupiter sees sensual riot. In Virgil Rumour has it that Dido and Aeneas are involved in a squalid affair and this is the version accepted by Iarbas. But Virgil's Jupiter sees only 'lovers forgetful of their better fame' (IV, 221), and Virgil allows us the thought that for such a love the world might well be lost. In Dryden, neither the conflict nor the sacrifice is intensely felt, so that where Virgil is most intense Dryden is most disappointing. As he had earlier clarified and simplified the issues of Shakespeare's *Antony and Cleopatra* in his play *All for Love*, so Dryden took a one-sided view of what was at issue between Dido and Aeneas in the fourth book of Virgil's *Aeneid* where he is too easily all for Rome.

No reader of Virgil can doubt that the Aeneid is pre-eminently a national epic, but Virgil is much less sanguine about the Roman destiny than a simple reading of the Roman passages might suggest. The artful way in which he has interwoven these prophecies of future time produces subtle and complicated effects.

To Jupiter grandly surveying world affairs from the viewpoint of eternity the whole of human history reaches a grand climax in the Augustan peace. The forward movement of the first half of the epic in which the Italian future is gradually revealed culminates in the revelation of the Roman destiny given to Aeneas by Anchises in Hades. Augustus is to restore to Italy the Golden Age of peace and virtue, and Rome's imperial mission is the art of government and rule, to subdue the proud and spare the conquered. Roman power is morally justified in the peace that it imposes. At the opening of the poem Jupiter had looked forward to the closing of the gates of the temple of Janus in the time of Augustus, yet the second half of the poem begins with the outbreak of the war signalled by the dramatic opening of these same gates by Juno, whereupon ploughshares are promptly forged into swords and the prospect of peace recedes, never fully to be envisaged again, for the poem does not quite come full circle. In the eighth book is a different kind of prophecy appropriate to the martial character of the last six books, a celebration of Roman manliness and military strength on the shield, beginning with the twin sons of Mars suckling the she-wolf, going on to the rape of the Sabines and the conquest of the Gauls, and concluding with the victory of Augustus and the gods of Rome against Antony and the forces of Cleopatra backed by the strange deities of the East. The final image is of the parade of Eastern peoples through the streets of Rome in the official triumph of Augustus, who appears not as civiliser but as the conqueror who victoriously asserts Roman power. The images on the shield triumphantly represent the still pictures of the relentless Roman will to power without the gloss put upon it in the Olympian vision of Jupiter and without the moral perspective of Anchises. In the present action of the poem, however, Aeneas is not a happy warrior and Virgil obliquely allows a view of events from the perspective of those who do not share the Roman view, whether it be that of Jupiter, or Anchises or what is celebrated on the shield.

In the personal history of Aeneas and Dido, Virgil skilfully foreshadowed the subsequent history of Rome and Carthage whose defeat in the struggle for supremacy in the Mediterranean was a decisive stage in the rise of Roman power. In cursing Aeneas, Dido hopes for everlasting hatred between the descendants of the two poeples with the coming of an avenger who will pursue the descendants of Troy. Her prophecy bears fruit in the career of Hannibal, but the greater prophecy is foreshadowed in Dido's own fate, the future doom of Carthage itself razed to the ground by the Romans in 146 B.C. 'Delenda est Carthago' ('Carthage must be destroyed') that inveterate old Roman Cato had chillingly and insistently declared. In pronouncing her own epitaph, Dido had hailed her achievements in founding a great city calling herself fortunate if only the Trojan ships had not touched the Carthaginian shore. When rumour of her death goes round the city, the women wail as if Carthage was falling before the invading enemy and being consumed by fire. In Dido's death, Virgil's sympathy is obliquely with the victims of relentless Roman power, and here is the germ of the famous aphorism put in the mouth of British opponents of Roman power by the imperial historian Tacitus 'ubi solitudinem faciunt, pacem appellant' ('where they make a desert, they call it peace' *Agricola* 30).

Later in the poem, the Italians might well have echoed Dido's words. The arrival of the Trojan ships destroys the peace and unleashes a furious war: 'heu frangimur fatis' ('we are shattered by the fates' VIII, 595) exclaims Latinus. Historical and artistic considerations alike dictate that the future allies of Rome be represented sympathetically. Their martial spirit is celebrated in the catalogue of forces with which book seven ends. The chief representatives of that spirit, Turnus, Mezentius and Camilla, even in defeat, embody the Italian strength and courage upon which Roman power is to depend: 'sit Romana potens Itala virtute propago' ('let Roman power draw on Italian strength' XII, 827). It may justly be argued that Virgil could scarcely have represented the victory of the Trojans over the Italians in the same manner in which he represented the conquest of Augustus over the peoples of the East on the shield, but Virgil has dramatised the conflict in such a way that in its climax attention is concentrated upon the final agony of Turnus who is sympathetically represented as the victim of a pitiless and inexorable fate.

Benignly addressing Venus in the opening book Jupiter had been serenely confident in his knowledge of the fates predicting that Aeneas would wage a mighty war in Italy, crushing proud nations in the process. Such is the long Olympian view. In the midst of things, however, after the war has broken out at the instigation of Juno, Olympian certainties fade and Jupiter claims to be baffled by the turn of events saying that he had forbidden the war in Italy. In the event he withdraws, leaving the fates to find their own way. Only in the final moment does he intervene to forbid Juno to pursue her opposition further, and then, admitting defeat, he yields to Juno's plea that the Trojans should lose their identity in Latium. After this compromise, divine support for the opposition to Aeneas is withdrawn and the fates find their way. But not before Jupiter has sent a horrid Fury to terrify Turnus. The gods play a part in the final combat of Achilles and Hector in the *Iliad*, but in Virgil the divine intervention is a particularly ugly manifestation of the malignant power of fate. To Aeneas's final taunt, Turnus replies that no words of Aeneas can frighten him:

di me terrent et Jupiter hostis

(XII, 895)

it is the gods and Jupiter's hostility that terrify me.

The god who guarantees no end to Roman dominion had made Aeneas dumb with fear at Carthage and now Turnus experiences the full terror of his might in Latium. The killing of Turnus, of course, answers Evander's prayer for vengeance, but in Virgil's presentation of it—Turnus has yielded and is begging for mercy on bended knee with suppliant hands in the name of Anchises—it is rather the fulfilment of anger than a pious duty performed, so that the poem ends not with the triumphant assertion of Roman power depicted on the shield nor with the magnanimous exercise of Roman power envisaged by Anchises, but on a bitter note—for Aeneas feels not the sweetness of revenge but the pain of loss—in which is emphasised the cost of it all to both victim and victor:

Tantae molis erat Romanam condere gentem.

That the poem should end thus, has always occasioned debate. In the Renaissance the Italian humanists, in rediscovering the lost grandeur of ancient Rome, shared all the enthusiasm of Anchises, and one of their number, Maphaeus Vegius, seeing something incomplete in the *Aeneid*, added a thirteenth book which was regularly reprinted in Renaissance editions of Virgil. Douglas translated it, though he felt the impropriety of so doing. In it, Aeneas is rewarded for his pains, celebrates his marriage to Lavinia and founds his city where he lives happily until he is received into the bosom of the gods. So Vegius imagined Virgil would have completed his poem had he lived to complete it. This impulse to reconcile the spirit of what happens in the present action of the poem with the spirit of the passages prophetic of the Roman future is understandable if we assume that Virgil's purpose is straightforwardly to raise admiration for the Roman achievement. But that so many readers holding this assumption have felt something incomplete in the poem must force us to question the assumption itself. Admiration for the Roman achievement is certainly felt in the *Aeneid*, but this is not all; the admiration is not without a measure of questioning and critical detachment. That this should be oblique is characteristically Virgilian and a consequence of the circumstances of the poem's composition.

From the beginning of his career it seems that Virgil had felt the promptings of the epic Muse:

> I first transferred to Rome Sicilian strains;
> Nor blushed the Doric Muse to dwell on Mantuan plains.
> But when I tried her tender voice, too young,
> And fighting kings and bloody battles sung,
> Apollo checked my pride, and bade me feed
> My fattening flocks, nor dare beyond the reed.
> *(The Sixth Pastoral, 1−6)*

Later Virgil declared his intention of singing Caesar's wars:

> A time will come, when my maturer muse
> In Caesar's wars a nobler theme shall choose,
> And through more ages bear my sovereign's praise,
> Than have from Tithon past to Caesar's days.
>
> Meantime we must pursue the sylvan lands
> (The abode of nymphs), untouched by former hands;
> For such, Maecenas, are thy hard commands.
> *(The Third Georgic, 79−82; 67−69)*

How hard the commands of Maecenas were we can only guess but Augustus we may be certain was not a disinterested patron and no doubt desired that the substance of his 'res gestae', which were later carved in stone throughout the empire, be celebrated in epic form. Some time after Virgil's death, Horace found it necessary modestly to decline to sing Caesar's praises in epic lays, leaving that task to his fellow poet Antonius:

> Thus, when the Theban swan attempts the skies,
> A nobler gale of rapture bids him rise;
> But like a bee which through the breezy groves
> With feeble wing and idle murmurs roves,
>   Sits on the bloom, and with unceasing toil
> From thyme sweet-breathing culls the flowery spoil;
> So I, weak bard! round Tiber's lucid spring,
> Of humbler strain laborious verses sing.
>   'Tis thine with deeper hand to strike the lyre,
> When Caesar shall his raptured bard inspire,
> And crowned with laurel, well earned mead of war,
> Drag the fierce Gaul at his triumphal car;

Than whom the gods ne'er gave, or bounteous fate,
To human kind a gift more good or great,
Nor from their treasures shall again unfold
Though time roll backward to this age of gold.
  Be thine the festal days, the city's joys,
The Forum silenced from litigious noise,
The public games for Caesar safe restored,
A blessing oft with pious vows implored.
                    (*Odes* IV, ii, 25–44 trans. Francis)[7]

Previous Roman poets, notably Cnaeus Naevius and Quintus Ennius, had made epics out of contemporary history. With such precedents in mind, Augustus might well have expected a poem centered upon his own achievements. In the event, Virgil did not venture the perilous enterprise of singing Caesar's wars, as Naevius and Ennius had sung of the wars of the Scipios. Fragments of their poems survive from which it is clear that they mixed myth and history as Virgil was to do later. Naevius in his *Punic War* used the myth of Aeneas to derive the Romans from Troy, described the Trojan wanderings and has the Trojans land at Carthage where they meet Dido. He also introduced Homer's gods, and has Venus complain to Jupiter about the treatment of her son in a storm raised by Juno. While Naevius seems to have moved quickly from myth to history and concentrated on the events that gave his poem its title, Ennius writing after him in his *Annales* dealt with the whole of Roman history up to his time as his title might suggest. He too used Homer's gods; Jupiter is closely associated with the Romans while Juno champions the cause of Carthage. Virgil, therefore, owed much to his Roman predecessors, but his master-stroke was to make the mythical material central to the whole of the present action of his poem, while history is referred to in future time. His epic is therefore set in a world seemingly remote and distant from the Roman present. This distance gave the poet greater freedom and detachment than was possible in dealing with contemporary material. As a matter of historical necessity, the conquered peoples of the East have to be paraded through the streets of Rome, but Virgil has considerable imaginative freedom with Dido and Turnus. Furthermore in his classic Aristotelian form there is a shifting perspective on things impossible in a straightforwardly linear narrative, so that he is not tied to the contemporary political world in the way that Dryden is, for example in *Absalom and Achitophel*.

Dryden gave the following account of Virgil's attitude to his contemporary political world:

> I say that Virgil having maturely weighed the condition of the times in which he lived; that an entire liberty was not to be retrieved; that the present settlement had the prospect of a long continuance in the same family, or those adopted into it; that he held his paternal estate from the bounty of the conqueror, by whom he was likewise enriched, esteemed and cherished; that this conqueror, though of a bad kind, was the very best of it; that the arts of peace flourished under him; that all men might be happy if they would be quiet; that, now he was in possession of the whole, yet he shared a great part of his authority with the Senate; that he would be chosen into the ancient offices of the Commonwealth, and ruled by the power which he derived from them; and prorogued his government from time to time, still, as it were, threatening to dismiss himself from public cares, which he exercised more for the common good than for any delight he took in greatness; these things, I say, being considered by the poet, he concluded it to be in the interest of his country to be so governed; to infuse an awful respect into the people towards such a prince; by that respect to confirm their obedience to him, and by that obedience to make them happy. This was the moral of his divine poem; honest in the poet; honourable to the Emperor, whom he derives from a divine extraction; and reflecting part of that honour on the Roman people, whom he derives also from the Trojans; and not only profitable, but necessary, to the present age, and likely to be such to their posterity.
>
> ('Dedication of the *Aeneis*', pp. 1014–15)

Striking in Dryden's prose is both the note of assurance on which he concludes and the sophisticated process of mature deliberation that leads him to his conclusion. The 'moral' is an orthodox reading of the poem derived from Le Bossu's *Traité du poème épique* of

1675. The reasoning that leads up to it may make us feel that Dryden is offering a spirited defence of his own conduct in accommodating himself to uncongenial realities under the regime of William III. But in this account the 'moral' (the truth of which in some form has always been accepted) is given a conclusive prominence that it does not quite have in the poem itself. It is not as if the *Aeneid* ends with the unambiguous and inescapable political message carried by the ending of *Absalom and Achitophel* when the speech of David/Charles is ratified by the assent of the Almighty. The form of Virgil's poem forces us to take a more detached and questioning view of any political moral the poem may be deemed to carry.

Virgil wrote under the patronage of Augustus to whom he was obliged and whom he must necessarily have pleased whether he wished to or not. Poets who incurred Caesar's displeasure were dealt with summarily as Ovid found to his cost. Virgil may genuinely have wished to please the Emperor. At any rate he seems to have succeeded since Augustus according to the ancient lives ordered that the *Aeneid* should be saved from the flames to which Virgil had committed it in the event of his death before completion. The same sources record that Virgil actually read parts of his poem in the presence of Augustus, and there is the famous anecdote that when Virgil read his lines on the death of Augustus's son-in-law and heir, who died young at the age of twenty in 23 B.C., Octavia fainted at the mention of her son Marcellus.

The inclusion of the figure of Marcellus is of course flattering to the imperial family, but few readers of Virgil think primarily of flattery when reading the famous lines on his doom and death. Marcellus, cruelly cut down before his prime, in whom ancient heroism was to be restored to Rome if the fates had allowed, has forever been a symbol of promise unfulfilled evoking feelings of sorrow for what might have been. But how characteristic of Virgil is the artful positioning of the lament to form the emotional climax of book six. Coming as it does immediately after Anchises's pageant of heroes in which the praise of Caesar figures prominently and after the triumphant assertion of the Roman imperial mission, it puts a perspective on the feeling of Roman pride and closes the book on a more universal note of sorrow appropriate to the subject matter and vision of book six. If Augustus had earlier glowed with pride, then perhaps he shed a tear at the end. Virgil is ringing changes like those brilliantly effected by Dryden's Timotheus in 'Alexander's Feast'. Immediately after the lament, Anchises dismisses Aeneas from Hades by way of the ivory gate, the gate of false dreams. The significance of this perplexing moment has often been debated. It is tempting to see much in the progress from the pomp of the pageant and the zeal of the mission to the lament for the loss of what was fated not to be and the hint of illusion. But the narrative is delicately orchestrated and any Virgilian irony is extremely fine. Nevertheless there is surely a teasing hint here that all is not quite as it might seem in the poem. If the hint is oblique then the circumstances in which Virgil wrote the poem made circumspection necessary. What is perhaps worth saying here is that Virgil's humanity transcends his Roman theme and is apparent in the ordering of the parts both in the larger structure and in particular instances such as this at the close of book six. Both the larger structure and the ordering of details cast an element of doubt on the assurance of Dryden's account of the poem's political moral.

The note of assurance that marks Dryden's prose is apparent in the translation. One example will suffice:

> At pater Aeneas, casu concussus acerbo,
> nunc huc ingentis, nunc illuc pectore curas
> mutabat versans, Siculisne resideret arvis,
> oblitus fatorum, Italasne capesseret oras.
> tum senior Nautes, unum Tritonia Pallas
> quem docuit multaque insignem reddidit arte,
> (haec responsa dabat, vel quae portenderet ira
> magna deum vel quae fatorum posceret ordo),
> isque his Aenean solatus vocibus infit:
> 'nate dea, quo fata trahunt retrahuntque sequamur;
> quidquid erit, superanda amnis fortuna ferendo est.'
> (V, 700–10)

> But doubtful thoughts the hero's heart divide,
> If he should still in Sicily reside,
> Forgetful of his fates,—or tempt the main,
> In hope the promised Italy to gain.

> Then Nautes, old and wise—to whom alone
> The will of Heaven by Pallas was foreshown;
> Versed in portents, experienced, and inspired
> To tell events, and what the Fates required—
> Thus, while he stood to neither part inclined,
> With cheerful words relieved his labouring mind:
> 'O goddess-born! resigned in every state,
> With patience bear, with prudence push your fate.
> By suffering well, our fortune we subdue;
> Fly when she frowns, and when she calls, pursue.'
> (V, 918–931)

In Virgil, Aeneas is in considerable confusion and remains so until Nautes's advice is confirmed for him by the spirit of Anchises in a dream. Dryden has played down the confusion felt by Aeneas, but more telling is the change in the tone of Nautes's advice. In the first line of Nautes's speech 'trahunt' can mean to draw in the sense of lead or drag; with 'retrahunt' the idea of dragging (or being dragged around by the fates) is inescapable. Given the movement of the line and the sound patterning the emphasis falls heavily upon dragging and redragging. In the second line the emphasis falls heavily upon 'ferendo', on *bearing*. Whatever happens we must endure and bear, being submissive to the will of heaven. In Dryden's recreation all the elements are there but they have been recast into something different. Dryden's version is much more dynamic. Aeneas must 'bear with patience' but also '*push* his fate'. There is nothing so active in Virgil. In the next line the climax is in the power of the individual to overcome in 'subdue'. In the final line the position of 'fly' and 'pursue' (a dynamic rendering of Virgil's 'following') again emphasises what the individual is to do. The domination of the fates is muted in Dryden whose version stresses by contrast the possibilities of individual effort.

Dryden's *Aeneid* affirms Roman greatness and the heroic effort that went into the building of Roman civilisation. This is his reading of the famous line beginning 'tantae molis'. Implicit in his interpretation of the poem and in his translation of this passage is the humanist idealism in which civilisation is the product of an heroic effort of individual will, the result of the best endeavours of the greatest spirits of whom Aeneas is the pattern and example. This was the humanist tradition inherited by Dryden, built upon an admiration for Roman greatness that extended from Petrarch to Gibbon.

> Rome was greater than I thought and so are its remains. Now I wonder not that the world was ruled by this city but that the rule came so late.

So wrote Petrarch on his first visit to the city that he had dreamed about. Later for Gibbon:

> the firm edifice of Roman power was raised and preserved by the wisdom of the ages.

Petrarch and Gibbon looked back across the centuries in admiration and awe to the lost Roman dominion. For Virgil, the present reality of the Roman dominion was something to be taken for granted; it was something that was fated to be, and there is no happy affirmation of the will to civilisation in the *Aeneid*. On the contrary, there is a sternness in Virgil that calls to mind Menenius on the inexorability of the historical process in *Coriolanus*:

>   For your wants,
> Your suffering in this dearth, you may as well
> Strike at the heaven with your staves, as lift them
> Against the Roman state, whose course will on
> The way it takes, cracking ten thousand curbs
> Of more strong link asunder than can ever
> Appear in your impediment.
>   (Act I, Sc.I, 64–70)

Aeneas is required above all to submit, endlessly to submit. He is more the passive instrument of the inscrutable fates than the heroic agent of a beneficent wisdom. In Virgil civilisation is not the product of anything that can be represented in the individual will, whether good or ill. It results from the collision of opposing forces hostile to the individual will in which the individual will is liable to be destroyed. This gloomy fatalism lies at the heart of the *Aeneid*.

But whatever the deeper reasons for Dryden's changes here, they are to some extent the product of a difference in temperament between the two poets that Dryden came to recognise when he later translated the first book of Homer's *Iliad* published in the *Fables* in 1700. In the preface he compares Homer and Virgil:

> But to return: our two great poets being so different in their tempers, one choleric and sanguine, the other phlegmatic and melancholic; that which makes them excel in their several ways is, that each of them has followed his own natural inclination, as well in forming the design, as in the execution of it. The very heroes shew their authors: Achilles is hot, impatient, revengeful—
>
> Impiger, iracundus, inexorabilis, acer, etc.,
>
> Aeneas patient, considerate, careful of his people, and merciful to his enemies; ever submissive to the will of heaven—
>
> ... quo fata trahunt retrahuntque sequamur.
>
> (p. 1449)

But where Virgil is melancholic and phlegmatic, Dryden is much more sanguine. Virgil's Nautes consoles, Dryden's offers 'cheerful words'. Dryden went on:

> This vehemence of his, I confess is more suitable to my temper: and therefore I have translated his first book with greater pleasure than any part of Virgil.

His own temperamental affinity with the vehement temper of Homer whom he appreciated as a poet of vigorous action led him to believe that he had been most successful in those parts of Virgil where the action is vigorous, particularly in the later books. Certainly no translator of Virgil has entered so successfully into the spirit of Virgil's *'Iliad'*. Let one representative moment illustrate the fighting spirit of Dryden's version:

> So stoops the yellow eagle from on high,
> And bears a speckled serpent through the sky,

Fastening his crooked talons on the prey:
The prisoner hisses through the liquid way;
Resists the royal hawk; and, though oppressed
She fights in volumes, and erects her crest:
Turned to her foe, she stiffens every scale,
And shoots her forky tongue, and whisks her threatening tail.
Against the victor, all defence is weak:
The imperial bird still plies her with his beak;
He tears her bowels, and her breast he gores,
Then claps his pinions, and securely soars.
                                              (XI, 1105—1116)

In such a passage there is Latin magnificence and Roman splendour, but overall the manner does not eclipse the matter. The tussle between the eagle and the snake is a real one; it is strangely exhilarating and indicative of the remorseless physical energy of the fight in the larger narrative. Dryden is good at stirring up the 'irascible appetite' and exciting 'the manly passions', an ability he admired in the author of the *Iliad*. But Virgil's *Iliad* is not any more than Homer's an unqualified vindication of 'the manly passions'. In Homer the war god is a distinctly unpleasant character, and in Virgil the war is caused by a Fury raised from Hades. Virgilian recoil from horror and brutality and Virgilian pity for the suffering of the weak and the defeated which had found open expression in his handling of the fate of the Trojans in the first half of the epic are also to be felt underlying the narrative in the last six books. Modern commentators also see in this narrative echoes of the troubled history of the last years of the Roman Republic which had seen a succession of civil wars and internal upheavals. As a poet who had lived through England's turbulance in the seventeenth century, Dryden represented the agonies as well as the fighting spirit of the final books. Here is a quiet moment in the indiscriminate fighting that precedes the final combat:

Peaceful Menoetes after these he killed,
Who long had shunned the dangers of the field:
On Lerna's lake a silent life he led,
And with his nets and angle earned his bread.
Nor pompous cares, nor palaces, he knew,

> But wisely from the infectious world withdrew.
> Poor was his house: his father's painful hand
> Discharged his rent, and ploughed another's land.
>
> (XII, 752–59)

There is sensitivity and pathos in the translation here which is all the more effectively conveyed because Dryden is not striving for effects. His language is simple and direct like the thought and feeling of the original with the result that the irony and injustice of Menoetes's death are conveyed artfully through the poet's restraint and control of language, matter and manner being in perfect harmony. Virgilian pathos may be muted in Dryden but it is not extinguished, and this control is surely preferable to the weepy sentimentality of the Romantic and post-Romantic Virgil.

Dryden's success in his translation is not limited to passages of vigorous action or to the speeches in which he could display his talent for dramatising speech in verse. As his success is variable so is it various. Those who know Dryden chiefly from his laureate poems, his satires and his heroic plays might be surprised that he is able to evoke so successfully the mysterious beauty of the Golden Bough or write poetry of such delicate and sensuous natural beauty as this:

> About the boughs an airy nation flew,
> Thick as the humming bees, that hunt the golden dew
> In summer's heat; on tops of lilies feed,
> And creep within their bells, to suck the balmy seed:
> The wingèd army roams the field around;
> The rivers and the rocks remurmur to the sound.
>
> (VI, 958–63)

If Dryden disappoints in book four, then he often exceeds expectation elsewhere, and nowhere more so than in book six. The painful encounters of Aeneas with Palinurus, Dido and Deiphobus, and the lament for the fate of Marcellus (of which there is a memorable echo in Dryden's fine poem on the death of the young poet John Oldham in 1685) show Dryden to be in sympathy with the Virgilian temper and prove him to be a poet who can command the pathetic as well as the sublime.

Finally the reader may wish to ponder the verdict of Dryden's most illustrious editor, Walter Scott:

He who sits down to Dryden's translation of Virgil, with the original text spread before him, will be at no loss to point out many passages that are faulty, many indifferently understood, many imperfectly translated, some in which dignity is lost, others in which bombast is substituted in its stead. But the unabated vigour and spirit of the version more than overbalances these and other deficiencies. A sedulous scholar might often approach more nearly to the dead letter of Virgil, and give an exact, distinct, sober-minded idea of the meaning and scope of particular passages. Trapp, Pitt, and others have done so. But the essential spirit of poetry is so volatile, that it escapes during such an operation, like the life of the poor criminal, whom the ancient anatomist is said to have dissected alive, in order to ascertain the seat of the soul. The carcase indeed is presented to the English reader, but the animating vigour is no more. It is in this art, of communicating the ancient poet's ideas with force and energy equal to his own, that Dryden has so completely exceeded all who have gone before, and all who have succeeded him.

Notes

1   Dryden's prefaces are included in *The Poems of John Dryden* edited by James Kinsley in four volumes Clarendon Press Oxford 1958, and all the page references in the introduction are to this edition. Dryden's translations of Virgil's *Pastorals* and *Georgics* (from which there are brief extracts in this introduction) are to be found in volume two. His *Aeneid* is in volume three. Dryden's prose is conveniently available in *John Dryden: Of Dramatic Poesy and Other Critical Essays* edited by George Watson in Everyman's Library (2 vols, London, 1962). This edition has notes and a useful index, but does not have 'The Dedication of the *Aeneis*' entire.
2   In 'The Character of St. Evremond' (Watson, op cit., p. 57). Dryden defends Virgil against French criticism here.

3   See, for example the close of *An Essay on Translated Verse* by the Earl of Roscommon (1685). Roscommon venerates Virgil as 'the sacred founder of our rules'.
4   From Tennyson's poem 'To Virgil' (Written at the Request of the Mantuans for the Nineteenth Centenary of Virgil's Death [1882: Virgil was born at Mantua in 19 B.C.]).
5   The fragments of Ennius are conveniently available in *Remains of Old Latin Vol I: Ennius and Caecilius* edited and translated by E.H. Warmington (Loeb Classical Library: Cambridge Mass. and London, 1967). The translation of the five line passage is by Warmington (p. 71).
6   Virgil has 'parcere subjectis et debellare superbos' ('to spare the conquered and to quell the proud').
7   *The Odes, Epodes and Carmen Seculare of Horace in Latin and English* By P. Francis (4 vols. 1743–46).

The Selection, the Text and the Notes

The intention in this edition has been to represent the most celebrated parts of the *Aeneid* as fully as possible while retaining a sufficiently general selection wherein the shape and design of the whole may be clear. What is offered is neither a series of 'highlights' nor a summary version but something of both.

Accordingly, books one and seven in which the action of the two halves of the poem is set in motion are generously represented as are the most famous books recounting the sack of Troy (two), the Dido episode (four), and the visit to Hades (six). In the intervening books three and five recounting the wanderings of Aeneas from Troy and the games in Sicily the selection is limited to highlights and representative episodes. In the war in Italy the basic pattern of events and relationships that constitutes the main plot is largely retained. Otherwise some narrative continuity has been sacrificed to allow inclusion of famous episodes. In book nine, for example, the night adventure of Nisus and Euryalus is included in its entirety at the expense of the siege of the Trojan camp which is its context. In book eleven the council of war has been sacrificed to allow generous representation of the episode of Camilla. In book twelve the final combat is given entire at the expense of the various manoeuvrings which lead up to it.

Many of the episodes are complete, but occasionally excisions within episodes have been made. In the description of the shield in book eight, for example, the more recondite allusions to Roman history have been removed. There are sometimes omissions too from Dryden's translation even where the original is being represented continuously. In fairness to Virgil, Dryden's infelicitous additions to the Dido episode (occasional couplets) have been removed. Such omissions and excisions are marked by a line of dots. The aim has been to represent Virgil through Dryden as attractively as possible, and to remove from the path of the first-time reader any obvious obstacles in the way of easy enjoyment.

To this end, both prose and verse texts have been standardised and modernised where possible. The text used here is an authorised reprint of that established for Dryden's Virgil in The World Classics Series. A complete text of Dryden's *Aeneid* retaining the printing conventions of the seventeenth century and including Dryden's prefatory material and his postscript can be found in volume three of *The Poetical Works of John Dryden* edited by James Kinsley (4 vols, Oxford, 1958).

To enhance the reader's pleasure, a selection of notes has been appended to the text drawn largely from eighteenth-century writers each of whom had a keen eye for local felicities in a particular narrative or for larger beauties in the ordering of the overall design. Their comments bear witness to the beauty of Virgil's art and the pleasure afforded by it, and also suggest the direction of its influence. Behind them is a long tradition of commentary on the text and a lively debate about the respective merits of Homer and Virgil that began in Roman times and had been renewed in the Renaissance.

The comments of Pope on Virgil are drawn from the notes he included in his translation of Homer's *Iliad* in 1715–1720 and *Odyssey* in 1723–6. They are conveniently available in volumes seven to ten of *The Twickenham Edition of the Poems of Alexander Pope*, (ed. Maynard Mack et al, London and New Haven, 1967). The remarks of Trapp are appended to his translation and can be found in *The Works of Virgil Translated into English Blank Verse* by Joseph Trapp (3 vols, London 1731). Warton's notes were made to accompany Christopher Pitt's translation of the *Aeneid* and can be found in *The Works of Virgil in Latin and English* (4 vols, London 1753). These authors draw upon the influential French commentary by J.R. de Segrais (also used by Dryden) to be found in *Traduction de l'Eneide de Virgile* par M. de Segrais (Paris 1668).

Otherwise notes have been kept to a minimum. Essential mythology and background information on the main characters either taken for granted by Virgil or included in parts of the poem not represented in the selection are given in the list of names and persons immediately following.

Names and Persons in the Aeneid

Achaemenides one of the companions of Odysseus mistakenly left behind in the cave of the Cyclops Polyphemus, the one-eyed giant (see *Odyssey* XI) when Odysseus escaped with the rest of his companions (book three).

Achates the faithful and silent companion of Aeneas 'fidus Achates'.

Achilles hero of the *Iliad*, the strongest of the Greek fighters at Troy and scourge of the Trojans. He killed most of the sons of Priam.

Aeneas son of Anchises and Venus. He is a direct descendant of Tros (whence Trojan) who was the grandfather of Priam so that he is a part of the Trojan royal family and a second or third cousin of the children of Priam. He played a prominent part in the fighting at Troy in encounters with Diomedes and Achilles. In the first he was saved by his mother (*Iliad* V) and in the second (*Iliad* XX) he was rescued by Poseidon (Neptune) who says that Aeneas is destined to survive so that the house of Dardanus, whom of all his children Zeus (Jupiter) loved most, might not perish now that Priam's line has fallen into disfavour. Aeneas and his children's children are to rule over the Trojans (*Iliad* XX, 302–308). According to some accounts, Dardanus, the product of an affair of Zeus with the Pleiad Electra daughter of Atlas, married the daughter of Teucer, the first king of Troy. Hence the Trojans are sometimes called Dardans, sometimes Teucrians. (Similarly the Greeks are called Argives, Achaeans or Danaans). Dardanus was born in Italy, so that the Trojans under Aeneas are returning to the country of their race's origin. One of the sons of Dardanus was Ilus (whence Ilium).

Allecto one of the three Furies raised from Hades by Juno to cause the war in Latium (book seven).

Amata queen of the Latins and wife of Latinus. She opposes the plan of Latinus that Aeneas should marry their daughter Lavinia, favouring the suit of Turnus her nephew. She hangs herself when it seems that Aeneas will triumph.

Anchises father of Aeneas, he was descended from Tros through Assaracus and Capys. He accompanied Aeneas on his seven year voyage interpreting omens and prophecies, as far as Sicily where he died. On his return to Sicily after being blown off course in a storm to Carthage, Aeneas makes libations at his tomb and institutes funeral games in his honour. Aeneas journeys to the underworld to meet his spirit in Hades (book six).

Andromache wife of Hector who became the slave of Pyrrhus, the son of Achilles, after the sack of Troy. Aeneas meets her after Pyrrhus has been killed and she is the wife of Helenus, a son of Priam (book three). Her son by Hector, Astyanax, was thrown from the battlements of Troy by the Greeks.

Ascanius son of Aeneas by Creusa who is to settle the Trojans in Alba Longa and rule for thirty years. He is also known as Iulus from which name the gens Iulia (notably Julius Caesar) claimed descent.

Augustus Caesar Caius Julius Caesar Octavianus, the nephew of Julius Caesar and his adopted heir. He took the name Augustus in 27 B.C. After he had defeated Mark Antony and Cleopatra at the battle of Actium in 31 B.C. he was sole ruler of the Roman world and celebrated a Roman triumph for victories in the eastern empire. His minister of the arts, Maecenas, was Virgil's patron. There is a tradition that he restored to Virgil his father's farm which had been expropriated in the civil wars. To inaugurate the new era of peace, the gates of the temple of Janus, open in time of war, were ceremonially closed early in his reign for only the third time in Roman history. Augustus secured the frontiers of the Roman empire and revised the constitution of the Roman state. The Augustan imperial settlement endured for four centuries. He is referred to in Jupiter's prophecy (book one) in the speech of Anchises (book six) and in the description of the shield (book eight).

Camilla daughter of Metabus expelled by his subjects for tyranny. In flight through a forest he came to a raging river. He attached a basket containing the infant Camilla to a spear, and as he cast the spear over the river he dedicated her to Diana, chaste goddess of the woods and hunting. Father and daughter survived, living a life apart from the society of men. Camilla appears to have been a Virgilian invention (book eleven).

Creusa wife of Aeneas and mother of Ascanius, lost in the departure from Troy (book two).

Deiphobus a son of Priam who married Helen after the death of Paris. To gain the favour of her former husband she betrayed him to Menelaus after the Greeks had broken into Troy. He tells his story to Aeneas in Hades (book six).

Dido also called Elissa, a Phoenician princess, sister of Pygmalion ruler of Tyre, and married to Sichaeus a man of secret wealth for which he was murdered while at the altar by Pygmalion who concealed the deed from his sister. But Sichaeus appeared to Dido in dreams warning her to flee and telling her where his secret treasure lay. Dido and her followers set sail from Tyre, and are building the new town of Carthage when Aeneas is shipwrecked on the African coast. Venus tells her history to Aeneas in book one.

Evander a son of Hermes (Mercury, also called Cyllenius) by the Arcadian nymph Carmenta who had prophetic powers. He was a Greek who sometime before the Trojan War had emigrated from Pallanteum in Arcadia (in the Greek Peloponnese) to Italy where he founded Pallanteum on the site of the future Rome. The Sibyl prophecies that Aeneas will seek aid from a Greek city and at the prompting of the river Tiber he sails to Pallanteum. Evander welcomes Aeneas, telling him that he had known Priam and Anchises before the Trojan War. He commits his son Pallas to the care of Aeneas, and puts Aeneas in charge of the Etruscan forces hostile to Turnus and the Rutulians (book eight).

Erato the muse of love poetry, mysteriously invoked by Virgil at the opening of the second half of the poem.

Euryalus the young friend of Nisus who features in the foot-race (book five) and in the night expedition in which he and Nisus go through enemy lines to alert Aeneas at Pallanteum to the plight of the besieged Trojans hard pressed by Turnus and the Rutulians (book nine).

Hector the oldest of Priam's sons and Troy's chief defender whose death at the hands of Achilles is the climax of the *Iliad*. Achilles fixed the corpse of Hector to his chariot and at dawn for several days after his death he repeatedly drove it round the funeral mound of his comrade Patroclus whom Hector had killed after

Achilles had foolishly allowed him to fight in his place and wearing his armour. His image thus wounded and desecrated comes to Aeneas on Troy's last night to warn him to flee from the city (book two).

Helen Zeus (Jupiter) gave Paris, the second son of Priam, the task of deciding which of the three senior goddesses was the fairest. Hera (Juno) offered him wealth and power if he chose her, Athene (Minerva) offered him renown in war, and Aphrodite (Venus) offered him the most beautiful woman in the world, Helen, wife of the Greek Menelaus, king of Sparta. Paris chose Venus and her gift. After he had abducted Helen from Sparta, the Greeks mounted an expedition against Troy under the leadership of Agamemnon, king of Mycenae and brother of Menelaus. The Greeks besieged Troy for ten years until they captured the city by the strategem of the wooden horse. As Troy burns, Aeneas catches sight of Helen cowering in a temple and is about to kill her when prevented by Venus (book two).

Helenus a son of Priam married to Andromache. He has prophetic powers and tells Aeneas of his coming destiny (book three).

Ilioneus the Trojan elder who petitions Dido in the absence of Aeneas (book one) and who is sent by Aeneas to make overtures to Latinus after the Trojans have landed in Italy (book seven).

Juno daughter of Saturn, sister and wife of Jupiter, queen of the Olympians. She is a goddess of power and authority, and as patroness of Carthage is naturally opposed to a people whose descendants according to the fates were to threaten the power of Carthage in a struggle for Mediterranean dominance. She hated the Trojans because of the judgement of Paris (see Helen). The founder of the Trojan race Dardanus was the product of one of Jupiter's amours. Ganymede, the beautiful youth beloved of Jupiter, was also a Trojan.

Jupiter son of Saturn and king of the gods, he is the most powerful of the Olympians and his special province is the upper air where he controls storms and clouds and sends rain. His brothers Neptune and Pluto rule the seas and the underworld respectively. His power is expressed in his thunderbolt. Another of his emblems is the eagle. The Romans built a temple to him on the highest of their seven hills, the Capitol, which overlooked their legislative assembly, the Forum, and the whole region of Latium. He is associated with dominion and power 'imperium' and with law and justice 'ius'. Hence his companion gods on the Capitol were Fides (Faithfulness or Fidelity) and Victoria (Victory).

Juturna a water nymph and sister of Turnus.

Latinus king of the Latins, son of Faunus (god of agriculture and cattle) and a Laurentine nymph Marica. He was the grandson of Picus and the great grandson of Saturn who had ruled Italy in the Golden Age of peace, simplicity and virtue. He was married to Amata. He had no male heir but a daughter named Lavinia. She was of marriageable age and many Italian princes, most notably Turnus, sought her hand in marriage. Oracles had foretold that she was destined to marry a stranger. When Aeneas lands in Italy Latinus recognises him as the stranger referred to in the oracle and offers him Lavinia in marriage. He opposes the war with the Trojans but is over-ruled (book seven).

Lausus young son of Mezentius q.v. killed by Aeneas (book ten).

Lavinia daughter of Latinus q.v. Aeneas is to marry her and names his city Lavinium after her.

Mars the god of war. Ilia, a descendant of Aeneas, gave birth to the twin sons of Mars, Romulus and Remus, so that the Romans (derived from Romulus the founder of the city of Rome) are descendants of the war god (see the description of the shield in book eight).

Mercury the messenger of the gods, called Cyllenius.

Mezentius king of the Tyrrhenians or Etruscans at Caere or Agylla and father of Lausus. He was expelled by his subjects because of his cruelty and took refuge with Turnus. The Etruscans demand the return of their king for punishment. Their forces are gathered when a prophet tells them that they are destined to be led by a foreign leader. They appeal to Evander (who is a Greek emigrant) but he is old and entrusts them to the command of Aeneas. In the action of the poem Mezentius is not guilty of any particular cruelty though he is consistently represented as one who scorned the gods. In one version of the legend he killed Aeneas before himself being killed by Ascanius (book ten).

Nisus see Euryalus.

52　NAMES AND PERSONS IN THE AENEID

Palinurus the helmsman of Aeneas mysteriously drowned on the voyage from Sicily to Italy. Aeneas meets his shade in Hades (book six).

Pallas young son of Evander killed by Turnus (book ten).

Priam king of Troy at the time of the Trojan War, and married to Hecuba (book two).

Pyrrhus also called Neoptolemus, son of Achilles who kills Priam (book two).

the Sibyl a generic name given to prophetic women. The Sibyl who acts as Aeneas's guide through the underworld is called Deiphobe. She lives in a cave and is inspired by Apollo god of prophecy, uttering truths when she is possessed by the god (book six).

Tarchon commander of the Etruscan forces committed to Aeneas (see Mezentius).

Turnus son of Daunus and king of the Rutulians. His mother was a sea nymph called Venilia so that like Aeneas he is goddess-born. He is the suitor of Lavinia whom he obviously expects to marry though he is not formally betrothed to her. In another version of the legend, Aeneas killed him before himself being killed by Mezentius. Virgil has rearranged the order of events so that the two suitors of Lavinia meet in single combat in the climax of the poem. In the Sibyl's prophecy of the war in Italy given to Aeneas in Hades, Turnus is identified with the Homeric Achilles.

Venus mother of Aeneas and goddess of love and beauty, known as Cytherea from the Aegean island of Cythera where she is supposed to have first landed after she had risen from the sea. She is also closely associated with Cyprus, in particular with Paphos and Idalium.

Checklist of Passages included in this Selection

Book I	1–61; 70–155; 159–161; 168–169; 176–244; 277–290; 308–327; 346–411; 420–470; 509–539; 556–573; 580–652; 684–708; 717–748; 751–759; 788–795; 801–802; 806–811; 824–859; 866–875; 886–892; 901–934; 969–1033; 1049–1051; 1056–end
Book II	1–428; 488–499; 619–624; 639–864; 958–1023; 1044–end
Book III	1–94; 378–455; 473–488; 561–597; 622–659; 744–907
Book IV	1–76; 93–128; 182–187; 194–222; 231–307; 320–321; 326–327; 350–353; 382–575; 591–598; 601–617; 620–700; 710–738; 757–770; 773–836; 847–906; 925–973; 984–996; 1003–end
Book V	373–475; 646–713; 783–790; 795–804; 808–828; 856–861; 896–979; 984–1000
Book VI	62–79; 120–175; 188–224; 271–272; 280–305; 336–353; 364–393; 410–456; 461–530; 538–539; 549–601; 610–645; 649–650; 655–712; 720–730; 739–783; 855–872; 895–904; 921–1040; 1055–1102; 1168–1242
Book VII	52–150; 203–210; 229–231; 266–281; 290–297; 302–320; 327–377; 393–413; 430–525; 538–543; 565–570; 578–657; 660–718; 724–754; 789–834; 840–870; 875–886; 895–906; 1071–1076; 1083–1084; 1094–end
Book VIII	27–140; 408–450; 457–466; 471–687; 772–790; 807–842; 867–878; 891–963; 973–end
Book IX	29–50; 199–670
Book X	1–14; 159–177; 609–746; 767–787; 878–973; 1071–end
Book XI	1–122; 139–146; 209–239; 250–260; 269–280; 733–814; 875–895; 962–996; 1003–1018; 1034–1262; 1293–end
Book XII	867–end

53

BOOK I

THE ARGUMENT

The Trojans, after a seven years' voyage, set sail for Italy, but are overtaken by a dreadful storm, which Æolus raises at Juno's request. The tempest sinks one ship, and scatters the rest. Neptune drives off the winds, and calms the sea. Æneas, with his own ship and six more, arrives safe at an African port. Venus complains to Jupiter of her son's misfortunes. Jupiter comforts her, and sends Mercury to procure him a kind reception among the Carthaginians. Æneas, going out to discover the country, meets his mother in the shape of a huntress, who conveys him in a cloud to Carthage, where he sees his friends whom he thought lost, and receives a kind entertainment from the queen. Dido, by a device of Venus, begins to have a passion for him, and after some discourse with him, desires the history of his adventures since the siege of Troy, which is the subject of the two following books.

ARMS, and the man I sing, who, forced by Fate,
And haughty Juno's unrelenting hate,
Expelled and exiled, left the Trojan shore.
Long labours, both by sea and land, he bore,
And in the doubtful war, before he won
The Latian realm, and built the destined town;
His banished gods restored to rites divine;
And settled sure succession in his line,
From whence the race of Alban fathers come,
And the long glories of majestic Rome.
    O muse! the causes and the crimes relate;
What goddess was provoked, and whence her hate;
For what offence the queen of heaven began
To persecute so brave, so just a man;
Involved his anxious life in endless cares,
Exposed to wants, and hurried into wars!
Can heavenly minds such high resentment show,
Or exercise their spite in human woe?
    Against the Tiber's mouth, but far away,
An ancient town was seated on the sea—
A Tyrian colony—the people made
Stout for the war, and studious for their trade:
Carthage the name—beloved by Juno more
Than her own Argos, or the Samian shore.

Here stood her chariot ; here, if heaven were **kind,**
The seat of awful empire she designed.
Yet she had heard an ancient rumour fly
(Long cited by the people of the sky),
That times to come should see the Trojan race
30 Her Carthage ruin, and her towers deface ;
Nor thus confined, the yoke of sovereign sway
Should on the necks of all the nations lay.
She pondered this, and feared it was in fate ;
Nor could forget the war she waged of late,
For conquering Greece, against the Trojan state,
Besides, long causes working in her mind,
And secret seeds of envy, lay behind :
Deep graven in her heart, the doom remained
Of partial Paris, and her form disdained ;
40 The grace bestowed on ravished Ganymed,
Electra's glories, and her injured bed.
Each was a cause alone ; and all combined
To kindle vengeance in her haughty mind.
For this, far distant from the Latian coast,
She drove the remnants of the Trojan host ;
And seven long years the unhappy wandering train
Were tossed by storms, and scattered through **the**
    main.
Such time, such toil, required the Roman name,
Such length of labour for so vast a frame !
50 Now scarce the Trojan fleet, with sails and **oars,**
Had left behind the fair Sicilian shores,
Entering with cheerful shouts the watery reign,
And ploughing frothy furrows in the main ;
When, lab'ring still with endless discontent,

1   Our author seems to sound a charge, and begins like the clangor of a trumpet:

   Arma virumque cano, Troiae qui primus ab oris—

   scarce a word without an *r*, and the vowels for the greater part sonorous.

                                                    Dryden 'Dedication'

10 The proposition of the *Aeneid* [Dryden 1–10] closes with dignity and magnificence not often found even in the poetry of Virgil.
                                                    Warton

DRYDEN'S AENEID

The queen of heaven did thus her fury vent:
'Then am I vanquished? must I yield? (said she)
And must the Trojans reign in Italy?
So Fate will have it; and Jove adds his force;
Nor can my power-divert their happy course.
60 Could angry Pallas, with revengeful spleen,
The Grecian navy burn, and drown the men?
. . .
70 But I, who walk in awful state above,
The majesty of heaven, the sister-wife of Jove,
For length of years my fruitless force employ
Against the thin remains of ruined Troy!
What nations now to Juno's power will pray,
Or offerings on my slighted altars lay?'
Thus raged the goddess; and with fury fraught,
The restless regions of the storms she sought,
Where, in a spacious cave of living stone,
The tyrant Æolus, from his airy throne,
80 With power imperial curbs the struggling winds,
And sounding tempests in dark prisons binds:
This way, and that, the impatient captives tend,
And, pressing for release, the mountains rend.
High in his hall the undaunted monarch stands,
And shakes his sceptre, and their rage commands;
Which did he not, their unresisted sway
Would sweep the world before them in their way;
Earth, air, and seas, through empty space would roll,
And heaven would fly before the driving soul.
90 In fear of this, the father of the gods
Confined their fury to those dark abodes,
And locked them safe within, oppressed with mountain loads:
Imposed a king with arbitrary sway,
To loose their fetters, or their force allay;
To whom the suppliant queen her prayers addressed,
And thus the tenor of her suit expressed:
'O Æolus!—for to thee the king of heaven
The power of tempests and of winds has given;
Thy force alone their fury can restrain,
100 And smooth the waves, or swell the troubled main—
A race of wandering slaves, abhorred by me,
With prosperous passage cut the Tuscan sea:
To fruitful Italy their course they steer,
And, for their vanquished gods design new temples there.

Raise all thy winds ; with night involve the skies ;
Sink or disperse my fatal enemies !
Twice seven—the charming daughters of the main,
Around my person wait, and bear my train :
Succeed my wish, and second my design ;
110 The fairest, Deiopeia, shall be thine,
And make thee father of a happy line.'
  To this the god : ' 'Tis yours, O queen ! to will
The work, which duty binds me to fulfil.
These airy kingdoms, and this wide command,
Are all the presents of your bounteous hand :
Yours is my sovereign's grace ; and as your guest,
I sit with gods at their celestial feast.
Raise tempests at your pleasure, or subdue ;
Dispose of empire, which I hold from you.'
120   He said, and hurled against the mountain side
His quivering spear, and all the god applied.
The raging winds rush through the hollow wound,
And dance aloft in air, and skim along the ground ;
Then, settling on the sea, the surges sweep,
Raise liquid mountains, and disclose the deep.
South, East, and West, with mixed confusion roar,
And roll the foaming billows to the shore.
The cables crack ; the sailors' fearful cries
Ascend ; and sable night involves the skies ;
130 And heaven itself is ravished from their eyes.
Loud peals of thunder from the poles ensue ;
Then flashing fires the transient light renew ;
The face of things a frightful image bears ;
And present death in various forms appears.
Struck with unusual fright, the Trojan chief,
With lifted hands and eyes, invokes relief ;
And, ' Thrice and four times happy those (he cried),
That under Ilian walls, before their parents, died !
Tydides, bravest of the Grecian train !
140 Why could not I by that strong arm be slain,
And lie by noble Hector on the plain,
Or great Sarpedon ; in those bloody fields,
Where Simoïs rolls the bodies and the shields
Of heroes, whose dismembered hands yet bear
The dart aloft, and clench the pointed spear ? '

145 The storm in both poets [Homer and Virgil] is described concisely,
but the images are full of terror. Homer leads the way and Virgil

DRYDEN'S AENEID

  Thus while the pious prince his fate bewails,
Fierce Boreas drove against his flying sails,
And rent the sheets : the raging billows rise,
And mount the tossing vessel to the skies ;
150 Nor can the shivering oars sustain the blow :
The galley gives her side, and turns her prow ;
While those astern, descending down the steep,
Through gaping waves behold the boiling deep.
Three ships were hurried by the southern blast,
And on the secret shelves with fury cast.

. . .

  Three more, fierce Eurus in his angry mood,
160 Dashed on the shallows of the moving sand,
And in mid ocean left them moored a-land.

. . .

168 And here and there above the waves were seen
Arms, pictures, precious goods, and floating men.

. . .

  Meantime imperial Neptune heard the sound
Of raging billows breaking on the ground.
Displeased, and fearing for his watery reign,
He reared his awful head above the main,
180 Serene in majesty,—then rolled his eyes
Around the space of earth, and seas, and skies.
He saw the Trojan fleet dispersed, distressed,
By stormy winds and wintry heaven oppressed.
Full well the god his sister's envy knew,
And what her aims and what her arts pursue.
He summoned Eurus and the western blast,
And first an angry glance on both he cast,
Then thus rebuked : ' Audacious winds ! from whence
This bold attempt, this rebel insolence ?
190 Is it for you to ravage seas and land,
Unauthorized by my supreme command ?
To raise such mountains on the troubled main ?
Whom I—but first 'tis fit the billows to restrain ;
And then you shall be taught obedience to my reign.
Hence ! to your lord my royal mandate bear—
The realms of ocean and the fields of air
Are mine, not his. By fatal lot to me
The liquid empire fell, and trident of the sea.
His power to hollow caverns is confined :
200 There let him reign the jailor of the wind,

With hoarse commands his breathing subjects call,
And boast and bluster in his empty hall.'
He spoke ; and while he spoke, he smoothed the sea,
Dispelled the darkness, and restored the day.
Cymothoë, Triton, and the sea-green train
Of beauteous nymphs, the daughters of the main,
Clear from the rocks the vessels with their hands :
The god himself with ready trident stands,
And opes the deep, and spreads the moving sands ;
210 Then heaves them off the shoals. — Where'er he guides
His finny coursers, and in triumph rides,
The waves unruffle, and the sea subsides.
As, when in tumults rise the ignoble crowd,
Mad are their motions, and their tongues are loud ;

follows in his footsteps without any deviation. Ulysses falls into lamentation, so does Aeneas; Ulysses wishes he had found a nobler death, so does Aeneas. This discovers a bravery of spirit; they lament not that they are to die, but only the inglorious manner of it. This fully answers an objection that has been made both against Homer and Virgil, who have been blamed for describing their heroes with such an air of mean-spiritedness. Drowning was esteemed by the ancients an accursed death, as it deprived their bodies of the rites of sepulture. It is no wonder that this kind of death was greatly dreaded, since it barred their entrance into the happy regions of the dead for many hundreds of years.

Pope on *Odyssey* V, 393

Note: references to Pope, here and elsewhere, are to the line numbers of his translation.

213 This I have observed of his similitudes in general, that they are not placed, as our unobserving critics tell us, in the heat of any action, but commonly in its declining. When he has warmed us in his description as much as he possibly can, then, lest that warmth should languish, he renews it by some apt similitude, which illustrates his subject, and yet palls not his audience. . . . While the storm was in its fury, any allusion had been improper; for the poet could have compared it to nothing more impetuous than itself; consequently he could have made no illustration.

Dryden 'Dedication'

And stones and brands in rattling volleys fly,
And all the rustic arms that fury can supply :
If then some grave and pious man appear,
They hush their noise, and lend a listening ear :
He soothes with sober words their angry mood,
220 And quenches their innate desire of blood :
So, when the father of the flood appears,
And o'er the seas his sovereign trident rears,
Their fury falls : he skims the liquid plains,
High on his chariot, and, with loosened reins,
Majestic moves along, and awful peace maintains.
The weary Trojans ply their shattered oars
To nearest land, and make the Libyan shores.
    Within a long recess there lies a bay :
An island shades it from the rolling sea,
230 And forms a port secure for ships to ride :
Broke by the jutting land, on either side,
In double streams the briny waters glide,
Betwixt two rows of rocks : a sylvan scene
Appears above, and groves for ever green :
A grot is formed beneath, with mossy seats,
To rest the Nereïds, and exclude the heats.
Down through the crannies of the living walls,
The crystal streams descend in murmuring falls.
No halsers need to bind the vessels here,
240 Nor bearded anchors ; for no storms they fear.
Seven ships within this happy harbour meet,
The thin remainders of the scattered fleet.
The Trojans, worn with toils, and spent with woes,
Leap on the welcome land, and seek their wished repose.

Aeneas cheers his troops

'Endure, and conquer ! Jove will soon dispose
To future good, our past and present woes.
With me, the rocks of Scylla you have tried ;
280 The inhuman Cyclops, and his den, defied.
What greater ills hereafter can you bear ?
Resume your courage, and dismiss your care :
An hour will come, with pleasure to relate
Your sorrows past, as benefits of fate.
Through various hazards and events, we move
To Latium, and the realms foredoomed by Jove.
Called to the seat (the promise of the skies)
Where Trojan kingdoms once again may rise,

Endure the hardships of your present state ;
290　Live, and reserve yourselves for better fate.'

Venus appeals to Jupiter on her son's behalf

When from aloft, almighty Jove surveys
Earth, air, and shores, and navigable seas :
310　At length, on Libyan realms he fixed his eyes :
Whom, pondering thus on human miseries,
When Venus saw, she with a lowly look,
Not free from tears, her heavenly sire bespoke :
' O king of gods and men ! whose awful hand
Disperses thunder on the seas and land ;
Disposes all with absolute command ;
How could my pious son thy power incense ?
Or what, alas ! is vanished Troy's offence ?
Our hope of Italy not only lost ;
320　On various seas by various tempests tossed,
But shut from every shore, and barred from every coast.
You promised once, a progeny divine,
Of Romans, rising from the Trojan line,
In after-times should hold the world in awe,
And to the land and ocean give the law.
How is your doom reversed, which eased my care
When Troy was ruined in that cruel war !
. . .

To whom the father of the immortal race,
Smiling, with that serene indulgent face
With which he drives the clouds and clears the skies—
First gave a holy kiss ; then thus replies :
350　' Daughter, dismiss thy fears : to thy desire,
The fates of thine are fixed, and stand entire.
Thou shalt behold thy wished Lavinian walls ;
And, ripe for heaven, when fate Æneas calls,
Then shalt thou bear him up, sublime, to me :

233　How delightful is the change of ideas from the hurry and horror of a tempest to such a sweet romantic scene. There never was a finer landscape than this charming description.

Trapp

No counsels have reversed my firm decree.
And, lest new fears disturb thy happy state,
Know, I have searched the mystic rolls of fate:
Thy son (nor is the appointed season far)
In Italy shall wage successful war:
360 Shall tame fierce nations in the bloody field;
And sovereign laws impose, and cities build;
Till, after every foe subdued, the sun
Thrice through the signs his annual race shall run
This is his time prefixed. Ascanius then,
Now called Iülus, shall begin his reign.
He, thirty rolling years the crown shall wear;
Then from Lavinium shall the seat transfer,
And with hard labour, Alba-longa build:
The throne with his succession shall be filled,
370 Three hundred circuits more: then shall be seen
Ilia the fair, a priestess and a queen,
Who, full of Mars, in time, with kindly throes,
Shall at a birth two goodly boys disclose.
The royal babes a tawny wolf shall drain:
Then Romulus his grandsire's throne shall gain,
Of martial towers the founder shall become,
The people Romans call, the city Rome.
To them no bounds of empire I assign,
Nor term of years to their immortal line.
380 E'en haughty Juno, who, with endless broils,
Earth, seas, and heaven, and Jove himself, turmoils,
At length atoned, her friendly power shall join,
To cherish and advance the Trojan line.
The subject world shall Rome's dominion own,
And, prostrate, shall adore the nation of the gown.
  An age is ripening in revolving fate,
When Troy shall overturn the Grecian state,
And sweet revenge her conquering sons shall call,
To crush the people that conspired her fall.
390 Then Cæsar from the Julian stock shall rise,
Whose empire ocean, and whose fame the skies
Alone shall bound; whom, fraught with eastern spoils,
Our heaven, the just reward of human toils,
Securely shall repay with rights divine;
And incense shall ascend before his sacred shrine.
Then dire debate, and impious war, shall cease,
And the stern age be softened into peace:
Then banished Faith shall once again return,
And Vestal fires in hallowed temples burn;

BOOK I   63

400 And Remus, with Quirinus shall sustain
    The righteous laws, and fraud and force restrain.
    Janus himself before his fane shall wait,
    And keep the dreadful issues of his gate
    With bolts and iron bars: within remains
    Imprisoned Fury, bound in brazen chains:
    High on a trophy raised, of useless arms,
    He sits, and threats the world with vain alarms.'
    He said, and sent Cyllenius with command
    To free the ports, and ope the Punic land
410 To Trojan guests; lest, ignorant of fate,
    The queen might force them from her town and state.
    . . .

420   Meantime, in shades of night Æneas lies:
    Care seized his soul, and sleep forsook his eyes.
    But when the sun restored the cheerful day,
    He rose, the coast and country to survey;
    Anxious and eager to discover more.
    It looked a wild uncultivated shore:
    But, whether human kind, or beasts alone
    Possessed the new-found region, was unknown.
    Beneath a ledge of rocks his fleet he hides:
    Tall trees surround the mountain's shady sides:
430 The bending brow above, a safe retreat provides.
    Armed with two pointed darts, he leaves his friends;
    And true Achates on his steps attends.
    Lo! in the deep recesses of the wood,
    Before his eyes his goddess mother stood:
    A huntress in her habit and her mien;
    Her dress, a maid, her air, confessed a queen.
    Bare were her knees, and knots her garments bind;
    Loose was her hair, and wantoned in the wind;
    Her hand sustained a bow; her quiver hung behind.
440 She seemed a virgin of the Spartan blood:
    With such array Harpalyce bestrode
    Her Thracian courser, and outstripped the rapid flood.

375 This is the first place where Virgil takes occasion to interweave a
    considerable part of the Roman history with his poem. It is here most
    judiciously introduced by way of prophecy, and the whole has at once
    such an elegant and majestic air as sufficiently distinguishes poetry
    from bare history.

                                                              Trapp

'Ho! strangers! have you lately seen (she said),
One of my sisters, like myself arrayed,
Who crossed the lawn, or in the forest strayed?
A painted quiver at her back she bore;
Varied with spots, a lynx's hide she wore;
And at full cry pursued the tusky boar.'
    Thus Venus: thus her son replied again:
450 'None of your sisters have we heard or seen,
O virgin! or what other name you bear
Above that style—O more than mortal fair!
Your voice and mien celestial birth betray.
If, as you seem, the sister of the day,
Or one at least of chaste Diana's train,
Let not an humble suppliant sue in vain;
But tell a stranger, long in tempests tossed,
What earth we tread, and who commands the coast?
Then on your name shall wretched mortals call,
460 And offered victims at your altars fall.'
    'I dare not (she replied) assume the name
Of goddess, or celestial honours claim;
For Tyrian virgins bows and quivers bear,
And purple buskins o'er their ankles wear.
Know, gentle youth, in Libyan lands you are
A people rude in peace, and rough in war.
The rising city, which from far you see,
Is Carthage, and a Tyrian colony.
Phœnician Dido rules the growing state;
470 Who fled from Tyre, to shun her brother's hate.
. . .
But whence are you? what country claims **your**
    birth?
510 What seek you, strangers, on our Libyan earth?'
    To whom, with sorrow streaming from his eyes,
And deeply sighing, thus her son replies:
'Could you with patience hear, or I relate,
O nymph! the tedious annals of our fate,
Through such a train of woes if I should run,
The day would sooner than the tale be done.
From ancient Troy, by force expelled, we came—
If you by chance have heard the Trojan name.
On various seas by various tempests tossed,
520 At length we landed on your Libyan coast.
The good Æneas am I called—a name,
While Fortune favoured, not unknown to **fame**.

BOOK I

My household gods, companions of my woes,
With pious care I rescued from our foes.
To fruitful Italy my course was bent;
And from the king of heaven is my descent.
With twice ten sail I crossed the Phrygian sea;
Fate and my mother-goddess led my way.
Scarce seven, the thin remainders of my fleet,
530 From storms preserved, within your harbour meet.
Myself distressed, an exile, and unknown,
Debarred from Europe, and from Asia thrown,
In Libyan deserts wander thus alone.'
  His tender parent could no longer bear,
But, interposing, sought to soothe his care.
'Whoe'er you are—not unbeloved by Heaven,
Since on our friendly shore your ships are driven—
Have courage: to the gods permit the rest,
And to the queen expose your just request.

. . .

  Thus having said, she turned, and made appear
Her neck refulgent, and dishevelled hair,
Which, flowing from her shoulders, reached the ground,
And widely spread ambrosial scents around.
560 In length of train descends her sweeping gown;
And by her graceful walk, the queen of love is known.
The prince pursued the parting deity
With words like these: 'Ah! whither do you fly?
Unkind and cruel! to deceive your son
In borrowed shapes, and his embrace to shun:
Never to bless my sight but thus, unknown;
And still to speak in accents not your own.'
Against the goddess these complaints he made,
But took the path, and her commands obeyed.
570 They march obscure; for Venus kindly shrouds
With mists their persons, and involves in clouds,
That, thus unseen, their passage none might stay,
Or force to tell the causes of their way.

. . .

556 The elegancy of this lovely description can never be too much admired, as well as the sudden and surprising turn of the discovery.
Trapp

580 They climb the next ascent, and, looking down,
Now at a nearer distance view the town.
The prince with wonder sees the stately towers
(Which late were huts, and shepherds' homely bowers),
The gates and streets ; and hears from every part
The noise and busy concourse of the mart.
The toiling Tyrians on each other call,
To ply their labour : some extend the wall ;
Some build the citadel ; the brawny throng
Or dig, or push unwieldy stones along.
590 Some for their dwellings choose a spot of ground,
Which, first designed, with ditches they surround.
Some laws ordain ; and some attend the choice
Of holy senates, and elect by voice.
Here some design a mole, while others there
Lay deep foundations for a theatre,
From marble quarries mighty columns hew,
For ornaments of scenes, and future view.
Such is their toil, and such their busy pains,
As exercise the bees in flowery plains,
600 When winter past, and summer scarce begun,
Invites them forth to labour in the sun ;
Some lead their youth abroad, while some condense
Their liquid store, and some in cells dispense :
Some at the gate stand ready to receive
The golden burden, and their friends relieve :
All, with united force, combine to drive
The lazy drones from the laborious hive.
With envy stung, they view each other's deeds :
The fragrant work with diligence proceeds.
610 'Thrice happy you, whose walls already rise !'
Æneas said, and viewed, with lifted eyes,
Their lofty towers : then entering at the gate,
Concealed in clouds (prodigious to relate),
He mixed, unmarked, among the busy throng,
Borne by the tide, and passed unseen along.
  Full in the centre of the town there stood,
Thick set with trees, a venerable wood :
The Tyrians, landing near this holy ground,
And digging here, a prosperous omen found :
620 From under earth a courser's head they drew,
Their growth and future fortune to foreshow :
This fated sign their foundress Juno gave,
Of a soil fruitful, and a people brave.
Sidonian Dido here with solemn state

BOOK I

Did Juno's temple build, and consecrate;
Enriched with gifts, and with a golden shrine;
But more the goddess made the place divine.
On brazen steps the marble threshold rose,
And brazen plates the cedar beams inclose :
630 The rafters are with brazen coverings crowned;
The lofty doors on brazen hinges sound.
What first Æneas in this place beheld,
Revived his courage, and his fears expelled.
For, while expecting there the queen, he raised
His wondering eyes, and round the temple gazed,
Admired the fortune of the rising town,
The striving artists, and their art's renown—
He saw, in order painted on the wall,
Whatever did unhappy Troy befall :
640 The wars that fame around the world had blown,
All to the life, and every leader known.
There Agamemnon, Priam here, he spies,
And fierce Achilles, who both kings defies.
He stopped, and weeping said : 'O friend, e'en here
The monuments of Trojan woes appear !
Our known disasters fill e'en foreign lands:
See there, where old unhappy Priam stands !
E'en the mute walls relate the warrior's fame,
And Trojan griefs the Tyrians' pity claim.'
650   He said—(his tears a ready passage find)
Devouring what he saw so well designed;
And with an empty picture fed his mind :
. . .

Himself he saw amidst the Grecian train,
Mixed in the bloody battle on the plain.
And swarthy Memnon in his arms he knew,
His pompous ensigns, and his Indian crew.
Penthesilea there, with haughty grace,
Leads to the wars an Amazonian race :

598 One may observe that though Homer sometimes takes his similitudes from the meanest and smallest things in nature, yet he orders it so as by their appearance to signalise and give lustre to his greatest heroes ... Virgil has imitated these humble comparisons as when he compares the builders of Carthage to bees.

Pope on *Iliad* XVI, 314

690 In their right hands a pointed dart they wield;
The left, for ward, sustains the lunar shield.
Athwart her breast a golden belt she throws,
Amidst the press alone provokes a thousand foes,
And dares her maiden arms to manly force oppose.
　Thus while the Trojan prince employs his eyes,
Fixed on the walls with wonder and surprise,
The beauteous Dido, with a numerous train,
And pomp of guards, ascends the sacred fane.
Such on Eurotas' banks, or Cynthus' height,
700 Diana seems; and so she charms the sight,
When in the dance the graceful goddess leads
The choir of nymphs, and overtops their heads.
Known by her quiver, and her lofty mien,
She walks majestic, and she looks their queen:
Latona sees her shine above the rest,
And feeds with secret joy her silent breast.
Such Dido was; with such becoming state,
Amidst the crowd, she walks serenely great.

. . .

　Another way by chance Æneas bends
His eyes, and unexpected sees his friends,
Antheus, Sergestus brave, Cloanthus strong,
720 And at their backs a mighty Trojan throng,
Whom late the tempest on the billows tossed,
And widely scattered on another coast.
The prince, unseen, surprised with wonder stands,
And longs, with joyful haste, to join their hands;
But, doubtful of the wished event, he stays,
And from the hollow cloud his friends surveys,
Impatient, till they told their present state,
And where they left their ships, and what their fate,
And why they came, and what was their request:
730 For these were sent commissioned by the rest,
To sue for leave to land their sickly men,
And gain admission to the gracious queen.
Entering, with cries they filled the holy fane;
Then thus, with lowly voice, Ilioneus began:
'O queen! indulged by favour of the gods
To found an empire in these new abodes;
To build a town; with statutes to restrain
The wild inhabitants beneath thy reign:
We wretched Trojans, tossed on every shore,
740 From sea to sea, thy clemency implore!

Forbid the fires our shipping to deface:
Receive the unhappy fugitives to grace,
And spare the remnant of a pious race!
We come not with design of wasteful prey,
To drive the country, force the swains away :
Nor such our strength, nor such is our desire:
The vanquished dare not to such thoughts aspire.
A land there is, Hesperia named of old—
. . .
751 Now called Italia, from the leader's name.
To that sweet region was our voyage bent,
When winds and every warring element
Disturbed our course, and, far from sight of land
Cast our torn vessels on the moving sand.
The sea came on ; the South, with mighty roar,
Dispersed and dashed the rest upon the rocky shore.
Those few you see, escaped the storm, and fear
(Unless you interpose) a shipwreck here.'
. . .
The modest queen awhile, with downcast eyes,
Pondered the speech, then briefly thus replies :
790 'Trojans ! dismiss your fears : my cruel fate,
And doubts attending an unsettled state,
Force me to guard my coast from foreign foes.
Who has not heard the story of your woes,
The name and fortune of your native place,
The fame and valour of the Phrygian race?
. . .
And would to heaven, the storm you felt would bring
On Carthaginian coasts your wandering king.
My people shall, by my command, explore
The ports and creeks of every winding shore,
810 And towns, and wilds, and shady woods, in quest
Of so renowned, and so desired a guest.'
. . .
The Trojan chief appeared in open sight,
August in visage, and serenely bright.
His mother-goddess, with her hands divine,
Had formed his curling locks, and made his temples shine,
And given his rolling eyes a sparkling grace,
And breathed a youthful vigour on his face ;
830 Like polished ivory, beauteous to behold,
Or Parian marble, when enchased in gold:

Thus radiant from the circling cloud he broke;
And thus with manly modesty he spoke:
'He whom you seek am I; by tempests tossed,
And saved from shipwreck on your Libyan coast
Presenting, gracious queen, before your throne,
A prince that owes his life to you alone:
Fair majesty! the refuge and redress
Of those whom fate pursues, and wants oppress!
840 You, who your pious offices employ
To save the relics of abandoned Troy;
Receive the shipwrecked on your friendly shore;
With hospitable rites relieve the poor;
Associate in your town a wandering train,
And strangers in your palace entertain.
What thanks can wretched fugitives return,
Who, scattered through the world in exile mourn?
The gods (if gods to goodness are inclined:
If acts of mercy touch their heavenly mind),
850 And, more than all the gods, your generous heart,
Conscious of worth, requite its own desert!
In you this age is happy, and this earth;
And parents more than mortal gave you birth.
While rolling rivers into seas shall run,
And round the space of heaven the radiant sun;
While trees the mountain-tops with shades supply,
Your honour, name, and praise, shall never die.
Whate'er abode my fortune has assigned,
Your image shall be present in my mind.'

. . .

The Tyrian queen stood fixed upon his face,
Pleased with his motions, ravished with his grace;
Admired his fortunes, more admired the man;
Then re-collected stood, and thus began:
870 'What fate, O goddess-born! what angry powers
Have cast you shipwrecked on our barren shores?
Are you the great Æneas, known to fame,
Who from celestial seed your lineage claim?
The same Æneas, whom fair Venus bore
To famed Anchises on the Idæan shore?

. . .

Enter, my noble guest! and you shall find,
If not a costly welcome, yet a kind:
For I myself, like you, have been distressed,

    Till Heaven afforded me this place of rest:
890 Like you, an alien in a land unknown,
    I learn to pity woes so like my own.'
    She said, and to the palace led her guest;
    . . .
    And sumptuous feasts are made in splendid halls:
    On Tyrian carpets, richly wrought, they dine;
    With loads of massy plate the sideboards shine,
    And antique vases all of gold, embossed
    (The gold itself inferior to the cost
    Of curious work), where on the sides were seen
    The fights and figures of illustrious men,
    From their first founder to the present queen.
        The good Æneas, whose paternal care
910 Iülus' absence could no longer bear,
    Dispatched Achates to the ships in haste,
    To give a glad relation of the past,
    And, fraught with precious gifts, to bring the boy,
    Snatched from the ruins of unhappy Troy.
    A robe of tissue, stiff with golden wire;
    An upper vest, once Helen's rich attire,
    From Argos by the famed adult'ress brought,
    With golden flowers and winding foliage wrought:
    Her mother Leda's present, when she came
920 To ruin Troy, and set the world on flame;
    The sceptre Priam's eldest daughter bore,
    Her orient necklace, and the crown she wore
    Of double texture, glorious to behold:
    One order set with gems, and one with gold.
    Instructed thus, the wise Achates goes,
    And, in his diligence, his duty shews.
        But Venus, anxious for her son's affairs,
    New counsels tries, and new designs prepares:
    That Cupid should assume the shape and face
930 Of sweet Ascanius, and the sprightly grace;
    Should bring the presents, in her nephew's stead,
    And in Eliza's veins the gentle poison shed:
    For much she feared the Tyrians, double-tongued:
    And knew the town to Juno's care belonged.
    . . .

        The goddess then to young Ascanius flies,
970 And in a pleasing slumber seals his eyes:
    Lulled in her lap, amidst a train of Loves,

She gently bears him to her blissful groves;
Then with a wreath of myrtle crowns his head,
And softly lays him on a flowery bed.
Cupid meantime assumed his form and face,
Following Achates with a shorter pace,
And brought the gifts. The queen already sat
Amidst the Trojan lords, in shining state,
High on a golden bed : her princely guest
980 Was next her side; in order sat the rest.
Then canisters with bread are heaped on high :
The attendants water for their hands supply,
And, having washed, with silken towels dry.
Next fifty handmaids in long order bore
The censers, and with fumes the gods adore;
Then youths and virgins, twice as many, join
To place the dishes, and to serve the wine.
The Tyrian train, admitted to the feast,
Approach, and on the painted couches rest.
990 All on the Trojan gifts with wonder gaze,
But view the beauteous boy with more amaze;
His rosy-coloured cheeks, his radiant eyes,
His motions, voice, and shape, and all the god's disguise;
Nor pass unpraised the vest and veil divine,
Which wandering foliage and rich flowers entwine.
But far above the rest, the royal dame
(Already doomed to love's disastrous flame),
With eyes insatiate, and tumultuous joy,
Beholds the presents, and admires the boy.
1000 The guileful god about the hero, long,
With children's play, and false embraces, hung;
Then sought the queen : she took him to her arms
With greedy pleasure, and devoured his charms.
Unhappy Dido little thought, what guest,
How dire a god she drew so near her breast.
But he, not mindless of his mother's prayer,
Works in the pliant bosom of the fair,
And moulds her heart anew, and blots her former care.
The dead is to the living love resigned ;
1010 And all Æneas enters in her mind.
 Now, when the rage of hunger was appeased,
The meat removed, and every guest was pleased,
The golden bowls with sparkling wine are crowned,
And through the palace cheerful cries resound.
From gilded roofs depending lamps display
Nocturnal beams, that emulate the day.

BOOK I

A golden bowl, that shone with gems divine,
The queen commanded to be crowned with wine—
The bowl that Belus used, and all the Tyrian line.
1020 Then, silence through the hall proclaimed, she spoke:
'O hospitable Jove! we thus invoke
With solemn rites, thy sacred name and power:
Bless to both nations this auspicious hour!
So may the Trojan and the Tyrian line
In lasting concord from this day combine.
Thou, Bacchus, god of joys and friendly cheer,
And gracious Juno, both, be present here!
And you, my lords of Tyre, your vows address
To heaven with mine, to ratify the peace.'
1030 The goblet then she took, with nectar crowned
(Sprinkling the first libations on the ground),
And raised it to her mouth with sober grace,
Then, sipping, offered to the next in place.
. . .
The unhappy queen with talk prolonged the night,
1050 And drank large draughts of love with vast delight:
Of Priam much inquired, of Hector more;
. . .

At length, as Fate and her ill stars required,
To hear the series of the war desired.
'Relate at large, my godlike guest (she said),
The Grecian stratagems, the town betrayed:
The fatal issue of so long a war,
Your flight, your wanderings, and your woes declare:
For, since on every sea, on every coast,
Your men have been distressed, your navy tossed,
Seven times the sun has either tropic viewed,
The winter banished, and the spring renewed.'

BOOK II

THE ARGUMENT

Æneas relates how the city of Troy was taken, after a ten years' siege, by the treachery of Sinon, and the stratagem of a wooden horse. He declares the fixed resolution he had taken not to survive the ruin of his country, and the various adventures he met with in the defence of it. At last, having been before advised by Hector's ghost, and now by the appearance of his mother Venus, he is prevailed upon to leave the town, and settle his household gods in another country. In order to this, he carries off his father on his shoulders, and leads his little son by the hand, his wife following him behind. When he comes to the place appointed for the general rendezvous, he finds a great confluence of people, but misses his wife, whose ghost afterwards appears to him, and tells him the land which was designed for him.

ALL were attentive to the godlike man,
When from his lofty couch he thus began:
'Great queen, what you command me to relate,
Renews the sad remembrance of our fate:
An empire from its old foundations rent,
And every woe the Trojans underwent;
A peopled city made a desert place;
All that I saw, and part of which I was;
Not e'en the hardest of our foes could hear,
10 Nor stern Ulysses tell, without a tear.
And now the latter watch of wasting night,
And setting stars, to kindly rest invite.
But since you take such interest in our woe,
And Troy's disastrous end desire to know,
I will restrain my tears, and briefly tell
What in our last and fatal night befell.
 By destiny compelled, and in despair,
The Greeks grew weary of the tedious war,
And by Minerva's aid, a fabric reared,
20 Which like a steed of monstrous height appeared:
The sides were planked with pine: they feigned it made
For their return, and this the vow they paid.
Thus they pretend; but in the hollow side,
Selected numbers of their soldiers hide:
With inward arms the dire machine they load;
And iron bowels stuff the dark abode.
In sight of Troy lies Tenedos, an isle
(While Fortune did on Priam's empire smile)
Renowned for wealth; but since, a faithless bay,
30 Where ships exposed to wind and weather lay.

There was their fleet concealed. We thought, for Greece,
Their sails were hoisted, and our fears release.
The Trojans, cooped within their walls so long,
Unbar their gates, and issue in a throng
Like swarming bees, and with delight survey
The camp deserted, where the Grecians lay :
The quarters of the several chiefs they showed :
Here Phœnix, here Achilles, made abode ;
Here joined the battles ; there the navy rode.
40 Part on the pile their wondering eyes employ—
The pile by Pallas raised to ruin Troy.
Thymœtes first ('tis doubtful whether hired,
Or so the Trojan destiny required)
Moved that the ramparts might be broken down,
To lodge the monster fabric in the town.
But Capys, and the rest of sounder mind,
The fatal present to the flames designed,
Or to the watery deep : at least to bore
The hollow sides, and hidden frauds explore.
50 The giddy vulgar, as their fancies guide,
With noise say nothing, and in parts divide.
Laocoön, followed by a numerous crowd,
Ran from the fort, and cried from far, aloud :

1   The destruction of an ancient, populous city, with all those scenes of devastation, sorrow and misery that must attend it, is one of the most striking objects in the world. Virgil accordingly chose it as the properest subject imaginable to move the passions of pity and terror, and surely he hath succeeded to his wish. One cannot but think that he was particularly pleased with this subject as it happened to be left untouched by Homer. Our poet however hath borrowed many fine hints and affecting circumstances from two tragedies of Euripides, the *Troades* and the *Hecuba*. Virgil in general seemeth to have been a great reader and lover of the works of this noble tragedian. And indeed these two writers seem to have nearly resembled each other in their genius and manner. Both were remarkable for brevity, and an elegant simplicity of style; both were of a tender temper and particularly skilled in moving the passions.

Warton

34– This is human nature in perfection. Nothing could be more proper in
39   the writer or more pleasant in the reader.

Trapp

"O wretched countrymen ! what fury reigns?
What more than madness has possessed your brains?
Think you the Grecians from your coasts are gone?
And are Ulysses' arts no better known?

This hollow fabric either must inclose
Within its blind recess, our secret foes ;
60 Or 'tis an engine raised above the town
To overlook the walls, and then to batter down.
Somewhat is sure designed by fraud or force :
Trust not their presents, nor admit the horse."
Thus having said, against the steed he threw
His forceful spear, which, hissing as it flew,
Pierced through the yielding planks of jointed wood.
And trembling in the hollow belly stood.
The sides, transpierced, return a rattling sound ;
And groans of Greeks inclosed come issuing through
    the wound.
70 And had not Heaven the fall of Troy designed,
Or had not men been fated to be blind,
Enough was said and done t' inspire a better mind.
Then had our lances pierced the treacherous wood,
And Ilian towers and Priam's empire stood.
  Meantime, with shouts, the Trojan shepherds bring
A captive Greek in bands, before the king—
Taken, to take—who made himself their prey
To impose on their belief, and Troy betray :
Fixed on his aim, and obstinately bent
80 To die undaunted, or to circumvent.
About the captive, tides of Trojans flow ;
All press to see, and some insult the foe.
Now hear how well the Greeks their wiles disguised :
Behold a nation in a man comprised !
Trembling the miscreant stood : unarmed and bound,
He stared, and rolled his haggard eyes around,
Then said, "Alas ! what earth remains, what sea,
Is open to receive unhappy me?
What fate a wretched fugitive attends,
90 Scorned by my foes, abandoned by my friends?"
He said, and sighed, and cast a rueful eye :
Our pity kindles, and our passions die.
We cheer the youth to make his own defence,
And freely tell us what he was, and whence :
What news he could impart we long to know,
And what to credit from a captive foe.

His fear at length dismissed, he said, "Whate'er
My fate ordains, my words shall be sincere;
I neither can nor dare my birth disclaim;
100 Greece is my country, Sinon is my name:
Though plunged by Fortune's power in misery,
'Tis not in Fortune's power to make me lie.
If any chance has hither brought the name
Of Palamedes, not unknown to fame,
Who suffered from the malice of the times,
Accused and sentenced for pretended crimes,
Because these fatal wars he would prevent:
Whose death the wretched Greeks too late lament.
Me, then a boy, my father, poor and bare
110 Of other means, committed to his care,
His kinsman and companion in the war.
While fortune favoured, while his arms support
The cause, and ruled the counsels of the court,
I made some figure there; nor was my name
Obscure, nor I without my share of fame.
But when Ulysses, with fallacious arts,
Had made impression in the people's hearts,
And forged a treason in my patron's name.
(I speak of things too far divulged by fame),
120 My kinsman fell. Then I, without support,
In private mourned his loss, and left the court.
Mad as I was, I could not bear his fate
With silent grief, but loudly blamed the state,
And cursed the direful author of my woes.—
'Twas told again; and hence my ruin rose.
I threatened, if indulgent Heaven once more
Would land me safely on my native shore,
His death with double vengeance to restore.
This moved the murderer's hate; and soon ensued

75   Here comes Sinon upon the stage, and the plot which is to be managed by his conduct. In describing his art Virgil has given sufficient proof of his own. I believe it may with truth be affirmed that there is not one single instance in any author, ancient or modern, which exceeds or even equals it. This may appear from a detail of particulars. We rarely suspect those who we heartily pity. Sinon therefore, by the first words he speaks endeavours to move compassion; and he does it most cunningly in that abrupt manner and by way of exclamation which is less suspicious than the formality of a set speech.
Trapp

130 The effects of malice from a man so proud.
Ambiguous rumours through the camp he spread,
And sought, by treason, my devoted head;
New crimes invented; left unturned no stone,
To make my guilt appear, and hide his own;
Till Calchas was by force and threatening wrought—
But why—why dwell I on that anxious thought?
If on my nation just revenge you seek.
(And 'tis to appear a foe, to appear a Greek);
Already you my name and country know:
140 Assuage your thirst of blood, and strike the blow:
My death will both the kingly brothers please,
And set insatiate Ithacus at ease."
This fair unfinished tale, these broken starts,
Raised expectations in our longing hearts;
Unknowing as we were in Grecian arts.
His former trembling once again renewed,
With acted fear, the villain thus pursued:
" Long had the Grecians (tired with fruitless care
And wearied with an unsuccessful war)
150 Resolved to raise the siege, and leave the town;
And had the gods permitted, they had gone.
But oft the wintry seas, and southern winds,
Withstood their passage home, and changed their minds,
Portents and prodigies their souls amazed;
But most, when this stupendous pile was raised;
Then flaming meteors, hung in air, were seen,
And thunders rattled through a sky serene.
Dismayed, and fearful of some dire event,
Eurypylus, to inquire their fate, was sent.
160 He from the gods this dreadful answer brought:
'O Grecians, when the Trojan shores you sought,
Your passage with a virgin's blood was bought:
So must your safe return be bought again,
And Grecian blood once more atone the main.'
The spreading rumour round the people ran;
All feared, and each believed himself the man.
Ulysses took the advantage of their fright;
Called Calchas, and produced in open sight;
Then bade him name the wretch, ordained by fate
170 The public victim, to redeem the state.
Already some presaged the dire event,
And saw what sacrifice Ulysses meant.
For twice five days, the good old seer withstood
The intended treason, and was dumb to blood,

Till, tired with endless clamours and pursuit
Of Ithacus, he stood no longer mute,
But, as it was agreed, pronounced that I
Was destined by the wrathful gods to die.
All praised the sentence, pleased the storm should fall
180 On one alone, whose fury threatened all.
The dismal day was come; the priests prepare
Their leavened cakes, and fillets for my hair.
I followed nature's laws, and must avow,
I broke my bonds, and fled the fatal blow.
Hid in a weedy lake all night I lay,
Secure of safety when they sailed away.
But now, what further hopes for me remain
To see my friends, or native soil again;
My tender infants, or my careful sire,
190 Whom they, returning, will to death require;
Will perpetrate on them their first design,
And take the forfeit of their heads for mine?
Which, O! if pity mortal minds can move,
If there be faith below, or gods above,
If innocence and truth can claim desert,
Ye Trojans, from an injured wretch avert!"
 False tears true pity move: the king commands
To loose his fetters, and unbind his hands;
Then adds these friendly words: "Dismiss thy fears;
200 Forget the Greeks; be mine as thou wert theirs;
But truly tell, was it for force or guile,
Or some religious end, you raised the pile?"
Thus said the king. He, full of fraudful arts,
This well-invented tale for truth imparts:

136 The art of breaking off in the middle of a sentence and interrupting himself with that question, to add to the impatience of his hearers, and his bidding them to take his life to gratify their mortal enemies, is admirable for reasons too plain to be insisted upon.
                 Trapp

148 This long formal story has such a mixture of religion and prodigy and distress, which last is exceedingly heightened by the solemn horror of an intended human sacrifice, that nothing could have been better calculated to amuse and confound the understanding of those who were already in great amazement.
                 Trapp

"Ye lamps of heaven! (he said, and lifted high
His hands, now free) Thou venerable sky!
Inviolable powers, adored with dread!
Ye fatal fillets, that once bound this head!
Ye sacred altars, from whose flames I fled!
Be all of you adjured; and grant I may
Without a crime, the ungrateful Greeks betray,
Reveal the secrets of the guilty state,
And justly punish whom I justly hate!
But you, O king! preserve the faith you gave,
If I to save myself, your empire save.
The Grecian hopes, and all the attempts they made,
Were only founded on Minerva's aid.
But from the time when impious Diomede,
And false Ulysses, that inventive head,
Her fatal image from the temple drew,
The sleeping guardians of the castle slew,
Her virgin statue with their bloody hands
Polluted, and profaned her holy bands;
From thence the tide of fortune left their shore,
And ebbed much faster than it flowed before:
Their courage languished, as their hopes decayed;
And Pallas, now averse, refused her aid.
Nor did the goddess doubtfully declare
Her altered mind, and alienated care.
When first her fatal image touched the ground,
She sternly cast her glaring eyes around,
That sparkled as they rolled, and seemed to threat:
Her heavenly limbs distilled a briny sweat.
Thrice from the ground she leaped, was seen to wield
Her brandished lance, and shake her horrid shield.
Then Calchas bade our host for flight prepare,
And hope no conquest from the tedious war,
Till first they sailed for Greece; with prayers besought
Her injured power, and better omens brought.
And now their navy ploughs the watery main,
Yet soon expect it on your shores again,
With Pallas pleased; as Calchas did ordain.
But first, to reconcile the blue-eyed maid
For her stolen statue and her tower betrayed,
Warned by the seer, to her offended name
We raised and dedicate this wondrous frame,
So lofty, lest through your forbidden gates
It pass, and intercept our better fates:
For, once admitted there, our hopes are lost;

250 And Troy may then a new Palladium boast:
For so religion and the gods ordain,
That, if you violate with hands profane
Minerva's gift, your town in flames shall burn;
(Which omen, O ye gods, on Græcia turn!)
But if it climb, with your assisting hands,
The Trojan walls, and in the city stands;
Then Troy shall Argos and Mycenæ burn,
And the reverse of fate on us return."
With such deceits he gained their easy hearts,
260 Too prone to credit his perfidious arts.
What Diomede, nor Thetis' greater son,
A thousand ships, nor ten years' siege, had done—
False tears and fawning words the city won.
A greater omen, and of worse portent,
Did our unwary minds with fear torment,
Concurring to produce the dire event.
Laocoön, Neptune's priest by lot that year,

258 He neither commends them for not having done the one, nor advises them to do the other. He only lays both before their eyes, and tells them the consequences of each, leaving the rest to their own choice and judgement. This is the more persuasive for not being in the form of a persuasion. There is a certain pride in human nature, which is flattered by being supposed to act of its own accord and by its own prudence rather than by advice. Besides Sinon having but a few minutes before been an enemy and a captive and being still a stranger, it would more especially have ill become him to be an adviser, and therefore he cunningly insinuates what he would have them do, not directly prescribes it.

Trapp

264 This amazing incident is extremely well timed and most properly introduced to confirm their belief and push them on to the immediate execution of Sinon's plot. And this very much contributes to salve the reputation of the Trojans, who otherwise, notwithstanding the exquisite art of Sinon's speeches and the plausible stories he had told them cannot well escape the censure of great weakness and credulity. Nor can it indeed even with this excuse unless we recur to the decrees of fate, which accordingly Virgil takes care in other places to mention.

Trapp

With solemn pomp then sacrificed a steer;
When (dreadful to behold!) from sea we spied
270 Two serpents, ranked abreast, the seas divide,
And smoothly sweep along the swelling tide.
Their flaming crests above the waves they shew;
Their bellies seem to burn the seas below;
Their speckled tails advance to steer their course,
And on the sounding shore the flying billows force.
And now the strand, and now the plain, they held:
Their ardent eyes with bloody streaks were filled;
Their nimble tongues they brandished as they came,
And licked their hissing jaws, that sputtered flame.
280 We fled amazed; their destined way they take,
And to Laocoön and his children make:
And first around the tender boys they wind,
Then with their sharpened fangs their limbs and bodies grind.
The wretched father, running to their aid
With pious haste, but vain, they next invade:
Twice round his waist their winding volumes rolled;
And twice about his gasping throat they fold.
The priest thus doubly choked—their crests divide,
And towering o'er his head in triumph ride.
290 With both his hands he labours at the knots;
His holy fillets the blue venom blots;
His roaring fills the flitting air around.
Thus, when an ox receives a glancing wound,
He breaks his bands, the fatal altar flies,
And with loud bellowings breaks the yielding skies.
Their tasks performed, the serpents quit their prey,
And to the tower of Pallas make their way:
Couched at her feet they lie, protected there
By her large buckler, and protended spear.
300   Amazement seizes all: the general cry
Proclaims Laocoön justly doomed to die,
Whose hand the will of Pallas had withstood,
And dared to violate the sacred wood.
All vote to admit the steed; that vows be paid,
And incense offered, to the offended maid.
A spacious breach is made: the town lies bare:
Some hoisting-levers, some the wheels prepare,
And fasten to the horse's feet: the rest
With cables haul along the unwieldy beast.
310 Each on his fellow for assistance calls:
At length, the fatal fabric mounts the walls,

Big with destruction.   Boys with chaplets crowned,
And choirs of virgins, sing and dance around.
Thus raised aloft, and then descending down,
It enters o'er our heads, and threats the town.
O sacred city, built by hands divine !
O valiant heroes of the Trojan line !
Four times he struck : as oft the clashing sound
Of arms was heard, and inward groans rebound.
320 Yet mad with zeal, and blinded with our fate,
We haul along the horse in solemn state ;
Then place the dire portent within the tower.
Cassandra cried, and cursed the unhappy hour ;
Foretold our fate ; but, by the god's decree,
All heard, and none believed the prophecy.
With branches we the fanes adorn, and waste
In jollity the day ordained to be the last.
    Meantime the rapid heavens rolled down the light,
And on the shaded ocean rushed the night :
330 Our men, secure, nor guards nor sentries held ;
But easy sleep their weary limbs compelled.
The Grecians had embarked their naval powers
From Tenedos, and sought our well-known shores,
Safe under covert of the silent night,
And guided by the imperial galley's light ;
When Sinon, favoured by the partial gods,
Unlocked the horse, and oped his dark abodes ;
Restored to vital air our hidden foes,
Who joyful from their long confinement rose.
340 Thessander bold, and Sthenelus their guide,
And dire Ulysses, down the cable slide :
Then Thoas, Athamas, and Pyrrhus, haste ;

282   This is one of the finest and noblest descriptions that ever was made. It is rarely if at all exceeded by Virgil himself and equalled by nobody else ... 'tis impossible to read without the most agreeable horror and astonishment. There is an ancient statue of Laocoon whence Virgil is supposed to have taken this description.

Trapp

323   An ordinary writer ... would probably have told us what she said, and that in a long speech too; but Virgil knew better.

Trapp

Nor was the Podalirian hero last,
Nor injured Menelaüs, nor the famed
Epeus, who the fatal engine framed.
A nameless crowd succeed ; their forces join
To invade the town, oppressed with sleep and wine.
Those few they find awake, first meet their fate ;
Then to their fellows they unbar the gate.
350 'Twas in the dead of night, when sleep repairs
Our bodies, worn with toils, our minds, with cares,
When Hector's ghost before my sight appears :
A bloody shroud he seemed, and bathed in tears ;
Such as he was, when, by Pelides slain,
Thessalian coursers dragged him o'er the plain.
Swoln were his feet, as when the thongs were thrust
Through the bored holes : his body black with dust :
Unlike that Hector who returned from toils
Of war, triumphant in Æacian spoils ;
360 Or him, who made the fainting Greeks retire,
And launched against their navy Phrygian fire.
His hair and beard stood stiffened with his gore ;
And all the wounds he for his country bore
Now streamed afresh, and with new purple ran.
I wept to see the visionary man,
And, while my trance continued, thus began :
"O light of Trojans, and support of Troy,
Thy father's champion, and thy country's joy !
O, long expected by thy friends ! from whence
370 Art thou so late returned for our defence ?
Do we behold thee, wearied as we are
With length of labours, and with toils of war ?
After so many funerals of thy own,
Art thou restored to thy declining town ?
But say, what wounds are these ? what new disgrace
Deforms the manly features of thy face ?"
To this, the spectre no reply did frame,
But answered to the cause for which he came ;
And, groaning from the bottom of his breast,
380 This warning, in these mournful words, expressed :
"O goddess-born ! escape, by timely flight,
The flames and horrors of this fatal night.
The foes already have possessed the wall :
Troy nods from high, and totters to her fall.
Enough is paid to Priam's royal name,
More than enough to duty and to fame.

> If by a mortal hand my father's throne
> Could be defended, 'twas by mine alone.
> Now Troy to thee commends her future state,
> And gives her gods companions of thy fate;
> From their assistance, happier walls expect,
> Which wand'ring long, at last thou shalt erect."

He said, and brought me, from their blest abodes,
The venerable statues of the gods;
With ancient Vesta from the sacred choir,
The wreaths and relics of the immortal fire.

    Now peals of shouts came thundering from afar,
Cries, threats, and loud laments, and mingled war:
The noise approaches, though our palace stood
Aloof from streets, encompassed with a wood.
Louder, and yet more loud, I hear the alarms
Of human cries, distinct, and clashing arms.
Fear broke my slumbers; I no longer stay,
But mount the terrace, thence the town survey,
And hearken, what the frightful sounds convey.
Thus, when a flood of fire by wind is borne,
Crackling it rolls, and mows the standing corn;
Or deluges, descending on the plains,
Sweep o'er the yellow year, destroy the pains
Of lab'ring oxen, and the peasant's gains;
Unroot the forest oaks, and bear away
Flocks, folds, and trees, an undistinguished prey:
The shepherd climbs the cliff, and sees from far
The wasteful ravage of the watery war.

    Then Hector's faith was manifestly cleared;
And Grecian frauds in open light appeared.
The palace of Deïphobus ascends

---

352 Whoever considers the character of Hector, the heroic virtue as well as heroic bravery, the conjugal, filial and paternal piety of that excellent prince, will be the more sensibly touched with the unutterable pathos of this description; with the questions which Aeneas asks and with the no reply which his friend makes. Such a spirit of sadness reigns through the whole, as is only to be felt but cannot be expressed. Then was there ever such a visionary scene to introduce such a real one? The dismal transition from the one to the other is inexpressibly affecting; the hero is waked from his frightful dream by that which fulfils it.

Trapp

In smoky flames, and catches on his friends'.
Ucalegon's burns next: the seas are bright
420 With splendour not their own, and shine with Trojan light.
New clamours and new clangours now arise,
The sound of trumpets mixed with fighting-cries.
With frenzy seized, I run to meet the alarms,
Resolved on death, resolved to die in arms,
But first to gather friends, with them to oppose
(If fortune favoured) and repel the foes:
Spurred by my courage, by my country fired
With sense of honour, and revenge inspired.

. . .

What tongue can tell the slaughter of that night?
What eyes can weep the sorrows and affright?
490 An ancient and imperial city falls;
The streets are filled with frequent funerals;
Houses and holy temples float in blood;
And hostile nations make a common flood.
Not only Trojans fall; but, in their turn,
The vanquished triumph, and the victors mourn.
Ours take new courage from despair and night.
Confused the fortune is, confused the fight.
All parts resound with tumults, plaints, and fears;
And grisly death in sundry shapes appears.

. . .

A postern-door, yet unobserved and free,
620 Joined by the length of a blind gallery,
To the king's closet led (a way well-known
To Hector's wife, while Priam held the throne—
Through which she brought Astyanax, unseen,
To cheer his grandsire, and his grandsire's queen).

. . .

Before the gate stood Pyrrhus, threatening loud,
640 With glittering arms conspicuous in the crowd.
So shines, renewed in youth, the crested snake
Who slept the winter in a thorny brake,
And casting off his slough when spring returns,
Now looks aloft, and with new glory burns,
Restored with poisonous herbs; his ardent sides
Reflect the sun; and, raised on spires, he rides
High o'er the grass: hissing he rolls along,
And brandishes by fits his forky tongue.

Proud Periphas, and fierce Automedon,
650 His father's charioteer, together run
To force the gate : the Scyrian infantry
Rush on in crowds, and the barred passage free.
Entering the court, with shouts the skies they rend,
And flaming firebrands to the roofs ascend.
Himself, among the foremost, deals his blows,
And with his axe repeated strokes bestows
On the strong doors : then all their shoulders ply,
Till from the posts the brazen hinges fly.
He hews apace : the double bars at length
660 Yield to his axe, and unresisted strength.
A mighty breach is made ; the rooms concealed,
Appear, and all the palace is revealed :
The halls of audience, and of public state,
And where the lonely queen in secret sat.
    Armed soldiers now by trembling maids are seen,
With not a door, and scarce a space between.
The house is filled with loud laments and cries ;
And shrieks of women rend the vaulted skies.
The fearful matrons run from place to place,
670 And kiss the thresholds, and the posts embrace.
The fatal work inhuman Pyrrhus plies ;
And all his father sparkles in his eyes.
No bars nor fighting guards his force sustain :
The bars are broken, and the guards are slain.
In rush the Greeks, and all the apartments fill ;
Those few defendants whom they find, they kill.
Not with so fierce a rage, the foaming flood
Roars when he finds his rapid course withstood,
Bears down the dams with unresisted sway,
680 And sweeps the cattle and the cots away.

623 This cool image of natural affection, brought in by the way, is very proper to vary the scene of warlike fire and fury. Monsieur Segrais has another, and that a very judicious and material remark upon it, viz. that the addition of this pathetical circumstance takes off from the littleness of such an idea as an entry and a back door, which is extremely artful in the poet. The same he says concerning that circumstance of the tower afterwards mentioned, that from thence they had a prospect of all the city and of the Grecian camp and navy. And these he produces as speciments of Virgil's skill and judgement in elevating little things and giving them an heroic turn.

Trapp

These eyes beheld him when he marched between
The brother-kings: I saw the unhappy queen,
The hundred wives, and where old Priam stood,
To stain his hallowed altar with his blood.
The fifty nuptial beds (such hopes had he,
So large a promise of a progeny),
The posts of plated gold, and hung with spoils.
Fell the reward of the proud victor's toils.
Where'er the raging fire had left a space,
690 The Grecians enter, and possess the place.
    Perhaps you may of Priam's fate inquire.
He, when he saw his regal town on fire,
His ruined palace, and his entering foes,
On every side, inevitable woes:
In arms disused invests his limbs, decayed
Like them with age: a late and useless aid.
His feeble shoulders scarce the weight sustain:
Loaded, not armed, he creeps along with pain,
Despairing of success, ambitious to be slain!
700 Uncovered but by heaven, there stood in view
An altar: near the hearth a laurel grew,
Doddered with age, whose boughs encompass round
The household gods, and shade the holy ground.
Here Hecuba, with all her helpless train
Of dames, for shelter sought, but sought in vain.
Driven like a flock of doves along the sky,
Their images they hug, and to their altars fly.
The queen, when she beheld her trembling lord,
And hanging by his side a heavy sword:
710 " What rage (she cried) has seized my husband's mind?
What arms are these, and to what use designed?
These times want other aids! Were Hector here,
E'en Hector now in vain, like Priam, would appear.
With us, one common shelter thou shalt find,
Or in one common fate with us be joined."
She said, and with a last salute embraced
The poor old man, and by the laurel placed.
Behold! Polites, one of Priam's sons,
Pursued by Pyrrhus, there for safety runs.
720 Through swords and foes, amazed and hurt, he flies
Through empty courts, and open galleries.
Him Pyrrhus, urging with his lance, pursues,
And often reaches, and his thrusts renews.
The youth, transfixed, with lamentable cries
Expires before his wretched parents' eyes:

Whom gasping at his feet when Priam saw,
The fear of death gave place to Nature's law ;
And, shaking more with anger than with age :
"The gods (said he) requite thy brutal rage !
730 (As sure they will, barbarian, sure they must,
If there be gods in heaven, and gods be just)
Who takest in wrongs an insolent delight ;
With a son's death to infect a father's sight.
Not he, whom thou and lying fame conspire
To call thee his—not he, thy vaunted sire
Thus used my wretched age : the gods he feared,
The laws of nature and of nations heard.
He cheered my sorrows, and, for sums of gold,
The bloodless carcase of my Hector sold ;
740 Pitied the woes a parent underwent,
And sent me back in safety from his tent."
   This said, his feeble hand a javelin threw,
Which, fluttering, seemed to loiter as it flew :
Just, and but barely, to the mark it held,
And faintly tinkled on the brazen shield.
   Then Pyrrhus thus : " Go thou from me to fate,
And to my father my foul deeds relate.
Now die !" With that he dragged the trembling sire,
Sliddering through clottered blood and holy mire
750 (The mingled paste his murdered son had made),
Hauled from beneath the violated shade,
And on the sacred pile the royal victim laid.
His right hand held his bloody falchion bare ;
His left he twisted in his hoary hair ;
Then, with a speeding thrust his heart he found :
The lukewarm blood came rushing through the wound,
And sanguine streams distained the sacred ground.
Thus Priam fell, and shared one common fate
With Troy in ashes, and his ruined state :
760 He, who the sceptre of all Asia swayed,
Whom monarchs like domestic slaves obeyed !

691   . . . the awful character of a great and good king; his hoary age which increases both our reverence for his person, and our pity for his misfortunes; his vain attempt to die with glory by putting on armour when he was scarce able to stand under the weight of it . . . the hot, rapid and insolent youth of Pyrrhus opposed to the venerable, pious and trembling age of Priam.

Trapp

On the bleak shore now lies the abandoned king,
A headless carcase, and a nameless thing!
  Then, not before, I felt my curdled blood
Congealed with fear; my hair with horror stood:
My father's image filled my pious mind,
Lest equal years might equal fortune find.
Again I thought on my forsaken wife,
And trembled for my son's abandoned life.
770 I looked about, but found myself alone,
Deserted at my need! My friends were gone!
Some spent with toil, some with despair oppressed
Leaped headlong from the heights; the flames consumed
      the rest
  Thus, wandering in my way without a guide,
The graceless Helen in the porch I spied
Of Vesta's temple; there she lurked alone;
Muffled she sat, and what she could, unknown;
But by the flames that cast their blaze around,
That common bane of Greece and Troy I found:
780 For Ilium burnt, she dreads the Trojan sword;
More dreads the vengeance of her injured lord:
E'en by those gods who refuged her, abhorred.
Trembling with rage, the strumpet I regard,
Resolved to give her guilt the due reward.
"Shall she triumphant sail before the wind,
And leave in flames unhappy Troy behind?
Shall she her kingdom and her friends review,
In state attended with a captive crew,
While unrevenged the good old Priam falls,
790 And Grecian fires consume the Trojan walls?
For this the Phrygian fields and Xanthian flood
Were swelled with bodies, and were drunk with blood!
'Tis true, a soldier can small honour gain,
And boast no conquest from a woman slain;
Yet shall the fact not pass without applause,
Of vengeance taken in so just a cause.
The punished crime shall set my soul at ease,
And murmuring manes of my friends appease."
  Thus while I rave, a gleam of pleasing light
800 Spread o'er the place; and, shining heavenly bright,
My mother stood revealed before my sight
(Never so radiant did her eyes appear;
Not her own star confessed a light so clear):
Great in her charms, as when on gods above
She looks, and breathes herself into their love.

BOOK II

She held my hand, the destined blow to break ;
Then from her rosy lips began to speak :
"My son ! from whence this madness, this neglect
Of my commands, and those whom I protect?
810 Why this unmanly rage? Recall to mind
Whom you forsake, what pledges leave behind.
Look if your helpless father yet survive,
Or if Ascanius or Creüsa live.
Around your house the greedy Grecians err ;
And these had perished in the nightly war
But for my presence, and protecting care.
Not Helen's face, nor Paris, was in fault ;
But by the gods was this destruction brought.
Now cast your eyes around, while I dissolve

763 This whole line is taken from Sir John Denham.

Dryden

775 It is no disgrace to the best or bravest man to be subject to such passions as betray him into no unworthy actions. A hero is not supposed to be insensible; he distinguishes himself as such if he restrains them within the bounds of reason. Both Aeneas and Ulysses [when watching the behaviour of the servants of Penelope] are fired with a just indignation, and this is agreeable to human nature; but both of them proceed to no outrageous action, and this shows that their passions are governed by superior reason. However the resentment of Ulysses is less liable to objection than that of Aeneas. Ulysses subdues his indignation by the reflection of his own reason, but Virgil introduces a machine to compose the spirit of Aeneas.

Pope on *Odyssey* XX, 12

819 For the perfection of poetical sublimity both in diction and sentiment there is perhaps nothing equal to them [lines 819-836] in the heathen world. What ideas can be more amazingly grand and awful than that of a mortal having his eyes opened by a divine power to see the gods in all the ensigns of terror and majesty, even then actually employed in the destruction of his country.

Trapp

When Venus opens the eyes of her son Aeneas to behold the gods ... we share the pleasure of that glorious vision (which Tasso has not ill

820 The mists and films that mortal eyes involve,
Purge from your sight the dross, and make you see
The shape of each avenging deity.
Enlightened thus, my just commands fulfil,
Nor fear obedience to your mother's will.
Where yon disordered heap of ruin lies,
Stones rent from stones—where clouds of dust arise,—
Amid that smother, Neptune holds his place,
Below the wall's foundation drives his mace,
And heaves the building from the solid base.
830 Look! where in arms, imperial Juno stands,
Full in the Scæan gate, with loud commands
Urging on shore the tardy Grecian bands.
See! Pallas, of her snaky buckler proud,
Bestrides the tower, refulgent through the cloud:
See! Jove new courage to the foe supplies,
And arms against the town the partial deities.
Haste hence, my son! this fruitless labour end:
Haste! where your trembling spouse and sire attend:
Haste! and a mother's care your passage shall befriend."
840 She said, and swiftly vanished from my sight,
Obscure in clouds, and gloomy shades of night.
 I looked, I listened! dreadful sounds I hear;
And the dire forms of hostile gods appear,
Troy sunk in flames I saw (nor could prevent),
And Ilium from its old foundations rent—
Rent like a mountain-ash, which dared the winds,
And stood the sturdy strokes of labouring hinds.
About the roots the cruel axe resounds;
The stumps are pierced with oft-repeated wounds:
850 The war is felt on high; the nodding crown
Now threats a fall, and throws the leafy honours down.
To their united force it yields, though late,
And mourns with mortal groans the approaching fate:
The roots no more their upper load sustain;
But down she falls, and spreads a ruin through the plain.
 Descending thence, I 'scape through foes and fire:
Before the goddess, foes and flames retire.
Arrived at home, he, for whose only sake,
Or most for his, such toils I undertake—
860 The good Anchises—whom, by timely flight,
I purposed to secure on Ida's height—
Refused the journey, resolute to die,
And add his funerals to the fate of Troy,
Rather than exile and old age sustain.

```
             . . .            the crackling flames appear on high,
                     And driving sparkles dance along the sky;
        960  With Vulcan's rage the rising winds conspire,
                     And near our palace roll the flood of fire.
                     "Haste, my dear father! ('tis no time to wait)
                     And load my shoulders with a willing freight.
                     Whate'er befalls, your life shall be my care;
                     One death, or one deliverance we will share.
                     My hand shall lead our little son; and you,
                     My faithful consort, shall our steps pursue.
                     Next, you my servants, heed my strict commands:
                     Without the walls a ruined temple stands,
        970  To Ceres hallowed once: a cypress nigh
                     Shoots up her venerable head on high,
                     By long religion kept: there bend your feet;
                     And in divided parties let us meet.
                     Our country gods, the relics, and the bands,
                     Hold you, my father, in your guiltless hands:
                     In me 'tis impious, holy things to bear,
                     Red as I am with slaughter, new from war,
                     Till in some living stream I cleanse the guilt
                     Of dire debate, and blood in battle spilt."
        980  Thus, ordering all that prudence could provide,
                     I clothe my shoulders with a lion's hide
                     And yellow spoils; then, on my bending back,
                     The welcome load of my dear father take;
                     While on my better hand Ascanius hung,
                     And with unequal paces tript along.
                     Creüsa kept behind: by choice we stray
                     Through every dark and every devious way.
```

copied in the sacking of Jerusalem): but the Greeks had done their business through neither Nepture, Juno nor Pallas had given them their divine assistance. The most crude machine which Virgil uses is in the episode of Camilla, where Opis, by the command of her mistress, kills Aruns.

Dryden 'Dedication'

856 With what variety has this narration already entertained us! And yet here is a new scene opened which with what follows in this book alone would be almost sufficient to furnish out a book of an heroic poem for any poet but Virgil.

Trapp

I, who so bold and dauntless, just before,
The Grecian darts and shock of lances bore,
990 At every shadow now, am seized with fear,
Not for myself, but for the charge I bear;
Till, near the ruined gate arrived at last,
Secure, and deeming all the danger past,
A frightful noise of trampling feet we hear.
My father, looking through the shades with fear,
Cried out, "Haste, haste, my son! the foes are nigh;
Their swords and shining armour I descry."
Some hostile god, for some unknown offence,
Had sure bereft my mind of better sense;
1000 For, while through winding ways I took my flight,
And sought the shelter of the gloomy night,
Alas! I lost Creüsa: hard to tell
If by her fatal destiny she fell,
Or weary sat, or wandered with affright;
But she was lost for ever to my sight.
I knew not, or reflected, till I meet
My friends at Ceres' now-deserted seat.
We met: not one was wanting; only she
Deceived her friends, her son, and wretched me.
1010 What mad expressions did my tongue refuse?
Whom did I not of gods or men accuse?
This was the fatal blow, that pained me more
Than all I felt from ruined Troy before.

Stung with my loss, and raving with despair,
Abandoning my now-forgotten care,
Of counsel, comfort, and of hope bereft,
My sire, my son, my country gods, I left.
In shining armour once again I sheath
My limbs, not feeling wounds, nor fearing death;
1020 Then headlong to the burning walls I run,
And seek the danger I was forced to shun.
I tread my former tracks, through night explore
Each passage, every street I crossed before.
. . .
Then, with ungoverned madness, I proclaim
Through all the silent streets Creüsa's name:
Creüsa still I call: at length she hears,
And sudden, through the shades of night, appears—
Appears, no more Creüsa, nor my wife,
But a pale spectre, larger than the life.
1050 Aghast, astonished, and struck dumb with fear
I stood: like bristles rose my stiffened hair.

Then thus the ghost began to soothe my grief:
"Nor tears, nor cries, can give the dead relief.
Desist, my much-loved lord, to indulge your pain;
You bear no more than what the gods ordain.
My fates permit me not from hence to fly;
Nor he, the great controller of the sky.
Long wand'ring ways for you the powers decree:
On land, hard labours, and a length of sea.
1060 Then, after many painful years are past,
On Latium's happy shore you shall be cast;
Where gentle Tiber from his bed beholds
The flowery meadows, and the feeding folds.
There, end your toils, and there your fates provide
A quiet kingdom, and a royal bride:
There Fortune shall the Trojan line restore;
And you for lost Creüsa weep no more.
Fear not that I shall watch, with servile shame,
The imperious looks of some proud Grecian dame;
1070 Or, stooping to the victor's lust, disgrace
My goddess-mother, or my royal race.
And now, farewell! the parent of the gods
Restrains my fleeting soul in her abodes.
I trust our common issue to your care."
She said, and gliding passed unseen in air.
I strove to speak; but horror tied my tongue;
And thrice about her neck my arms I flung,
And thrice deceived, on vain embraces hung:
Light as an empty dream at break of day,
1080 Or as a blast of wind, she rushed away.
  Thus having passed the night in fruitless pain,
I to my longing friends return again

1022 Aeneas returns into the city, and with him the poet artfully returns to finish the description of the sack and ruin of it when we thought he could add no more upon that subject but had entirely dismissed it.
Trapp

1082 It was necessary that Aeneas should have a considerable force to attend him besides his own family, and to tell this in general, to slide it in by the by, without a particular account how they came thither, which would have been needless and tedious, is another instance of Virgil's elegant and judicious brevity.
Trapp

(Amazed the augmented number to behold,
Of men and matrons mixed, of young and old):
A wretched exiled crew together brought,
With arms appointed, and with treasure fraught,
Resolved, and willing, under my command
To run all hazards both of sea and land.
The Morn begun, from Ida, to display
1090 Her rosy cheeks; and Phosphor led the day:
Before the gates the Grecians took their post,
And all pretence of late relief was lost.
I yield to Fate, unwillingly retire,
And, loaded, up the hill convey my sire.

This instance of filial piety, a great prince and hero's bearing his old feeble father on his shoulders, is highly pleasing. A modern leader or general would never submit to so laborious a task, but would order their servants or soldiers to undertake it.

Warton

BOOK III

THE ARGUMENT

Æneas proceeds in his relation: he gives an account of the fleet with which he sailed, and the success of his first voyage to Thrace. From thence he directs his course to Delos, and asks the oracle what place the gods had appointed for his habitation. By a mistake of the oracle's answer, he settles in Crete. His household gods give him the true sense of the oracle in a dream. He follows their advice, and makes the best of his way for Italy. He is cast on several shores, and meets with very surprising adventures, till at length he lands on Sicily, where his father Anchises dies. This is the place which he was sailing from, when the tempest rose, and threw him upon the Carthaginian coast.

'WHEN Heaven had overturned the Trojan state
And Priam's throne, by too severe a fate;
When ruined Troy became the Grecian's prey,
And Ilium's lofty towers in ashes lay;
Warned by celestial omens, we retreat,
To seek in foreign lands a happier seat.
Near old Antandros, and at Ida's foot,
The timber of the sacred groves we cut,
And build our fleet—uncertain yet to find
10 What place the gods for our repose assigned.
Friends daily flock; and scarce the kindly spring
Began to clothe the ground, and birds to sing,
When old Anchises summoned all to sea:
The crew, my father and the Fates obey.
With sighs and tears I leave my native shore,
And empty fields, where Ilium stood before.
My sire, my son, our less and greater gods,
All sail at once, and cleave the briny floods.
   Against our coast appears a spacious land,
20 Which once the fierce Lycurgus did command

1   This book is one of those and I believe the very one, of the whole *Aeneid*, which is least read and admired. This neglect I believe is as much owing to the disadvantage of its situation as to any other reason; for the second book, containing the destruction and burning of Troy presents so great an object to the reader that he disdains the third; and the fourth is so charming and interesting by the tenderness and passion which it contains, that one has naturally an impatience to read it.... What appears to be admirable in this great work is that everything in it is beautiful but nothing alike.
                                                                                    Warton

(Thracia the name—the people bold in war—
Vast are their fields, and tillage is their care),
A hospitable realm while Fate was kind,
With Troy in friendship and religion joined.
I land with luckless omens ; then adore
Their gods, and draw a line along the shore :
I lay the deep foundations of a wall,
And Ænos, named from me, the city call.
To Dionæan Venus vows are paid,
30 And all the powers that rising labours aid ;
A bull on Jove's imperial altar laid.
Not far, a rising hillock stood in view .
Sharp myrtles on the sides, and cornels grew.
There, while I went to crop the sylvan scenes,
And shade our altar with their leafy greens,
I pulled a plant (with horror I relate
A prodigy so strange, and full of fate),
The rooted fibres rose, and from the wound,
Black bloody drops distilled upon the ground.
40 Mute and amazed, my hair with terror stood ;
Fear shrunk my sinews, and congealed my blood.
Manned once again, another plant I try ;
That other gushed with the same sanguine dye.
Then fearing guilt for some offence unknown,
With prayers and vows the Dryads I atone,
With all the sisters of the woods, and most
The god of arms, who rules the Thracian coast—
That they, or he, these omens would avert,
Release our fears, and better signs impart.
50 Cleared, as I thought, and fully fixed at length
To learn the cause, I tugged with all my strength :
I bent my knees against the ground : once more
The violated myrtle ran with gore.
Scarce dare I tell the sequel : from the womb
Of wounded earth, and caverns of the tomb,
A groan, as of a troubled ghost, renewed
My fright, and then these dreadful words ensued :
"Why dost thou thus my buried body rend ?
O ! spare the corpse of thy unhappy friend !
60 Spare to pollute thy pious hands with blood :
The tears distil not from the wounded wood ;
But every drop this living tree contains,
Is kindred blood, and ran in Trojan veins.
O ! fly from this unhospitable shore,
Warned by my fate ; for I am Polydore !

>   Here loads of lances, in my blood embrued,
>   Again shoot upward, by my blood renewed."
>   My faltering tongue and shivering limbs declare
>   My horror, and in bristles rose my hair.
> 70 When Troy with Grecian arms was closely pent,
>   Old Priam, fearful of the war's event,
>   This hapless Polydore to Thracia sent:
>   Loaded with gold, he sent his darling far
>   From noise and tumults, and destructive war:
>   Committed to the faithless tyrant's care;
>   Who, when he saw the power of Troy decline,
>   Forsook the weaker, with the strong to join:
>   Broke every bond of nature and of truth,
>   And murdered, for his wealth, the royal youth.
> 80 O sacred hunger of pernicious gold!
>   What bands of faith can impious lucre hold?
>   Now, when my soul had shaken off her fears,
>   I call my father, and the Trojan peers—
>   Relate the prodigies of heaven—require
>   What he commands, and their advice desire.
>   All vote to leave that execrable shore,
>   Polluted with the blood of Polydore;
>   But, ere we sail, his funeral rites prepare;
>   Then to his ghost, a tomb and altars rear.
> 90 In mournful pomp the matrons walk the round,
>   With baleful cypress and blue fillets crowned,
>   With eyes dejected, and with hair unbound.
>   Then bowls of tepid milk and blood we pour,
>   And thrice invoke the soul of Polydore.

Aeneas encounters Andromache and Helenus

>   Then to Chaonia's port our course we bend,
>   And, landed, to Buthrotus' heights ascend.
> 380 **Here wondrous things were loudly blazed by Fame:**
>   **How Helenus revived the Trojan name,**

80 This sententious acclamation is very judiciously placed by the poet ... this poet is indeed admirable in the art and propriety of introducing what the critics call sentences, or moral reflections on life and manners. They should be but sparingly introduced in an epic poem, and require great delicacy and judgement in the management of them.

Warton

And reigned in Greece ; that Priam's captive son
Succeeded Pyrrhus in his bed and throne ;
And fair Andromache, restored by fate,
Once more was happy in a Trojan mate.
I leave my galleys riding in the port,
And long to see the new Dardanian court.
    By chance, the mournful queen, before the gate,
Then solemnized her former husband's fate.
390 Green altars, raised of turf, with gifts she crowned ;
And sacred priests in order stand around,
And thrice the name of hapless Hector sound.
The grove itself resembles Ida's wood ;
And Simoïs seemed the well-dissembled flood.
But when, at nearer distance, she beheld
My shining armour and my Trojan shield,
Astonished at the sight, the vital heat
Forsakes her limbs, her veins no longer beat :
She faints, she falls, and scarce recovering strength,
400 Thus, with a faltering tongue, she speaks at length :
" Are you alive, O goddess-born ! (she said)
Or, if a ghost, then where is Hector's shade ?"
At this she cast a loud and frightful cry.
With broken words I made this brief reply :
" All of me that remains, appears in sight ;
I live ; if living be to loathe the light—
No phantom ; but I drag a wretched life ;
My fate resembling that of Hector's wife.
What have you suffered since you lost your lord ?
410 By what strange blessing are you now restored?
Still are you Hector's ? or is Hector fled,
And his remembrance lost in Pyrrhus' bed ?"
With eyes dejected, in a lowly tone,
After a modest pause, she thus begun :
"O only happy maid of Priam's race,
Whom death delivered from the foe's embrace !
Commanded on Achilles' tomb to die,
Not forced, like us, to hard captivity,
Or in a haughty master's arms to lie.
420 In Grecian ships, unhappy we were borne,
Endured the victor's lust, sustained the scorn :
Thus I submitted to the lawless pride
Of Pyrrhus, more a handmaid than a bride.
Cloyed with possession, he forsook my bed,
And Helen's lovely daughter sought to wed ;
Then, me to Trojan Helenus resigned,

And his two slaves in equal marriage joined ;
Till young Orestes, pierced with deep despair,
And longing to redeem the promised fair,
430 Before Apollo's altar slew the ravisher.
By Pyrrhus' death the kingdom we regained :
At least one half with Helenus remained.
Our part, from Chaon, he Chaonia calls ;
And names, from Pergamus, his rising walls.
But you, what fates have landed on our coast?
What gods have sent you, or what storms have tossed?
Does young Ascanius life and health enjoy,
Saved from the ruins of unhappy Troy?
O ! tell me how his mother's loss he bears,
440 What hopes are promised from his blooming years,
How much of Hector in his face appears?"
She spoke ; and mixed her speech with mournful cries;
And fruitless tears came trickling from her eyes.
At length her lord descends upon the plain,
In pomp, attended with a numerous train ;
Receives his friends, and to the city leads,
And tears of joy amidst his welcome sheds.
Proceeding on, another Troy I see,
Or in less compass, Troy's epitome.
450 A rivulet by the name of Xanthus ran ;
And I embrace the Scæan gate again.
My friends in porticoes were entertained ;
And feasts and pleasures through the city reigned.
The tables filled the spacious hall around ;
And golden bowls with sparkling wine were crowned.

. . .

The prophet first with sacrifice adores
The greater gods ; their pardon then implores ;
Unbinds the fillet from his holy head ;
To Phœbus, next, my trembling steps he led,

388 But what scene is there ... at once so moving and surprising and therefore so truly tragical as this wonderful meeting of Aeneas with Andromache ... she is paying the funeral ceremonies to the memory of Hector her first husband. This is an image of the coolest sadness; and the sudden turn from this to the surprise that follows is to the last degree affecting and will be so as long as human nature and Virgil's works are in being.

Trapp

Full of religious doubts and awful dread.
Then, with his god possessed, before the shrine
These words proceeded from his mouth divine:
480 "O goddess-born! (for heaven's appointed will,
With greater auspices of good than ill,
Foreshows thy voyage, and thy course directs;
Thy fates conspire, and Jove himself protects),
Of many things, some few I shall explain,
Teach thee to shun the dangers of the main,
And how at length the promised shore to gain.
The rest, the fates from Helenus conceal,
And Juno's angry power forbids to tell.

. . .

Arrived at Cumæ, when you view the flood
Of black Avernus, and the sounding wood,
The mad prophetic Sibyl you shall find,
Dark in a cave, and on a rock reclined.
She sings the fates, and in her frantic fits,
The notes and names, inscribed, to leaves commits.
What she commits to leaves, in order laid,
Before the cavern's entrance are displayed:
Unmoved they lie; but, if a blast of wind
570 Without, or vapours issue from behind,
The leaves are borne aloft in liquid air,
And she resumes no more her museful care;
Nor gathers from the rocks her scattered verse,
Nor sets in order what the winds disperse.
Thus, many not succeeding, most upbraid
The madness of the visionary maid,
And with loud curses leave the mystic shade.
Think it not loss of time awhile to stay,
Though thy companions chide thy long delay;
580 Though summoned to the seas; though pleasing gales
Invite thy course, and stretch thy swelling sails;
But beg the sacred priestess to relate
With willing words, and not to write, thy fate.
The fierce Italian people she will show,
And all thy wars, and all thy future woe;
And what thou may'st avoid, and what must undergo.
She shall direct thy course, instruct thy mind,
And teach thee how the happy shores to find.
This is what heaven allows me to relate:
590 Now part in peace; pursue thy better fate,
And raise, by strength of arms, the Trojan state."

This when the priest with friendly voice declared,
He gave me license, and rich gifts prepared :
Bounteous of treasure, he supplied my want
With heavy gold, and polished elephant ;
Then Dodonæan caldrons put on board ;
And every ship with sums of silver stored.

. . .

    Nor less the queen our parting thence deplored,
Nor was less bounteous than her Trojan lord.
A noble present to my son she brought,
A robe with flowers on golden tissue wrought :
A Phrygian vest ; and loads with gifts beside
Of precious texture, and of Asian pride.
"Accept (she said) these monuments of love,
Which in my youth with happier hands I wove :
630 Regard these trifles for the giver's sake :
'Tis the last present Hector's wife can make.
Thou call'st my lost Astyanax to mind :
In thee, his features and his form I find ;
His eyes so sparkled with a lively flame ;
Such were his motions ; such was all his frame ;
And ah ! had heaven so pleased, his years had been the
    With tears I took my last adieu, and said : [same."
"Your fortune, happy pair, already made,
Leaves you no farther wish. My different state,
640 Avoiding one, incurs another fate.
To you a quiet seat the gods allow :
You have no shores to search, no seas to plough ;
Nor fields of flying Italy to chase—
Deluding visions and a vain embrace !
You see another Simoïs, and enjoy
The labours of your hands, another Troy,
With better auspice than her ancient towers ;
And less obnoxious to the Grecian powers.
If e'er the gods whom I with vows adore,
650 Conduct my steps to Tiber's happy shore :
If ever I ascend the Latian throne,
And build a city I may call my own :
As both of us our birth from Troy derive ;
So let our kindred lines in concord live ;
And both in acts of equal friendship strive.
Our fortunes, good or bad, shall be the same :
The double Troy shall differ but in name :
That what we now begin, may never end,
But long to late posterity descend."

Aeneas encounters Achaemenides and the Cyclopes

    The flagging winds forsook us, with the sun;
And, wearied, on Cyclopean shores we run.
    The port, capacious and secure from wind,
Is to the foot of thundering Ætna joined.
By turns a pitchy cloud she rolls on high;
By turns hot embers from her entrails fly,
750 And flakes of mountain flames, that lick the sky.
Oft from her bowels massy rocks are thrown,
And shivered by the force, come piece-meal down:
Oft liquid lakes of burning sulphur flow,
Fed from the fiery springs that boil below.
Enceladus, they say, transfixed by Jove,
With blasted limbs came tumbling from above;
And where he fell, the avenging father drew
This flaming hill, and on his body threw.
As often as he turns his weary sides,
760 He shakes the solid isle, and smoke, the heavens hides.
In shady woods we pass the tedious night,
Where bellowing sounds and groans our souls affright,
Of which no cause is offered to the sight;
For not one star was kindled in the sky;
Nor could the moon her borrowed light supply;
For misty clouds involved the firmament:
The stars were muffled, and the moon was pent.
    Scarce had the rising sun the day revealed;
Scarce had his heat the pearly dews dispelled;
770 When from the woods there bolts, before our sight,
Somewhat betwixt a mortal and a sprite,
So thin, so ghastly meagre, and so wan,
So bare of flesh, he scarce resembled man.
This thing, all tattered, seemed from far to implore
Our pious aid, and pointed to the shore.
We look behind; then view his shaggy beard:
His clothes were tagged with thorns, and filth his limbs
    besmeared;
The rest, in mien, in habit, and in face,
Appeared a Greek: and such indeed he was.
780 He cast on us, from far, a frightful view,
Whom soon for Trojans and for foes he knew:
Stood still, and paused; then all at once began
To stretch his limbs, and trembled as he ran.
Soon as approached, upon his knees he falls,
And thus with tears and sighs for pity calls:

"Now, by the powers above, and what we share
From nature's common gift, this vital air,
O Trojans, take me hence! I beg no more;
But bear me far from this unhappy shore.
790 'Tis true I am a Greek, and farther own,
Among your foes besieged the imperial town.
For such demerits if my death be due,
No more for this abandoned life I sue:
This only favour let my tears obtain,
To throw me headlong in the rapid main:
Since nothing more than death my crime demands,
I die content, to die by human hands."
　　He said; and on his knees my knees embraced:
I bade him boldly tell, his fortune past,
800 His present state, his lineage, and his name,
The occasion of his fears, and whence he came.
The good Anchises raised him with his hand;
Who thus encouraged, answered our demand:
"From Ithaca, my native soil, I came
To Troy; and Achæmenides my name.
Me my poor father with Ulysses sent;
(O! had I stayed, with poverty content!)
But, fearful for themselves, my countrymen
Left me forsaken in the Cyclop's den.
810 The cave, though large, was dark; the dismal floor
Was paved with mangled limbs and putrid gore.
Our monstrous host, of more than human size
Erects his head and stares within the skies:
Bellowing, his voice, and horrid is his hue.
Ye gods, remove this plague from mortal view!
The joints of slaughtered wretches are his food;
And for his wine, he quaffs the streaming blood.

744　Virgil has borrowed this episode of Polyphemus [the Cyclops], and inserted it into the third of the *Aeneis*. I will not presume to decide which author has the greatest success; they both have their peculiar excellences ... in Homer we find a greater variety of natural incidents than in Virgil, but in Virgil a greater pomp of verse. Homer is not uniform in his description, but sometimes stoops perhaps below the dignity of epic poetry; Virgil walks along with an even, grave and majestic pace. They both raise our admiration, mixed with delight and terror.

　　　　　　　　　　　Pope on *Odyssey* IX, concluding remark

These eyes beheld, when with his spacious hand
He seized two captives of our Grecian band;
820 Stretched on his back, he dashed against the stones
Their broken bodies, and their crackling bones :
With spouting blood the purple pavement swims,
While the dire glutton grinds the trembling limbs.
　Not unrevenged Ulysses bore their fate,
Nor thoughtless of his own unhappy state;
For, gorged with flesh, and drunk with human wine,
While fast asleep the giant lay supine
(Snoring aloud, and belching from his maw
His indigested foam, and morsels raw);
830 We pray, we cast the lots, and then surround
The monstrous body stretched along the ground.
Each, as he could approach him, lends a hand
To bore his eye-ball with a flaming brand.
Beneath his frowning forehead lay his eye;
For only one did the vast frame supply—
But that a globe so large, his front it filled,
Like the sun's disk, or like a Grecian shield.
The stroke succeeds; and down the pupil bends.
This vengeance followed for our slaughtered friends
840 But haste, unhappy wretches ! haste to fly !
Your cables cut, and on your oars rely !
Such, and so vast as Polypheme appears,
A hundred more this hated island bears :
Like him, in caves they shut their woolly sheep;
Like him, their herds on tops of mountains keep;
Like him, with mighty strides they stalk from steep to
　　steep.
And now three moons their sharpened horns renew,
Since thus in woods and wilds, obscure from view,
I drag my loathsome days with mortal fright,
850 And in deserted caverns lodge by night.
Oft from the rocks a dreadful prospect see
Of the huge Cyclops, like a walking tree :
From far I hear his thundering voice resound,
And trampling feet that shake the solid ground.
Cornels and savage berries of the wood,
And roots and herbs have been my meagre food.
While all around my longing eyes I cast,
I saw your happy ships appear at last.
On those I fixed my hopes, to these I run :
860 'Tis all I ask, this cruel race to shun :
What other death you please, yourselves bestow."

Scarce had he said, when on the mountain's brow,
We saw the giant shepherd stalk before
His following flock, and leading to the shore:
A monstrous bulk, deformed, deprived of sight;
His staff a trunk of pine, to guide his steps aright.
His ponderous whistle from his neck descends;
His woolly care their pensive lord attends:
This only solace his hard fortune sends.
870 Soon as he reached the shore and touched the waves,
From his bored eye the gutt'ring blood he laves:
He gnashed his teeth and groaned: through seas he strides;
And scarce the topmost billows touched his sides.
 Seized with a sudden fear, we run to sea,
The cables cut, and silent haste away;
The well-deserving stranger entertain;
Then, buckling to the work, our oars divide the main.
The giant hearkened to the dashing sound;
But, when our vessels out of reach he found,
880 He strided onward, and in vain essayed
The Ionian deep, and durst no farther wade.
With that he roared aloud: the dreadful cry
Shakes earth and air and seas; the billows fly
Before the bellowing noise to distant Italy,
The neighbouring Ætna trembling all around,
The winding caverns echo to the sound.
 His brother Cyclops hear the yelling roar,
And rushing down the mountains, crowd the shore.
We saw their stern distorted looks, from far,

840   This break in Achaemenides's speech is of an exquisite beauty. In the midst of his narration, the fear of the Cyclops, and the dangers he had just escaped, break in upon his mind and stop him for a moment from finishing his account, to give the Trojans advice to fly immediately. The circumstances that follow of his hearing the giant's footsteps and the loud voices while he lay hid in dens and caves are strongly imagined.

Warton

882   This is a most noble hyperbole and by no means too bold as some will have it. They forget not only the prerogative of poetry, but the real nature of fear which always swells and heightens its object.

Trapp

890 And one-eyed glance, that vainly threatened war—
A dreadful council ! with their heads on high
(The misty clouds about their foreheads fly)
Not yielding to the towering tree of Jove,
Or tallest cypress of Diana's grove.
New pangs of mortal fear our minds assail:
We tug at every oar, and hoist up every sail,
And take the advantage of the friendly gale.
Forewarned by Helenus, we strive to shun
Charybdis' gulf, nor dare to Scylla run.
900 An equal fate on either side appears:
We, tacking to the left, are free from fears;
For, from Pelorus' point, the north arose,
And drove us back where swift Pantagias flows.
His rocky mouth we pass; and make our way
By Thapsus, and Megara's winding bay.
This passage Achæmenides had shown,
Tracing the course which he before had run.

. . .

BOOK IV

THE ARGUMENT

Dido discovers to her sister her passion for Æneas, and her thoughts of marrying him. She prepares a hunting match for his entertainment. Juno, by Venus's consent, raises a storm which separates the hunters, and drives Æneas and Dido into the same cave, where their marriage is supposed to be completed. Jupiter despatches Mercury to Æneas, to warn him from Carthage. Æneas secretly prepares for his voyage. Dido finds out his design, and, to put a stop to it, makes use of her own and her sister's entreaties, and discovers all the variety of passions that are incident to a neglected lover. When nothing would prevail upon him, she contrives her own death, with which this book concludes.

But anxious cares already seized the queen;
She fed within her veins a flame unseen:
The hero's valour, acts, and birth, inspire
Her soul with love, and fan the secret fire.
His words, his looks, imprinted in her heart,
Improve the passion, and increase the smart.
Now, when the purple morn had chased away
The dewy shadows, and restored the day,
Her sister first with early care she sought,
10 And thus in mournful accents eased her thought:
'My dearest Anna ! what new dreams affright
My labouring soul ! what visions of the night
Disturb my quiet, and distract my breast
With strange ideas of our Trojan guest !
His worth, his actions, and majestic air,

1 This fourth book is entirely devoted to the pathetic. . . . The origin and progress of the passion of love, its various effects on the mind, its doubts and hopes, and fears and jealousies, its pleasures and pains till it end in the deepest despair, were never so forcibly, so elegantly, or naturally described.

Warton

11 Admirable is the art and nature of this speech in the mouth of a woman, expressing both her love and her modesty, arguing against what she passionately desires, and wanting to be advised to do that which she already half (if not quite) resolves to do, whether she be advised or no.

Trapp

A man descended from the gods, declare
Fear ever argues a degenerate kind :
His birth is well asserted by his mind.
Then, what he suffered, when by fate betrayed !
What brave attempts for falling Troy he made !
Such were his looks, so gracefully he spoke,
That, were I not resolved against the yoke
Of hapless marriage—never to be cursed
With second love, so fatal was my first—
To this one error I might yield again ;
For, since Sichæus was untimely slain,
This only man is able to subvert
The fixed foundations of my stubborn heart.
And, to confess my frailty, to my shame,
Somewhat I find within, if not the same,
Too like the sparkles of my former flame.
But first let yawning earth a passage rend,
And let me through the dark abyss descend—
First let avenging Jove, with flames from high,
Drive down this body to the nether sky,
Condemned with ghosts in endless night to lie—
Before I break the plighted faith I gave !
No ! he who had my vows, shall ever have ;
For, whom I loved on earth, I worship in the grave.'
   She said : the tears ran gushing from her eyes,
And stopped her speech.   Her sister thus replies :
'O dearer than the vital air I breathe !
Will you to grief your blooming years bequeath,
Condemned to waste in woes your lonely life,
Without the joys of mother or of wife?
Think you these tears, this pompous train of woe,
Are known or valued by the ghosts below?
I grant, that, while your sorrows yet were green,
It well became a woman, and a queen,
The vows of Tyrian princes to neglect ;
To scorn Iärbas and his love reject ;
With all the Libyan lords of mighty name :
But will you fight against a pleasing flame?
This little spot of land, which heaven bestows,
On every side is hemmed with warlike foes :
Gætulian cities here are spread around,
And fierce Numidians there your frontiers bound :
Here lies a barren waste of thirsty land,
And there the Syrtes raise the moving sand :
Barcæan troops besiege the narrow shore ;

BOOK IV   111

    And from the sea Pygmalion threatens more.
Propitious heaven, and gracious Juno, lead
This wandering navy to your needful aid :
How will your empire spread, your city rise,
From such a union, and with such allies !
Implore the favour of the powers above ;
And leave the conduct of the rest to love.
Continue still your hospitable way,
And still invent occasions of their stay,
70 Till storms and winter winds shall cease to threat,
And planks and oars repair their shattered fleet.'
    These words, which from a friend and sister came
With ease resolved the scruples of her fame,
And added fury to the kindled flame.
Inspired with hope, the project thèy pursue ;
On every altar sacrifice renew ;
. . .
    Sick with desire, and seeking him she loves,
From street to street the raving Dido roves.
So, when the watchful shepherd, from the blind,
Wounds with a random shaft the careless hind,
Distracted with her pain she flies the woods,
Bounds o'er the lawn, and seeks the silent floods—
With fruitless care ; for still the fatal dart
100 Sticks in her side, and rankles in her heart.
And now she leads the Trojan chief along
The lofty walls, amidst the busy throng ;
Displays her Tyrian wealth, and rising town,
Which love, without his labour makes his own.
This pomp she shows, to tempt her wandering guest :
Her faltering tongue forbids to speak the rest.
When day declines and feasts renew the night,

32 There are some delicate strokes of nature in the cautious manner in which Dido reveals her new-born passion to her sister. But what follows in the solemn protestation she makes, that she was immoveably resolved never to marry again, is inimitably just and natural, and the true picture of a widow's resolutions. The reader of taste will likewise be charmed with the arguments her sister uses to persuade her to indulge her passion and marry again: 'tis impossible to think of more strong and weighty ones.

                                                        Warton

Still on his face she feeds her famished sight;
She longs again to hear the prince relate
110 His own adventures, and the Trojan fate.
He tells it o'er and o'er ; but still in vain ;
For still she begs to hear it once again.
The hearer on the speaker's mouth depends ;
And thus the tragic story never ends.
    Then, when they part, when Phœbe's paler light
Withdraws, and falling stars to sleep invite,
She last remains ; when every guest is gone,
Sits on the bed he pressed, and sighs alone ;
Absent, her absent hero sees and hears ;
120 Or in her bosom young Ascanius bears,
And seeks the father's image in the child,
If love by likeness might be so beguiled.
    Meantime the rising towers are at a stand ;
No labours exercise the youthful band,
Nor use of arts, nor toils of arms they know :
The mole is left unfinished to the foe ;
The mounds, the works, the walls neglected lie,
Short of their promised height, that seemed to threat the sky.

Juno and Venus agree to bring about the consummation of the love of Dido and Aeneas

182   The rosy morn was risen from the main ;
And horns and hounds awake the princely train :
They issue early through the city gate,
Where the more wakeful huntsmen ready wait,
With nets, and toils, and darts, beside the force
Of Spartan dogs, and swift Massylian horse.

. . .

The queen at length appears : on either hand,
The brawny guards in martial order stand.
A flowered cymar with golden fringe she wore,
And at her back a golden quiver bore ;
Her flowing hair a golden caul restrains ;
A golden clasp the Tyrian robe sustains.
200 Then young Ascanius, with a sprightly grace
Leads on the Trojan youth to view the chase.
But far above the rest in beauty shines
The great Æneas, when the troop he joins ;

Like fair Apollo, when he leaves the frost
Of wintry Xanthus, and the Lycian coast;
When to his native Delos he resorts,
Ordains the dances, and renews the sports;
Where painted Scythians, mixed with Cretan bands,
Before the joyful altars join their hands:
210 Himself, on Cynthus walking, sees below
The merry madness of the sacred show.
Green wreaths of bays his length of hair inclose;
A golden fillet binds his awful brows;
His quiver sounds.—Not less the prince is seen
In manly presence, or in lofty mien.
 Now had they reached the hills, and stormed the seat
Of savage beasts, in dens, their last retreat.
The cry pursues the mountain-goats; they bound
From rock to rock, and keep the craggy ground:
220 Quite otherwise the stags, a trembling train
In herds unsingled, scour the dusty plain,
And a long chase, in open view maintain.
. . .

 Meantime, the gathering clouds obscure the skies;
From pole to pole the forky lightning flies;
The rattling thunders roll; and Juno pours
A wintry deluge down, and sounding showers.
The company, dispersed, to coverts ride,
And seek the homely cots, or mountain's hollow side.
The rapid rains, descending from the hills,
To rolling torrents raise the creeping rills.
The queen and prince, as love or fortune guides,
240 One common cavern in her bosom hides,

204 ... this divine beauty of his and his motion are the two principal points aimed at by Virgil in this similitude, and the two things that strike one in viewing the Apollo Belvedere.
Warton quoting Spence Polymetis Dialogue VIII

239 Sir R. Steele in the Tatlers observes the great judgement and exactness of Virgil in dropping the epithet he usually applies to his hero, 'pius Aeneas', and calling him only 'Dux Trojanus' now he is entering upon the adventure of the cave.
Warton

Then first the trembling earth the signal gave;
And flashing fires enlighten all the cave:
Hell from below, and Juno from above,
And howling nymphs, were conscious to their love.
From this ill-omened hour, in time arose
Debate and death, and all succeeding woes.
    The queen, whom sense of honour could not move,
No longer made a secret of her love,
But called it marriage; by that specious name
250 To veil the crime, and sanctify the shame.
    The loud report through Libyan cities goes.
Fame, the great ill, from small beginnings grows—
Swift from the first; and every moment brings
New vigour to her flights, new pinions to her wings.
Soon grows the pigmy to gigantic size;
Her feet on earth, her forehead in the skies.
Enraged against the gods, revengeful Earth
Produced her, last of the Titanian birth:
Swift is her walk, more swift her wingèd haste:
260 A monstrous phantom, horrible and vast.
As many plumes as raise her lofty flight;
So many piercing eyes enlarge her sight;
Millions of opening mouths to fame belong,
And every mouth is furnished with a tongue;
And round, with listening ears the flying plague is hung.
She fills the peaceful universe with cries
No slumbers ever close her wakeful eyes.
By day, from lofty towers her head she shows,
And spreads through trembling crowds disastrous news;
270 With court-informers, haunts, and royal spies;
Things done, relates; not done, she feigns, and mingles
    truth with lies.
Talk is her business; and her chief delight
To tell of prodigies, and cause affright.
She fills the people's ears with Dido's name,
Who, lost to honour and the sense of shame,
Admits into her throne and nuptial bed
A wandering guest, who from his country fled.
Whole days with him she passes in delights;
And wastes in luxury long winter nights,
280 Forgetful of her fame, and royal trust,
Dissolved in ease, abandoned to her lust.
    The goddess widely spreads the loud report,
And flies at length to king Iärbas' court.
When first possessed with this unwelcome news,

BOOK IV

    Whom did he not of men and gods accuse?
This prince, from ravished Garamantis born,
A hundred temples did with spoils adorn
In Ammon's honour, his celestial sire ;
A hundred altars fed with wakeful fire ;
290 And, through his vast dominions, priests ordained,
Whose watchful care these holy rites maintained.
The gates and columns were with garlands crowned,
And blood of victim beasts enriched the ground.
    He, when he heard a fugitive could move
The Tyrian princess, who disdained his love,
His breast with fury burned, his eyes with fire—
Mad with despair, impatient with desire—
Then on the sacred altars pouring wine,
He thus with prayers implored his sire divine :
300 'Great Jove ! propitious to the Moorish race,
Who feast on painted beds, with offerings grace
Thy temples, and adore thy power divine
With blood of victims, and with sparkling wine ;
Seest thou not this ! or do we fear in vain
Thy boasted thunder, and thy thoughtless reign?
Do thy broad hands the forky lightnings lance?
Thine are the bolts, or the blind work of chance?
. . .
320   His vows, in haughty terms, he thus preferred,
And held his altar's horns: the mighty Thunderer heard,
. . .
326 He calls Cyllenius ; and the god attends ;
By whom this menacing command he sends :
. . .

---

241 If ever Virgil (says M. Segrais) showed his address in making things understood only by glancing at and lightly touching upon them, it is doubtless in this passage, at which it was so easy to make a false step. All the commentators praise his modesty and his delicacy.
Warton

251 This description of Fame (says M. Segrais) ought to be considered as one of the greatest ornaments of the *Aeneis*.
Trapp

350   Hermes obeys; with golden pinions binds
His flying feet, and mounts the western winds:
And, whether o'er the seas or earth he flies,
With rapid force they bear him down the skies.
. . .

    Arriving there, he found the Trojan prince
New ramparts raising for the town's defence.
A purple scarf, with gold embroidered o'er
(Queen Dido's gift), about his waist he wore;
A sword, with glittering gems diversified,
For ornament, not use, hung idly by his side.
Then thus, with wingèd words, the god began
(Resuming his own shape): 'Degenerate man!
390 Thou woman's property! what mak'st thou here,
These foreign walls and Tyrian towers to rear?—
Forgetful of thy own! All-powerful Jove,
Who sways the world below and heaven above,
Has sent me down with this severe command:
What means thy lingering in the Libyan land?
If glory cannot move a mind so mean,
Nor future praise from flitting pleasure wean,
Regard the fortunes of thy rising heir:
The promised crown let young Ascanius wear,
400 To whom the Ausonian sceptre, and the state
Of Rome's imperial name, is owed by fate.'
So spoke the god; and, speaking, took his flight
Involved in clouds; and vanished out of sight.
    The pious prince was seized with sudden fear:
Mute was his tongue, and upright stood his hair.
Revolving in his mind the stern command,
He longs to fly, and loathes the charming land.
What should he say, or how should he begin?
What course, alas! remains, to steer between
410 The offended lover and the powerful queen?
This way, and that, he turns his anxious mind;
And all expedients tries, and none can find.
Fixed on the deed, but doubtful of the means;
After long thought, to this advice he leans:
Three chiefs he calls, commands them to repair
The fleet, and ship their men, with silent care.
Some plausible pretence he bids them find,
To colour what in secret he designed.
Himself, meantime, the softest hours would choose,
420 Before the love-sick lady heard the news,

And move her tender mind, by slow degrees
To suffer what the sovereign power decrees:
Jove will inspire him, when, and what to say.
They hear with pleasure, and with haste obey.
 But soon the queen perceives the thin disguise:
(What arts can blind a jealous woman's eyes?)
She was the first to find the secret fraud,
Before the fatal news was blazed abroad:
Love the first motions of the lover hears,
430 Quick to presage, and e'en in safety fears.
Nor impious Fame was wanting, to report
The ships repaired, the Trojans' thick resort,
And purpose to forsake the Tyrian court.
Frantic with fear, impatient of the wound,
And impotent of mind, she roves the city round.
Less wild the Bacchanalian dames appear,
When, from afar, their nightly god they hear,
And howl about the hills, and shake the wreathy spear
At length she finds the dear perfidious man;
440 Prevents his formed excuse, and thus began:
'Base and ungrateful! could you hope to fly,
And undiscovered 'scape a lover's eye?
Nor could my kindness your compassion move,
Nor plighted vows, nor dearer bands of love?
Or is the death of a despairing queen
Not worth preventing, though too well foreseen?
E'en when the wintry winds command your stay,
You dare the tempests, and defy the sea.
False as you are, suppose you were not bound
450 To lands unknown, and foreign coasts to sound;
Were Troy restored, and Priam's happy reign,
Now durst you tempt, for Troy, the raging main?
See, whom you fly! am I the foe you shun?
Now, by those holy vows, so late begun,
By this right hand (since I have nothing more
To challenge, but the faith you gave before),
I beg you by these tears too truly shed,
By the new pleasures of our nuptial bed;
If ever Dido, when you most were kind,
460 Were pleasing in your eyes, or touched your mind;
By these my prayers, if prayers may yet have place,
Pity the fortunes of a falling race!
For you I have provoked a tyrant's hate,
Incensed the Libyan and the Tyrian state,
For you alone, I suffer in my fame,

Bereft of honour, and exposed to shame!
Whom have I now to trust, ungrateful guest?
(That only name remains of all the rest!)
What have I left? or whither can I fly?
470 Must I attend Pygmalion's cruelty,
Or, till Iärbas shall in triumph lead
A queen that proudly scorned his proffered bed?
Had you deferred, at least, your hasty flight,
And left behind some pledge of our delight;
Some babe to bless the mother's mournful sight;
Some young Æneas to supply your place,
Whose features might express his father's face;
I should not then complain to live bereft
Of all my husband, or be wholly left.'
480   Here paused the queen. Unmoved he holds his eyes,
By Jove's command; nor suffered love to rise
Though heaving in his heart; and thus at length replies:
'Fair queen, you never can enough repeat
Your boundless favours, or I own my debt;
Nor, can my mind forget Eliza's name
While vital breath inspires this mortal frame.
This only let me speak in my defence—
I never hoped a secret flight from hence,
Much less pretended to the lawful claim
490 Of sacred nuptials, or a husband's name.
For, if indulgent heaven would leave me free,
And not submit my life to fate's decree,
My choice would lead me to the Trojan shore,
Those relics to review, their dust adore;
And Priam's ruined palace to restore.
But now the Delphian oracle commands,
And fate invites me to the Latian lands.
That is the promised place to which I steer;
And all my vows are terminated there.
500 If you, a Tyrian and a stranger born,
With walls and towers a Libyan town adorn,
Why may not we—like you, a foreign race—
Like you, seek shelter in a foreign place?
As often as the night obscures the skies
With humid shades, or twinkling stars arise,
Anchises' angry ghost in dreams appears,
Chides my delay, and fills my soul with fears;
And young Ascanius justly may complain,
Defrauded of his fate and destined reign.
510 E'en now the herald of the gods appeared—

Waking I saw him, and his message heard.
From Jove he came commissioned, heavenly **bright**
With radiant beams, and manifest to sight
(The sender and the sent I both attest):
These walls he entered, and those words expressed.
Fair queen, oppose not what the gods command:
Forced by my fate, I leave your happy land.'
   Thus while he spoke, already she began
With sparkling eyes to view the guilty man;
520 From head to foot surveyed his person o'er;
Nor longer these outrageous threats forbore:
'False as thou art, and more than false, forsworn!
Not sprung from noble blood, nor goddess born,
But hewn from hardened entrails of a rock!
And rough Hyrcanian tigers gave thee suck!
Why should I fawn? what have I worse to fear?
Did he once look, or lend a listening ear,
Sighed when I sobbed, or shed one kindly tear?
All, symptoms of a base ungrateful mind,
530 So foul, that which is worse, 'tis hard to find.
Of man's injustice why should I complain?
The gods, and Jove himself, behold in vain
Triumphant treason: yet no thunder flies;
Nor Juno views my wrongs with equal eyes:
Faithless is earth, and faithless are the skies!
Justice is fled, and truth is now no more!
   I saved the shipwrecked exile on my shore:
With needful food his hungry Trojans fed:
I took the traitor to my throne and bed.
540 Fool that I was! 'tis little to repeat
The rest: I stored and rigged his ruined fleet.

483 The truth is I am no great admirer of this speech in the main. Though Aeneas does not appear insensible, yet a little more tenderness might not have misbecome him.

Trapp

527 Most elegant and pathetical is this transition from the second person to the third. It implies two things; first, her aversion: she will not speak *to* him but *of* him; secondly an appeal as it were to the standers by, which the impotence of rage and distress is always apt to make.

Trapp

I rave, I rave ! A god's command he pleads,
And makes heaven accessory to his deeds.
Now Lycian lots, and now the Delian god,
Now Hermes is employed from Jove's abode,
To warn him hence ; as if the peaceful state
Of heavenly powers were touched with human fate !
But go ! thy flight no longer I detain—
Go ! seek thy promised kingdom through the main !
550 Yet, if the heavens will hear my pious vow,
The faithless waves, not half so false as thou,
Or secret sands, shall sepulchres afford
To thy proud vessels, and their perjured lord !
Then shalt thou call on injured Dido's name :
Dido shall come in a black sulphury flame,
When death has once dissolved her mortal frame—
Shall smile to see the traitor vainly weep :
Her angry ghost, arising from the deep,
Shall haunt thee waking, and disturb thy sleep !
560 At least my shade thy punishment shall know ;
And fame shall spread the pleasing news below.

Abruptly here she stops ; then turns away
Her loathing eyes, and shuns the sight of day.
Amazed he stood, revolving in his mind
What speech to frame, and what excuse to find.
Her fearful maids their fainting mistress led,
And softly laid her on her ivory bed.

But good Æneas, though he much desired
To give that pity which her grief required
570 (Though much he mourned, and laboured with **his love**);
Resolved at length, obeys the will of Jove :
Reviews his forces : they with early care
Unmoor their vessels, and for sea prepare.
The fleet is soon afloat, in all its pride ;
And well-caulked galleys in the harbour ride.

. . .

591 What pangs the tender breast of Dido tore,
When, from the tower, she saw the covered shore,
And heard the shouts of sailors from afar,
Mixed with the murmurs of the watery war !
All-powerful Love ! what changes canst thou cause
In human hearts, subjected to thy laws !
Once more her haughty soul the tyrant bends
To prayers and mean submissions she descends.

. . .

BOOK IV

'Look, Anna! look! the Trojans crowd to sea;
They spread their canvas, and their anchors weigh;
The shouting crew their ships with garlands bind,
Invoke the sea-gods, and invite the wind.
Could I have thought this threatening blow so near,
My tender soul had been forewarned to bear.
But do not you my last request deny;
With yon perfidious man your interest try;
And bring me news, if I must live or die.
610 You are his favourite; you alone can find
The dark recesses of his inmost mind;
In all his trusted secrets you have part,
And know the soft approaches to his heart.
Haste then, and humbly seek my haughty foe;
Tell him, I did not with the Grecians go,
Nor did my fleet against his friends employ,
Nor swore the ruin of unhappy Troy,
. . .
620 Whom does he shun? and whither would he fly?
Can he this last, this only prayer deny?
Let him at least his dangerous flight delay,
Wait better winds, and hope a calmer sea.
The nuptials he disclaims, I urge no more:
Let him pursue the promised Latian shore.
A short delay is all I ask him now—
A pause of grief, an interval from woe;
Till my soft soul be tempered to sustain
Accustomed sorrows, and inured to pain.
630 If you in pity grant this one request,
My death shall glut the hatred of his breast.'
This mournful message pious Anna bears,
And seconds with her own, her sister's tears:
But all her arts are still employed in vain:
Again she comes, and is refused again.
His hardened heart nor prayers nor threat'nings move;
Fate and the god, had stopped his ears to love.
As, when the winds their airy quarrel try,

638 Few similes, if any at all, even in Virgil himself, are more noble and beautiful than this. It gives us a perfect image of the great and deep impressions which are made upon the hero, and yet of his steadfastness in not being subdued by them. The ideas are entirely correspondent, and the expressions altogether admirable.

Trapp

Justling from every quarter of the sky;
640 This way and that the mountain oak they bend;
His boughs they shatter, and his branches rend;
With leaves and falling mast they spread the ground;
The hollow valleys echo to the sound;
Unmoved, the royal plant their fury mocks,
Or, shaken, clings more closely to the rocks:
Far as he shoots his towering head on high,
So deep in earth his fixed foundations lie.
No less a storm the Trojan hero bears;
Thick messages and loud complaints he hears,
650 And bandied words, still beating on his ears.
Sighs, groans, and tears, proclaim his inward pains;
But the firm purpose of his heart remains.
    The wretched queen, pursued by cruel Fate,
Begins at length the light of heaven to hate;
And loathes to live. Then dire portents she sees,
To hasten on the death her soul decrees—
Strange to relate! for when, before the shrine
She pours in sacrifice the purple wine,
The purple wine is turned to putrid blood;
660 And the white offered milk, converts to mud.
This dire presage, to her alone revealed,
From all, and e'en her sister, she concealed.
A marble temple stood within the grove,
Sacred to death, and to her murdered love;
That honoured chapel she had hung around
With snowy fleeces, and with garlands crowned.
Oft, when she visited this lonely dome,
Strange voices issued from her husband's tomb;
She thought she heard him summon her away,
670 Invite her to his grave, and chide her stay.
Hourly 'tis heard, when with a boding note
The solitary skreech-owl strains her throat,
And on a chimney's top, or turret's height,
With songs obscene, disturbs the silence of the night.
Besides, old prophecies augment her fears;
And stern Æneas in her dreams appears,
Disdainful as by day: she seems, alone,
To wander in her sleep, through ways unknown,
Guideless and dark; or, in a desert plain
680 To seek her subjects, and to seek in vain—
Like Pentheus, when, distracted with his fear
He saw two suns, and double Thebes, appear;
Or mad Orestes, when his mother's ghost

Full in his face infernal torches tossed,
And shook her snaky locks : he shuns the sight,
Flies o'er the stage, surprised with mortal fright :
The Furies guard the door, and intercept his flight.
   Now, sinking underneath a load of grief,
From death alone she seeks her last relief :
690 The time and means resolved within her breast,
She to her mournful sister thus addressed
(Dissembling hope, her cloudy front she clears,
And a false vigour in her eyes appears) :
'Rejoice ! (she said) instructed from above,
My lover I shall gain, or lose my love.
Nigh rising Atlas, next the falling sun,
Long tracts of Æthiopian climates run :
There, a Massylian priestess I have found,
Honoured for age, for magic arts renowned.
700 The Hesperian temple was her trusted care ;
. . .
710 Witness ye gods, and thou, my better part,
How loth I am to try this impious art !
Within the secret court, with silent care,
Erect a lofty pile, exposed in air :
Hang on the topmost part, the Trojan vest,
Spoils, arms, and presents, of my faithless guest.
Next, under these, the bridal bed be placed,
Where I my ruin in his arms embraced.
All relics of the wretch are doomed to fire ;
For so the priestess and her charms require.'
720   Thus far she said, and farther speech forbears.
A mortal paleness in her face appears :
Yet the mistrustless Anna could not find
The secret funeral in these rites designed ;
Nor thought so dire a rage possessed her mind.
Unknowing of a train concealed so well,
She feared no worse than when Sichæus fell ;
Therefore obeys.   The fatal pile they rear
Within the secret court, exposed in air,
The cloven holms and pines are heaped on **high :**

657— If it be possible to determine which passage in the *Aeneis* is the very
687 best of all, surely it is this. The dreadful and the wonderful joined
with the pathetical reign through the whole to a degree unutterable.
Trapp

730 And garlands on the hollow spaces lie :
Sad cypress, vervain, yew, compose the **wreath** ;
And every baleful green denoting death.
The queen, determined to the fatal deed,
The spoils and sword he left, in order spread,
And the man's image on the nuptial bed.
　　And now (the sacred altars placed around)
The priestess enters, with her hair unbound,
And thrice invokes the powers below the ground.

. . .

　　'Twas dead of night, when weary bodies close
Their eyes in balmy sleep, and soft repose :
The winds no longer whisper through the woods ;
760 Nor murmuring tides disturb the gentle floods.
The stars in silent order moved around ;
And Peace, with downy wings was brooding **on the**
　　ground.
The flocks and herds, and particoloured fowl
Which haunt the woods or swim the weedy pool,
Stretched on the quiet earth, securely lay,
Forgetting the past labours of the day.
All else, of Nature's common gift partake ;
Unhappy Dido was alone awake :
Nor sleep nor ease the furious queen can find :
770 Sleep fled her eyes, as quiet fled her mind.

. . .

　　Then thus she said within her secret mind :
' What shall I do ? what succour can I find ?
Become a suppliant to Iärbas' pride,
And take my turn to court, and be denied ?
Shall I with this ungrateful Trojan go,
Forsake an empire, and attend a foe ?
Himself I refuged, and his train relieved—
780 'Tis true—but am I sure to be received ?
Can gratitude in Trojan souls have place ?
Laomedon still lives in all his race !
Then shall I seek alone the churlish crew,
Or with my fleet their flying sails pursue ?
What force have I but those, whom scarce **before**
I drew reluctant from their native shore ?
Will they again embark at my desire,
Once more sustain the seas, and quit their **second Tyre?**
Rather with steel thy guilty breast invade,
790 And take the fortune thou thyself hast made.

Your pity, sister, first seduced my mind;
Or seconded too well what I designed.
These dear-bought pleasures had I never known;
Had I continued free, and still my own
(Avoiding love), I had not found despair,
But shared with savage beasts the common air:
Like them, a lonely life I might have led;
Not mourned the living, nor disturbed the dead.'
These thoughts she brooded in her anxious breast.—
800 On board, the Trojan found more easy rest.
Resolved to sail, in sleep he passed the night;
And ordered all things for his early flight.

To whom, once more the wingèd god appears:
His former youthful mien and shape he wears;
And with this new alarm invades his ears:
'Sleep'st thou, O goddess-born? and canst thou **drown**
Thy needful cares, so near a hostile town,
Beset with foes; nor hear'st the western gales
Invite thy passage, and inspire thy sails?
810 She harbours in her heart a furious hate
(And thou shalt find the dire effects too late),
Fixed on revenge, and obstinate to die.—
Haste swiftly hence, while thou hast power to fly!
The sea with ships will soon be covered o'er,
And blazing firebrands kindle all the shore.
Prevent her rage, while night obscures the skies;
And sail before the purple morn arise.
Who knows what hazards thy delay may bring?
Woman's a various and a changeful thing!'
820 Thus, Hermes in the dream; then took his flight
Aloft in air, unseen, and mixed with night.

Twice warned by the celestial messenger,
The pious prince arose with hasty fear;
Then roused his drowsy train without delay:

757 This exquisite description can never be sufficiently admired. Virgil describes minutely and at length the profound calm, quiet and stillness of the night, in order to render the cruel disturbancies and agonies of the restless queen more affecting by such a contrast. . . . Virgil never makes a description for the sake of the fine verses it may contain, or to show his talent of painting well, but always in order to heighten some passion, and further the action of the poem.

Warton

'Haste to your banks! your crooked anchors weigh,
And spread your flying sails, and stand to sea!
A god commands! he stood before my sight,
And urged us once again to speedy flight.
O sacred power! what power soe'er thou art,
830 To thy blessed orders I resign my heart.
Lead thou the way; protect thy Trojan bands;
And prosper the design thy will commands.'
He said; and, drawing forth his flaming sword,
His thundering arm divides the many-twisted cord.
An emulating zeal inspires his train:
They run; they snatch; they rush into the main.

. . .

'And shall the ungrateful traitor go (she said),
My land forsaken, and my love betrayed?
Shall we not arm? not rush from every street,
850 To follow, sink, and burn, his perjured fleet?
Haste! haul my galleys out! pursue the foe!
Bring flaming brands! set sail, and swiftly row!
What have I said? Where am I? Fury turns
My brain; and my distempered bosom burns.
Then, when I gave my person and my throne,
This hate, this rage, had been more timely shown.
See now the promised faith, the vaunted name,
The pious man, who, rushing through the flame,
Preserved his gods, and to the Phrygian shore
860 The burden of his feeble father bore!
I should have torn him piece-meal—strewed in floods
His scattered limbs, or left exposed in woods:
Destroyed his friends, and son; and from the fire
Have set the reeking boy before the sire!
Events are doubtful, which on battle wait;
Yet where's the doubt, to souls secure of fate?
My Tyrians, at their injured queen's command,
Had tossed their fires amid the Trojan band:
At once extinguished all the faithless name;
870 And I myself, in vengeance of my shame,
Had fall'n upon the pile, to mend the funeral flame.
Thou Sun, who view'st at once the world below!
Thou Juno, guardian of the nuptial vow!
Thou Hecate, hearken from thy dark abodes!
Ye Furies, fiends, and violated gods!
All powers invoked with Dido's dying breath,
Attend her curses, and avenge her death!

If so the Fates ordain, and Jove commands,
The ungrateful wretch should find the Latian lands,
880　Yet let a race untamed, and haughty foes,
His peaceful entrance with dire arms oppose:
Oppressed with numbers in the unequal field,
His men discouraged, and himself expelled,
Let him for succour sue from place to place,
Torn from his subjects, and his son's embrace.
First, let him see his friends in battle slain,
And their untimely fate lament in vain:
And when at length, the cruel war will cease,
On hard conditions may he buy his peace;
890　Nor let him then enjoy supreme command;
But fall, untimely, by some hostile hand;
And lie unburied on the barren sand!
These are my prayers, and this my dying will;
And you, my Tyrians, every curse fulfil:
Perpetual hate and mortal wars proclaim
Against the prince, the people, and the name.
These grateful offerings on my grave bestow;
Nor league, nor love, the hostile nations know!
Now, and from hence in every future age,
900　When rage excites your arms, and strength supplies
　　　the rage,
Rise some avenger of our Libyan blood;
With fire and sword pursue the perjured brood:
Our arms, our seas, our shores, opposed to theirs;
And the same hate descend on all our heirs!'
　　This said, within her anxious mind she weighs
The means of cutting short her odious days.
. . .

Ghastly she gazed; with pain she drew her breath;
And nature shivered at approaching death.
　　Then swiftly to the fatal place she passed,
And mounts the funeral pile with furious haste;
Unsheaths the sword the Trojan left behind
930　(Not for so dire an enterprise designed).
But when she viewed the garments loosely spread,
Which once he wore, and saw the conscious bed,
She paused, and with a sigh, the robes embraced;
Then on the couch her trembling body cast,
Repressed her ready tears, and spoke her last:
'Dear pledges of my love, while heaven so pleased,
Receive a soul, of mortal anguish eased.

My fatal course is finished ; and I go,
A glorious name, among the ghosts below.
940 A lofty city by my hands is raised ;
Pygmalion punished, and my lord appeased.
What could my fortune have afforded more,
Had the false Trojan never touched my shore?'
Then kissed the couch ; and 'Must I die (she said),
And unrevenged? 'tis doubly to be dead !
Yet e'en this death with pleasure I receive :
On any terms, 'tis better than to live.
These flames, from far, may the false Trojan view ;
These boding omens his base flight pursue !'
950 She said, and struck : deep entered in her side
The piercing steel, with reeking purple dyed.
Clogged in the wound the cruel weapon stands ;
The spouting blood came streaming on her hands.
   Her sad attendants saw the deadly stroke,
And with loud cries the sounding palace shook.
Distracted, from the fatal sight they fled,
And through the town the dismal rumour spread.
First from the frighted court the yell began ;
Redoubled, thence from house to house it ran :
960 The groans of men, with shrieks, laments, and cries
Of mixing women, mount the vaulted skies.
Not less the clamour, than if—ancient Tyre,
Or the new Carthage, set by foes on fire—
The rolling ruin, with their loved abodes,
Involved the blazing temple of their gods.
   Her sister hears : and furious with despair,
She beats her breast, and rends her yellow hair ;
And, calling on Eliza's name aloud,
Runs breathless to the place, and breaks the crowd,
970 'Was all that pomp of woe for this prepared,
These fires, this funeral pile, these altars reared?
Was all this train of plots contrived (said she),
All, only to deceive unhappy me?'
. . .
This said, she mounts the pile with eager haste,
And in her arms the gasping queen embraced ;
Her temples chafed ; and her own garments tore
To stanch the streaming blood, and cleanse the gore.
Thrice Dido tried to raise her drooping head,
And, fainting, thrice fell grovelling on the bed :
990 Thrice oped her heavy eyes, and saw the light ;
But, having found it, sickened at the sight,

And closed her lids at last in endless night.
   Then Juno, grieving that she should sustain
A death so lingering, and so full of pain,
Sent Iris down to free her from the strife
Of labouring nature, and dissolve her life.

. . .

1003 Downward the various goddess took her flight,
And drew a thousand colours from the light.
Then stood above the dying lover's head,
And said : 'I thus devote thee to the dead :
This offering to the infernal gods I bear.'
Thus while she spoke, she cut the fatal hair :
The struggling soul was loosed, and life dissolved in air.

BOOK V

THE ARGUMENT

Æneas, setting sail from Afric, is driven by a storm on the coasts of Sicily, where he is hospitably received by his friend Acestes, king of part of the island, and born of Trojan parentage. He applies himself to celebrate the memory of his father with divine honours, and accordingly institutes funeral games, and appoints prizes for those who should conquer in them. While these ceremonies were performing, Juno sends Iris to persuade the Trojan women to burn the ships, who upon her instigation set fire to them; which burned four, and would have consumed the rest, had not Jupiter by a miraculous shower extinguished it. Upon this, Æneas, by the advice of one of his generals, and a vision of his father, builds a city for the women, old men, and others, who were either unfit for war, or weary of the voyage, and sails for Italy. Venus procures of Neptune a safe voyage for him and all his men, excepting only his pilot Palinurus, who was unfortunately lost.

The foot-race

From thence his way the Trojan hero bent
Into the neighbouring plain, with mountains pent,
Whose sides were shaded with surrounding wood.
Full in the midst of this fair valley, stood
A native theatre, which, rising slow
By just degrees, o'erlooked the ground below.
High on a sylvan throne the leader sat;
380 A numerous train attend in solemn state.
Here those, that in the rapid course delight,
Desire of honour, and the prize, invite.
The rival runners without order stand;
The Trojans, mixed with the Sicilian band.
First Nisus, with Euryalus, appears—
Euryalus a boy of blooming years,
With sprightly grace and equal beauty crowned—
Nisus, for friendship to the youth, renowned.
Diores next, of Priam's royal race,
390 Then Salius, joined with Patron, took their place;
(But Patron in Arcadia had his birth,
And Salius, his from Acarnanian earth;)
Then two Sicilian youths—the names of these
Swift Helymus, and lovely Panopes
(Both jolly huntsmen, both in forests bred,
And owning old Acestes for their head),
With several others of ignobler name,
Whom time has not delivered o'er to fame.

BOOK V   131

　　　To these the hero thus his thoughts explained,
400　In words which general approbation gained :
　　'One common largess is for all designed
　　(The vanquished and the victor shall be joined):
　　Two darts of polished steel and Gnossian wood,
　　A silver-studded axe, alike bestowed.

I have frequently wondered at the judgement of the celebrated Montaigne who says he esteemed this book of the *Aeneid* to be the most perfect and beautiful of the whole twelve. 'Tis not to be disputed that it contains many and various beauties, but being purely descriptive and not at all applying to the passions, it can never interest the reader so deeply, nor engage his attention so strongly, as several other parts of the poem must do if he has any feeling or sensibility.

　　　　　　　　　　　　　　　　　　　　　　　　Warton

The poet, judicious in everything having conceived the representation of these sports as a great embellishment to his work because it is a subject capable of much ornament, judged further that he could nowhere better insert it than in this place, to make an agreeable opposition to what he had treated of in the fourth book, not doubting but that it was requisite to recreate the spirits of his reader grieved and afflicted by the tragical death of Dido. That beautiful order which is remarkable through this whole poem discovers itself particularly in the detail of this book. These sports, varied by the diversity of their own nature, are still more so by his manner of relating them, by the different scene, and the different success, and by the rewards proportioned to the dignity of the contention and the quality of the contenders. The actions of the hero are conducted with no less judgement. The poet considered that the person whom he would propose as a pattern to others ought not to be regarded in the most sublime and important actions only. He thought fit after the example of Homer to humanise his hero a little and to show him in sports and diversions as in the other occurrences of civil life. Let any one then consider the equity and humanity which accompanies all his actions, and all the decencies which he is made to observe.

　　　　　　　　　　　　　　　　　　　Trapp translating Segrais

385　A good preparatory hint to the episode of Nisus and Euryalus in the
　　ninth book.

'The foremost three have olive-wreaths decreed
The first of these obtains a stately steed
Adorned with trappings; and the next in fame,
The quiver of an Amazonian dame,
With feathered Thracian arrows well supplied:
410 A golden belt shall gird his manly side,
Which with a sparkling diamond shall be tied.
The third this Grecian helmet shall content.'
He said. To their appointed base they went;
With beating hearts the expected sign receive,
And, starting all at once, the barrier leave.
Spread out, as on the wingèd winds, they flew,
And seized the distant goal with greedy view.
Shot from the crowd, swift Nisus all o'er-passed;
Nor storms, nor thunder, equal half his haste.
420 The next, but, though the next, yet far disjoined,
Came Salius; and Euryalus behind;
Then Helymus, whom young Diores plied,
Step after step, and almost side by side,
His shoulders pressing—and, in longer space,
Had won, or left at least a dubious race.
Now, spent, the goal they almost reach at last,
When eager Nisus, hapless in his haste,
Slipped first, and, slipping, fell upon the plain,
Soaked with the blood of oxen newly slain.
430 The careless victor had not marked his way;
But, treading where the treacherous puddle lay,
His heels flew up; and on the grassy floor
He fell, besmeared with filth and holy gore.
Not mindless then, Euryalus, of thee,
Nor of the sacred bonds of amity,
He strove the immediate rival's hope to cross,
And caught the foot of Salius as he rose:
So Salius lay extended on the plain :
Euryalus springs out, the prize to gain,
440 And leaves the crowd :—applauding peals attend
The victor to the goal, who vanquished by his friend.
Next Helymus; and then Diores came,
By two misfortunes made the third in fame.
But Salius enters, and, exclaiming loud
For justice, deafens and disturbs the crowd ;
Urges his cause may in the court be heard ;
And pleads the prize is wrongfully conferred.
But favour for Euryalus appears ;
His blooming beauty, with his tender years,

450   Had bribed the judges for the promised prize;
Besides, Diores fills the court with cries,
Who vainly reaches at the last reward,
If the first palm on Salius be conferred.
Then thus the prince : ' Let no disputes arise :
Where Fortune placed it, I award the prize.
But Fortune's errors give me leave to mend,
At least to pity my deserving friend.'
He said, and, from among the spoils, he draws
(Ponderous with shaggy mane and golden paws)
460   A lion's hide ; to Salius this he gives :
Nisus with envy sees the gift, and grieves.
' If such rewards to vanquished men are due
(He said), and falling is to rise by you,
What prize may Nisus from your bounty claim,
Who merited the first rewards and fame?
In falling, both an equal fortune tried ;
Would Fortune for my fall so well provide !'
With this he pointed to his face, and showed
His hands and all his habit smeared with blood.
470   The indulgent father of the people smiled,
And caused to be produced an ample shield,
Of wondrous art, by Didymaon wrought,
Long since from Neptune's bars in triumph brought.
This given to Nisus, he divides the rest,
And equal justice in his gifts expressed.

The archery contest

450   I am of the opinion that in this foot-race [*Iliad* XXIII] has shown more judgement and morality than Virgil. Nisus in the latter is unjust to his adversary, in favour of his friend Euryalus, so that Euryalus wins the race by palpable fraud, yet the poet gives him the first prize, whereas Homer makes Ulysses victorious, purely through the mischance of Ajax, and his own piety in invoking Minerva.

Pope on *Iliad* XXIII concluding remark

However this may be, one cannot but be charmed at the manner with which Virgil keeps up the characters of all the persons he introduces. Of which this action of Nisus in striving to be as serviceable to his friend as he possibly could is a beautiful instance.

Warton (having quoted Pope)

This done, Æneas orders, for the close,
The strife of archers, with contending bows.
The mast, Sergestus' shattered galley bore,
With his own hands he raises on the shore.
650 A fluttering dove upon the top they tie,
The living mark at which their arrows fly.
The rival archers in a line advance,
Their turn of shooting to receive from chance:
A helmet holds their names: the lots are drawn;
On the first scroll was read Hippocoön:
The people shout. Upon the next was found
Young Mnestheus, late with naval honours crowned.
The third contained Eurytion's noble name,
Thy brother, Pandarus, and next in fame,
660 Whom Pallas urged the treaty to confound,
And send among the Greeks a feathered wound.
Acestes, in the bottom, last remained,
Whom not his age from youthful sports restrained.
Soon all with vigour bend their trusty bows;
And from the quiver each his arrow chose,
Hippocoön's was the first: with forceful sway
It flew, and, whizzing, cut the liquid way.
Fixed in the mast the feathered weapon stands:
The fearful pigeon flutters in her bands;
670 And the tree trembled; and the shouting cries
Of the pleased people rend the vaulted skies.
Then Mnestheus to the head his arrow drove,
With lifted eyes, and took his aim above,
But made a glancing shot, and missed the dove,
Yet missed so narrow, that he cut the cord
Which fastened by the foot, the flitting bird.
The captive thus released, away she flies,
And beats with clapping wings the yielding skies.
His bow already bent, Eurytion stood;
680 And, having first invoked his brother-god,
His wingèd shaft with eager haste he sped.
The fatal message reached her as she fled:
She leaves her life aloft; she strikes the ground,
And renders back the weapon in the wound.
Acestes, grudging at his lot, remains
Without a prize to gratify his pains.
Yet, shooting upward, sends his shaft, to shew
An archer's art, and boast his twanging bow.
The feathered arrow gave a dire portent,
690 And latter augurs judge from this event.

Chafed by the speed, it fired ; and, as it flew,
A train of following flames, ascending, drew :
Kindling they mount, and mark the shiny way ;
Across the skies as falling meteors play,
And vanish into wind, or in a blaze decay.
The Trojans and Sicilians wildly stare,
And trembling, turn their wonder into prayer.
The Dardan prince put on a smiling face,
And strained Acestes with a close embrace ;
700 Then honouring him with gifts above the rest,
Turned the bad omen, nor his fears confessed.
' The gods (said he) this miracle have wrought,
And ordered you the prize without the lot.
Accept this goblet, rough with figured gold,
Which Thracian Cisseus gave my sire of old :
This pledge of ancient amity receive,
Which to my second sire I justly give.'
He said, and, with the trumpet's cheerful sound,
Proclaimed him victor, and with laurel crowned.
710 Nor good Eurytion envied him the prize,
Though he transfixed the pigeon in the skies.
Who cut the line, with second gifts was graced ;
The third was his whose arrow pierced the mast.

The Trojan women burn the ships

    Thus far the sacred sports they celebrate ;
But Fortune soon resumed her ancient hate ;
For, while they pay the dead his annual dues,
Those envied rites Saturnian Juno views ;
And sends the goddess of the various bow,
To try new methods of revenge below :
Supplies the winds to wing her airy way,
790 Where in the port secure the navy lay.
. . .

783 From sports and diversions here is a sudden change to the most disastrous incident imaginable. Virgil shows his judgement in nothing more than in transitions, in diversifying his scenes, and alternately raising and depressing the mind of his reader.
                                                                                   Trapp

The Trojan matrons, on the sands alone,
With sighs and tears Anchises' death bemoan:
Then, turning to the sea their weeping eyes,
Their pity to themselves renews their cries.
' Alas ! (said one) what oceans yet remain
800 For us to sail ! what labours to sustain !'
All take the word, and, with a general groan
Implore the gods for peace, and places of their own.
The goddess, great in mischief, views their pains,
And in a woman's form her heavenly limbs restrains.

. . .

Thus changed, amidst the crying crowd she ran,
Mixed with the matrons, and these words began:
810 ' O wretched we ! whom not the Grecian power
Nor flames destroyed, in Troy's unhappy hour !
O wretched we ! reserved by cruel Fate
Beyond the ruins of the sinking state !
Now, seven revolving years are wholly run,
Since this improsperous voyage we begun ;
Since, tossed from shores to shores, from lands to
    lands,
Inhospitable rocks and barren sands.
Wandering in exile, through the stormy sea,
We search in vain for flying Italy.
820 Now cast by Fortune on this kindred land,
What should our rest and rising walls withstand ;
Or hinder, here, to fix our banished band?
O country lost, and gods redeemed in vain,
If still in endless exile we remain !
Shall we no more the Trojan walls renew.
Or streams of some dissembled Simoïs view ?
Haste ! join with me ! the unhappy fleet consume !
Cassandra bids ; and I declare her doom.

. . .

Struck with the sight, and seized with rage divine,
The matrons prosecute their mad design:
They shriek aloud : they snatch with impious hands
The food of altars : firs and flaming brands,
860 Green boughs and saplings, mingled in their haste,
And smoking torches, on the ships they cast.

. . .

The fire descends or mounts, but still prevails ;
Nor buckets poured, nor strength of human hand,

BOOK V

Can the victorious element withstand.
The pious hero rends his robe, and throws
900 To heaven his hands, and, with his hands, his vows.
'O Jove! (he cried) if prayers can yet have place;
If thou abhorr'st not all the Dardan race;
If any spark of pity still remain;
If gods are gods, and not invoked in vain;
Yet spare the relics of the Trojan train!
Yet from the flames our burning vessels free!
Or let thy fury fall alone on me:
At this devoted head thy thunder throw,
And send the willing sacrifice below.'
910 Scarce had he said, when southern storms arise:
From pole to pole the forky lightning flies:
Loud rattling shakes the mountains and the plain:
Heaven bellies downward, and descends in rain:
Whole sheets of water from the clouds are sent,
Which, hissing through the planks, the flames prevent,
And stop the fiery pest. Four ships alone
Burn to the waist, and for the fleet atone.
  But doubtful thoughts the hero's heart divide,
If he should still in Sicily reside,
920 Forgetful of his fates,—or tempt the main,
In hope the promised Italy to gain.
Then Nautes, old and wise—to whom alone
The will of Heaven by Pallas was foreshown;
Versed in portents, experienced, and inspired
To tell events, and what the Fates required—
Thus, while he stood to neither part inclined,
With cheerful words relieved his labouring mind:
'O goddess-born! resigned in every state,
With patience bear, with prudence push your fate.
930 By suffering well, our fortune we subdue;
Fly when she frowns, and when she calls, pursue.
Your friend Acestes is of Trojan kind;
To him disclose the secrets of your mind;
Trust in his hands your old and useless train,
Too numerous for the ships which yet remain—
The feeble, old, indulgent of their ease,
The dames, who dread the dangers of the seas,
With all the dastard crew, who dare not stand
The shock of battle with your foes by land.
940 Here you may build a common town for all,
And, from Acestes' name, Acesta call.'
The reasons, with his friend's experience joined,

Encouraged much, but more disturbed his mind,
 'Twas dead of night; when, to his slumbering eyes
His father's shade, descended from the skies,
And thus he spoke: 'O, more than vital breath
Loved while I lived, and dear e'en after death!
O son, in various toils and troubles tossed!
The king of heaven employs my careful ghost
On his commands—the god who saved from fire
Your flaming fleet, and heard your just desire.
The wholesome counsel of your friend receive,
And here, the coward train and women, leave.
The chosen youth, and those who nobly dare,
Transport, to tempt the dangers of the war:
The stern Italians will their courage try:
Rough are their manners, and their minds are high.
But first to Pluto's palace you shall go,
And seek my shade among the blest below;
For not with impious ghosts my soul remains;
Nor suffers, with the damned, perpetual pains;
But breathes the living air and soft Elysian plains.
The chaste Sibylla shall your steps convey,
And blood of offered victims free the way.
There shall you know what realms the gods assign,
And learn the fates and fortunes of your line.
But now farewell! I vanish with the night,
And feel the blast of heaven's approaching light.'
He said, and mixed with shades, and took his airy
    flight.
'Whither so fast? (the filial duty cried)
And why, ah! why the wished embrace denied?'
    He said, and rose; as holy zeal inspires,
He rakes hot embers, and renews the fires;
His country gods and Vesta then adores
With cakes and incense, and their aid implores.
Next, for his friends and royal host he sent,
Revealed his vision, and the god's intent,
With his own purpose. All, without delay,
The will of Jove, and his desires, obey.'

. . .

The prince designs a city with the plough:
The lots their several tenements allow.
This part, is named from Ilium, that, from Troy;
And the new king ascends the throne with joy;

      A chosen senate from the people draws;
      Appoints the judges, and ordains the laws.
990 Then, on the top of Eryx, they begin
      A rising temple to the Paphian queen.
      Anchises, last, is honoured as a god:
      A priest is added; annual gifts bestowed;
      And groves are planted round his blest abode.
      Nine days they pass in feasts, their temples crowned;
      And fumes of incense in the fanes abound.
      Then from the south arose a gentle breeze,
      That curled the smoothness of the glassy seas;
      The rising winds a ruffling gale afford,
1000 And call the merry mariners aboard.

      . . .

BOOK VI

THE ARGUMENT

The Sibyl foretells Æneas the adventures he should meet with in Italy. She attends him to hell; describing to him the various scenes of that place, and conducting him to his father Anchises, who instructs him in those sublime mysteries of the soul of the world, and the transmigration; and shows him that glorious race of heroes, which was to descend from him and his posterity.

The Trojans land at Cumae where Aeneas seeks the cave of the Sibyl

    A spacious cave, within its farmost part,
Was hewed and fashioned by laborious art,
Through the hill's hollow sides: before the place,
A hundred doors a hundred entries grace;
As many voices issue, and the sound
Of Sibyl's words as many times rebound.
Now to the mouth they come. Aloud she cries:
'This is the time! inquire your destinies!
70 He comes! behold the god!' Thus while she said
(And shivering at the sacred entry stayed),
Her colour changed; her face was not the same;
And hollow groans from her deep spirit came.
Her hair stood up; convulsive rage possessed
Her trembling limbs, and heaved her labouring breast.
Greater than human kind she seemed to look;
And with an accent more than mortal, spoke:
Her staring eyes with sparkling fury roll;
When all the god came rushing on her soul.

. . .

120   Struggling in vain, impatient of her load,
And labouring underneath the ponderous god,
The more she strove to shake him from her breast,
With more, and far superior force he pressed;
Commands his entrance, and, without control,
Usurps her organs, and inspires her soul.
Now, with a furious blast, the hundred doors
Ope of themselves; a rushing whirlwind roars
Within the cave, and Sibyl's voice restores:
'Escaped the dangers of the watery reign,
130 Yet more and greater ills by land remain.
The coast so long desired (nor doubt the event),

Thy troops shall reach, but, having reached, repent.
Wars! horrid wars, I view!—a field of blood,
And Tiber rolling with a purple flood.
Simoïs nor Xanthus shall be wanting there:
A new Achilles shall in arms appear;
And he too, goddess-born. Fierce Juno's hate
Added to hostile force, shall urge thy fate.
To what strange nations shalt not thou resort;
140 Driven to solicit aid at every court!
The cause, the same which Ilium once oppressed:
A foreign mistress, and a foreign guest.
But thou, secure of soul, unbent with woes,
The more thy fortune frowns, the more oppose.
The dawnings of thy safety shall be shown,
From whence thou least shalt hope—a Grecian town.'
    Thus, from the dark recess, the Sibyl spoke;
And the resisting air the thunder broke;
The cave rebellowed, and the temple shook.
150 The ambiguous god, who ruled her labouring breast,
In these mysterious words his mind expressed:
Some truth revealed, in terms involved the rest.
At length her fury fell: her foaming ceased,
And, ebbing in her soul, the god decreased.
    Then thus the chief: 'No terror to my view,
No frightful face of danger, can be new.
Inured to suffer, and resolved to dare,
The Fates, without my power, shall be without my care.
This let me crave—since near your grove the road

It [book six] contains such a treasure of various learning, so much theology, philosophy and history, such excellent reflections and discourses upon the immortality of the soul, and the happiness and misery of a future state, all adorned with such living descriptions and animated with such an inexpressible spirit of poetry, as are all in conjunction who where else to be met with, and can never be sufficiently admired. It is certainly the most noble and perhaps the most elegant of all the *Aeneis*. But it is more particularly marked by its piety and religion, and yet more by its wonders and surprises. For as the fourth book has far more of the pathetical than of the marvellous, though a great deal even of that, so this has far more of the marvellous than of the pathetical, though something too even of that.

Trapp

160   To hell lies open, and the dark abode
     Which Acheron surrounds, the innavigable flood—
     Conduct me through the regions void of light,
     And lead me longing to my father's sight.
     For him, a thousand dangers I have sought,
     And, rushing where the thickest Grecians fought,
     Safe on my back the sacred burden brought.
     He, for my sake, the raging ocean tried,
     And wrath of heaven (my still auspicious guide),
     And bore, beyond the strength decrepit age supplied.
170   Oft, since he breathed his last, in dead of night,
     His reverend image stood before my sight;
     Enjoined to seek, below, his holy shade—
     Conducted there by your unerring aid.
     But you, if pious minds by prayers are won,
     Oblige the father, and protect the son.
. . .

      So prayed the Trojan prince, and, while he prayed,
     His hand upon the holy altar laid.
190   Then, thus replied the prophetess divine:
     'O goddess-born, of great Anchises' line!
     The gates of hell are open night and day;
     Smooth the descent, and easy is the way:
     But to return, and view the cheerful skies,
     In this, the task and mighty labour lies.
     To few, great Jupiter imparts this grace,
     And those of shining worth, and heavenly race.
     Betwixt those regions and our upper light,
     Deep forests and impenetrable night
200   Possess the middle space: the infernal bounds,
     Cocytus, with his sable waves surrounds.
     But, if so dire a love your soul invades,
     As twice below to view the trembling shades;
     If you so hard a toil will undertake,
     As twice to pass the innavigable lake;
     Receive my counsel. In the neighbouring grove
     There stands a tree: the queen of Stygian Jove
     Claims it her own; thick woods and gloomy night
     Conceal the happy plant from human sight.
210   One bough it bears; but (wondrous to behold!)
     The ductile rind and leaves of radiant gold:
     This, from the vulgar branches must be torn,
     And to fair Proserpine, the present borne,
     Ere leave be given to tempt the nether skies.

BOOK VI

    The first thus rent, a second will arise;
And the same metal the same room supplies.
Look round the wood, with lifted eyes, to see
The lurking gold upon the fatal tree;
Then rend it off, as holy rites command:
220 The willing metal will obey thy hand,
Following with ease, if, favoured by thy fate,
Thou art foredoomed to view the Stygian state;
If not, no labour can the tree constrain;
And strength of stubborn arms and steel, are vain.

. . .

271   Thus while he wrought, involving in his mind
The ways to compass what his wish designed,

. . .

280 Two doves, descending from their airy flight,
Secure upon the grassy plain alight.
He knew his mother's birds; and thus he prayed:
'Be you my guides, with your auspicious aid,
And lead my footsteps, till the branch be found,
Whose glittering shadow gilds the sacred ground.
And thou, great parent! with celestial care,
In this distress, be present to my prayer.'
Thus having said, he stopped, with watchful sight
Observing still the motions of their flight,
290 What course they took, what happy signs they show.
They fed, and, fluttering, by degrees withdrew
Still farther from the place, but still in view:
Hopping and flying, thus they led him on
To the slow lake, whose baleful stench to shun,
They winged their flight aloft; then, stooping low,
Perched on the double tree that bears the golden bough.
Through the green leaves the glittering shadows glow;
As, on the sacred oak, the wintry misletoe,
Where the proud mother views her precious brood,
300 And happier branches, which she never sowed.
Such was the glittering; such the ruddy rind,
And dancing leaves, that wantoned in the wind.
He seized the shining bough with griping hold,
And rent away with ease, the lingering gold;
Then to the Sibyl's palace bore the prize.

. . .

    These rites performed, the prince, without delay,
Hastes to the nether world, his destined way.

Deep was the cave ; and, downward as it went
From the wide mouth, a rocky, rough descent :
340 And here the access a gloomy grove defends ;
And here the innavigable lake extends,
O'er whose unhappy waters, void of light,
No bird presumes to steer his airy flight :
Such deadly stenches from the depth arise,
And steaming sulphur, that infects the skies.
From hence, the Grecian bards their legends make,
And give the name Avernus, to the lake.
Four sable bullocks, in the yoke untaught,
For sacrifice the pious hero brought.
350 The priestess pours the wine betwixt their horns ;
Then cuts the curling hair ; that first oblation burns,
Invoking Hecate hither to repair—
A powerful name in hell and upper air,

. . .

Late the nocturnal sacrifice begun,
Nor ended till the next returning sun.
Then earth began to bellow, trees to dance,
And howling dogs in glimmering light advance,
Ere Hecate came : ' Far hence be souls profane !
(The Sibyl cried) and from the grove abstain !
370 Now, Trojan, take the way thy fates afford ;
Assume thy courage, and unsheath thy sword.'
She said, and passed along the gloomy space ;
The prince pursued her steps with equal pace.
 Ye realms yet unrevealed to human sight !
Ye gods who rule the regions of the night !
Ye gliding ghosts ! permit me to relate
The mystic wonders of your silent state.
 Obscure they went through dreary shades, that led
Along the waste dominions of the dead.
380 Thus wander travellers in woods by night,
By the moon's doubtful and malignant light,
When Jove in dusky clouds involves the skies,
And the faint crescent shoots by fits before their eyes.
 Just in the gate, and in the jaws of hell,
Revengeful Cares and sullen Sorrows dwell ;
And pale Diseases, and repining Age,
Want, Fear, and Famine's unresisted rage ;
Here Toils, and Death, and Death's half-brother **Sleep**
(Forms terrible to view), their sentry keep ;

390 With anxious Pleasures of a guilty mind;
Deep Frauds before, and open Force behind;
The Furies' iron beds; and Strife, that shakes
Her hissing tresses, and unfolds her snakes.

. . .

410   Hence to deep Acheron they take their way,
Whose troubled eddies, thick with ooze and clay,
Are whirled aloft, and in Cocytus lost:
There, Charon stands, who rules the dreary coast—
A sordid god : down from his hoary chin
A length of beard descends, uncombed, unclean :
His eyes, like hollow furnaces on fire;
A girdle foul with grease, binds his obscene attire.
He spreads his canvas; with his pole he steers;
The freights of flitting ghosts in his thin bottom bears
420 He looked in years; yet, in his years were seen
A youthful vigour, and autumnal green.
An airy crowd came rushing where he stood,
Which filled the margin of the fatal flood :

380 This simile of three lines both for its natural ideas and elegant expressions is one of the most beautiful in nature.
                                              Trapp

384 Virgil has not only borrowed the general design from Homer [*Odyssey* XI], but imitated many particular incidents. ... In the *Aeneid* there is a magnificent description of the descent and entrance into hell, and the diseases cares and terrors that Aeneas sees in his journey are very happily imagined as an introduction into the regions of death, whereas there is nothing so noble in Homer. We are scarce able to discover the place where the poet lays his scene, or whether Ulysses continues below or above the ground.
                  Pope on *Odyssey* XI introductory remark

    The subterreanean world as the poet has described it, may be divided into four parts: first, the porch or entrance; secondly the space between the entrance and the river's side, possessed by those who wander unburied and those who wait to be ferried over; thirdly the river itself with Charon and his boat; fourthly the regions beyond the river, which last may be divided into three parts: first, the mansions of those who are in a middle state; secondly Tartarus or the place of the damned; thirdly Elysium or the place of the blessed.
                                              Trapp

Husbands and wives, boys and unmarried maids,
And mighty heroes' more majestic shades ;
And youths, intombed before their fathers' eyes,
With hollow groans, and shrieks, and feeble cries.
Thick as the leaves in autumn strew the woods,
Or fowls by winter forced, forsake the floods,
430 And wing their hasty flight to happier lands—
Such, and so thick, the shivering army stands,
And press for passage, with extended hands.
   Now these, now those, the surly boatman bore :
The rest he drove to distance from the shore.
The hero, who beheld with wondering eyes,
The tumult mixed with shrieks, laments, and cries,
Asked of his guide, what the rude concourse meant?
Why to the shore the thronging people bent?
What forms of law among the ghosts were used?
440 Why some were ferried o'er, and some refused?
'Son of Anchises ! offspring of the gods !
(The Sibyl said) you see the Stygian floods !
The sacred streams which heaven's imperial state
Attests in oaths, and fears to violate.
The ghosts rejected are the unhappy crew
Deprived of sepulchres and funeral due :
The boatman, Charon : those, the buried host,
He ferries over to the farther coast ;
Nor dares his transport vessel cross the waves
450 With such whose bones are not composed in graves.
A hundred years they wander on the shore ;
At length, their penance done, are wafted o'er.'
   The Trojan chief his forward pace repressed,
Revolving anxious thoughts within his breast.
He saw his friends, who, whelmed beneath the waves,
Their funeral honours claimed, and asked their quiet graves.

. . .

Amidst the spirits, Palinurus pressed,
Yet fresh from life, a new-admitted guest.
Who, while he steering viewed the stars, and bore
His course from Afric to the Latian shore,
Fell headlong down. The Trojan fixed his view,
And scarcely through the gloom the sullen shadow knew.
Then thus the prince : ' What envious power, O friend !
Brought your loved life to this disastrous end?
For Phœbus, ever true in all he said,
470 Has in your fate alone, my faith betrayed.

The god foretold you should not die before
You reached, secure from seas, the Italian shore.
Is this the unerring power?' The ghost replied:
'Nor Phœbus flattered, nor his answers lied;
Nor envious gods have sent me to the deep;
But, while the stars and course of heaven I keep,
My wearied eyes were seized with fatal sleep.
I fell; and with my weight the helm, constrained,
Was drawn along, which yet my gripe retained.
480 Now by the winds and raging waves I swear,
Your safety, more than mine, was then my care;
Lest, of the guide bereft, the rudder lost,
Your ship should run against the rocky coast.
Three blustering nights, borne by the southern blast,
I floated, and discovered land at last:
High on a mounting wave my head I bore,
Forcing my strength, and gathering to the shore:
Panting, but past the danger, now I seized
The craggy cliffs, and my tired members eased.
490 While, cumbered with my dropping clothes I lay,
The cruel nation, covetous of prey,
Stained with my blood the unhospitable coast;
And now, by winds and waves, my lifeless limbs are
    tossed;
Which, O! avert, by yon ethereal light,
Which I have lost for this eternal night.
Or, if by dearer ties you may be won,
By your dead sire, and by your living son,
Redeem from this reproach my wandering ghost.
Or with your navy seek the Velin coast,
500 And in a peaceful grave my corpse compose;
Or, if a nearer way your mother shows
(Without whose aid, you durst not undertake
This frightful passage o'er the Stygian lake),
Lend to this wretch your hand, and waft him o'er
To the sweet banks of yon forbidden shore.'
Scarce had he said; the prophetess began:
'What hopes delude thee, miserable man?
Thinkest thou, thus unintombed to cross the floods,
To view the Furies and infernal gods,
510 And visit without leave, the dark abodes?
Attend the term of long revolving years;
Fate, and the dooming gods, are deaf to tears.
This comfort of thy dire misfortune take—
The wrath of heaven, inflicted for thy sake,

With vengeance shall pursue the inhuman coast,
Till they propitiate thy offended ghost;
And raise a tomb, with vows and solemn prayer;
And Palinurus' name the place shall bear.'
This calmed his cares—soothed with his future fame,
520 And pleased to hear his propagated name.
    Now nearer to the Stygian lake they draw:
Whom, from the shore the surly boatman saw;
Observed this passage through the shady wood,
And marked their near approaches to the flood:
Then thus he called aloud, inflamed with wrath:
' Mortal, whate'er, who this forbidden path
In arms presum'st to tread ! I charge thee, stand,
And tell thy name, and business in the land !
Know, this the realm of night—the Stygian shore:
530 My boat conveys no living bodies o'er .
. . .
    To whom the Sibyl thus : ' Compose thy mind :
Nor frauds are here contrived, nor force designed.
. . .
Then showed the shining bough, concealed within her
    vest.
550 No more was needful ; for the gloomy god
Stood mute with awe, to see the golden rod ;
Admired the destined offering to his queen—
A venerable gift, so rarely seen.
His fury thus appeased, he puts to land :
The ghosts forsake their seats at his command :
He clears the deck, receives the mighty freight ;
The leaky vessel groans beneath the weight.
Slowly she sails, and scarcely stems the tides ;
560 The pressing water pours within her sides.
His passengers at length are wafted o'er,
Exposed, in muddy weeds upon the miry shore.
    No sooner landed, in his den they found
The triple porter of the Stygian sound,
Grim Cerberus ; who soon began to rear
His crested snakes, and armed his bristling hair.
The prudent Sibyl had before prepared
A sop, in honey steeped, to charm the guard ;
Which, mixed with powerful drugs, she cast before
His greedy grinning jaws, just oped to roar.
570 With three enormous mouths he gapes, and straight,
With hunger pressed, devours the pleasing bait.
Long draughts of sleep his monstrous limbs enslave ;

He reels, and falling, fills the spacious cave.
The keeper charmed, the chief without delay
Passed on, and took the irremeable way.
Before the gates, the cries of babes new-born,
Whom Fate had from their tender mothers torn,
Assault his ears : then, those whom form of laws
Condemned to die, when traitors judged their cause.
580 Nor want they lots, nor judges to review
The wrongful sentence, and award a new.
Minos, the strict inquisitor, appears ;
And lives and crimes, with his assessors, hears.
Round, in his urn, the blended balls he rolls,
Absolves the just, and dooms the guilty souls.
The next, in place and punishment, are they
Who prodigally threw their souls away :
Fools, who, repining at their wretched state,
And loathing anxious life, suborned their fate.
590 With late repentance, now they would retrieve
The bodies they forsook, and wish to live ;
Their pains and poverty desire to bear,
To view the light of heaven, and breathe the vital air :
But Fate forbids ; the Stygian floods oppose,
And, with nine circling streams, the captive souls inclose.
  Not far from thence, the Mournful Fields appear,
So called from lovers that inhabit there.
The souls whom that unhappy flame invades,
In secret solitude and myrtle shades
600 Make endless moans, and, pining with desire,
Lament too late their unextinguished fire.
. . .
610 Not far from these Phœnician Dido stood,
Fresh from her wound, her bosom bathed in blood ;
Whom when the Trojan hero hardly knew,
Obscure in shades, and with a doubtful view
(Doubtful as he who sees, through dusky night,
Or thinks he sees, the moon's uncertain light),
With tears he first approached the sullen shade;
And as his love inspired him, thus he said :
'Unhappy queen ! then is the common breath
Of rumour true, in your reported death,
620 And I, alas ! the cause ?—By Heaven, I vow,
And all the powers that rule the realms below,
Unwilling I forsook your friendly state,
Commanded by the gods, and forced by Fate !

Those gods, that Fate, whose unresisted might
Have sent me to these regions void of light,
Through the vast empire of eternal night!
Nor dared I to presume, that, pressed with grief,
My flight should urge you to this dire relief.
Stay, stay your steps, and listen to my vows!
630 'Tis the last interview that Fate allows!'
In vain he thus attempts her mind to move
With tears and prayers, and late repenting love.
Disdainfully she looked; then turning round,
She fixed her eyes unmoved upon the ground;
And, what he says and swears, regards no more
Than the deaf rocks, when the loud billows roar:
But whirled away, to shun his hateful sight,
Hid in the forest, and the shades of night:
Then sought Sichæus through the shady grove,
640 Who answered all her cares, and equalled all her love.
 Some pious tears the pitying hero paid,
And followed with his eyes the flitting shade;
Then took the forward way, by Fate ordained,
And, with his guide, the farther fields attained,
Where, severed from the rest, the warrior souls remained.
. . .
Of Trojan chiefs he viewed a numerous train,
All much lamented, all in battle slain:
. . .
The gladsome ghosts, in circling troops, attend,
And with unwearied eyes behold their friend;
Delight to hover near, and long to know
What business brought him to the realms below.
 But Argive chiefs, and Agamemnon's train,
660 When his refulgent arms flashed through the shady plain,
Fled from his well-known face with wonted fear;
As when his thundering sword and pointed spear
Drove headlong to their ships, and gleaned the routed rear.
They raised a feeble cry, with trembling notes,
But the weak voice deceived their gasping throats.
Here Priam's son, Deïphobus, he found,
Whose face and limbs were one continued wound;
Dishonest, with lopped arms, the youth appears,
Spoiled of his nose, and shortened of his ear.
670 He scarcely knew him, striving to disown
His blotted form, and blushing to be known;
And therefore first began: 'O Teucer's race!

BOOK VI

Who durst thy faultless figure thus deface?
What heart could wish, what hand inflict this dire disgrace?
'Twas famed, that in our last and fatal night,
Your single prowess long sustained the fight;
Till tired, not forced, a glorious fate you chose,
And fell upon a heap of slaughtered foes.
But, in remembrance of so brave a deed,
680 A tomb and funeral honours I decreed;
Thrice called your manes on the Trojan plains:
The place your armour and your name retains.
Your body too I sought, and, had I found,
Designed for burial in your native ground.'
    The ghost replied: 'Your piety has paid
All needful rites to rest my wandering shade;
But cruel Fate, and my more cruel wife,
To Grecian swords betrayed my sleeping life.
These are the monuments of Helen's love:
690 The shame I bear below, the marks I bore above.
You know in what deluding joys, we past
The night that was by heaven decreed our last.
For, when the fatal horse, descending down
Pregnant with arms o'erwhelmed the unhappy town,
She feigned nocturnal orgies; left my bed;
And, mixed with Trojan dames, the dances led;
Then, waving high her torch, the signal made,
Which roused the Grecians from their ambuscade.
With watching over-worn, with cares oppressed,
700 Unhappy I had laid me down to rest;
And heavy sleep my weary limbs possessed.
Meantime my worthy wife our arms mislaid,
And, from beneath my head, my sword conveyed;
The door unlatched, and, with repeated calls
Invites her former lord within my walls.
Thus, in her crime her confidence she placed,
And with new treasons would redeem the past.
What need I more? Into the room they ran,

633 'Tis well known that this silence of Dido is copied from that of Ajax in ... the *Odyssey*, which is nobly imagined. Longinus in his ninth section produces it as one of the examples of the true sublime. ... Dido in Virgil behaves with the same greatness and majesty as Homer's Ajax.

                                                  Warton

And meanly murdered a defenceless man.
710 Ulysses, basely born, first led the way.—
Avenging powers! with justice if I pray,
That fortune be their own another day!

. . .

720 While thus, in talk the flying hours they pass,
The sun had finished more than half his race;
And they, perhaps, in words and tears had spent
The little time of stay which heaven had lent:
But thus the Sibyl chides their long delay:
'Night rushes down, and headlong drives the day:
'Tis here, in different paths, the way divides;
The right to Pluto's golden palace guides;
The left to that unhappy region tends,
Which to the depth of Tartarus descends:
730 The seat of night profound, and punished fiends.'

. . .

The hero, looking on the left, espied
740 A lofty tower, and strong on every side
With treble walls, which Phlegethon surrounds,
Whose fiery flood the burning empire bounds;
And, pressed betwixt the rocks, the bellowing noise
    resounds.
Wide is the fronting gate, and raised on high
With adamantine columns, threats the sky.
Vain is the force of man, and heaven's as vain,
To crush the pillars which the pile sustain.
Sublime on these, a tower of steel is reared;
And dire Tisiphonè there keeps the ward,
750 Girt in her sanguine gown, by night and day
Observant of the souls that pass the downward way.
From hence are heard the groans of ghosts, the pains
Of sounding lashes, and of dragging chains.
The Trojan stood astonished at their cries;
And asked his guide, from whence those yells arise,
And what the crimes, and what the tortures were,
And loud laments that rent the liquid air?
She thus replied: 'The chaste and holy race
Are all forbidden this polluted place.
760 But Hecate, when she gave to rule the woods,
Then led me trembling through these dire abodes,
And taught the tortures of the avenging gods.
These are the realms of unrelenting Fate;
And awful Rhadamanthus rules the state:

He hears and judges each committed crime;
Inquires into the manner, place, and time.
The conscious wretch must all his acts reveal
(Loth to confess, unable to conceal),
From the first moment of his vital breath,
770 To his last hour of unrepenting death.
Straight o'er the guilty ghost, the Fury shakes
The sounding whip, and brandishes her snakes,
And the pale sinner, with her sisters, takes.'
Then, of itself, unfolds the eternal door;
With dreadful sounds the brazen hinges roar.
'You see, before the gate, what stalking ghost
Commands the guard, what sentries keep the post.
More formidable Hydra stands within,
Whose jaws with iron teeth severely grin.
780 The gaping gulf low to the centre lies,
And twice as deep, as earth is distant from the skies.
The rivals of the gods, the Titan race,
Here, singed with lightning, roll within the unfathomed
    space.
. . .

But let us haste our voyage to pursue:
The walls of Pluto's palace are in view;
The gate, and iron arch above it, stands,
On anvils laboured by the Cyclops' hands.
Before our farther way the Fates allow,
860 Here must we fix on high the golden bough.'
She said: and through the gloomy shades they past,
And chose the middle path.—Arrived at last,
The prince, with living water sprinkled o'er
His limbs and body; then approached the door,
Possessed the porch, and on the front above
He fixed the fatal bough, required by Pluto's love.
    These holy rites performed, they took their way,

739 There is something strangely terrifying to the imagination in
    Aeneas's and the Sibyl's standing before the adamantine gates, and
    listening to the clank of chains and the noise of iron whips that were
    heard in those regions of pain and sorrow.
                                                                Warton

Where long extended plains of pleasure lay.
The verdant fields with those of heaven may vie,
870 With ether vested, and a purple sky—
The blissful seats of happy souls below :
Stars of their own, and their own suns, they know.

. . .

Here patriots live, who, for their country's good,
In fighting fields, were prodigal of blood :
Priests of unblemished lives here make abode,
And poets worthy their inspiring god ;
And searching wits, of more mechanic parts,
900 Who graced their age with new invented arts ;
Those who, to worth their bounty did extend,
And those who knew that bounty to commend.
The heads of these with holy fillets bound,
And all their temples were with garlands crowned.

. . .

But old Anchises, in a flowery vale,
Reviewed his mustered race, and took the tale—
Those happy spirits, which, ordained by Fate,
For future being and new bodies wait :
With studious thought observed the illustrious throng,
In nature's order, as they passed along :
Their names, their fates, their conduct, and their care,
In peaceful senates, and successful war.
He, when Æneas on the plain appears,
930 Meets him with open arms, and falling tears :
' Welcome (he said), the gods, undoubted race !
O long expected, to my dear embrace !
Once more 'tis given me to behold your face !
The love and pious duty which you pay,
Have passed the perils of so hard a way.
'Tis true, computing times, I now believed
The happy day approached, nor are my hopes deceived.
What length of lands, what oceans have you passed,
What storms sustained, and on what shores been cast !
940 How have I feared your fate ! but feared it most,
When love assailed you on the Libyan coast.'
To this, the filial duty thus replies :
' Your sacred ghost, before my sleeping eyes
Appeared, and often urged this painful enterprise.
After long tossing on the Tyrrhene sea,
My navy rides at anchor in the bay.

But reach your hand, oh parent shade ! nor shun
The dear embraces of your longing son !'
He said ; and falling tears his face bedew ;
950 Then thrice, around his neck, his arms he threw ;
And thrice the flitting shadow slipped away,
Like winds, or empty dreams, that fly the day.
   Now, in a secret vale, the Trojan sees
A separate grove, through which a gentle breeze
Plays with a passing breath, and whispers through the
      trees ;
And, just before the confines of the wood,
The gliding Lethe leads her silent flood.
About the boughs an airy nation flew,
Thick as the humming bees, that hunt the golden dew
960 In summer's heat ; on tops of lilies feed,
And creep within their bells, to suck the balmy seed :
The wingèd army roams the field around ;
The rivers and the rocks remurmur to the sound.
Æneas wondering stood, then asked the cause
Which to the stream the crowding people draws.
Then thus the sire : 'The souls that throng the flood,
Are those to whom, by Fate, are other bodies owed ;
In Lethe's lake they long oblivion taste,
Of future life secure, forgetful of the past.
970 Long has my soul desired this time and place,
To set before your sight your glorious race ;
That this presaging joy may fire your mind,
To seek the shores by destiny designed.'
'O father ! can it be, that souls sublime
Return, to visit our terrestrial clime ;
And that the generous mind, released by death,
Can covet lazy limbs, and mortal breath ?'
Anchises, then, in order, thus begun
To clear those wonders to his godlike son :
980 'Know, first, that heaven and earth's compacted frame,
And flowing waters, and the starry flame,
And both the radiant lights, one common soul
Inspires and feeds, and animates the whole.
This active mind, infused through all the space,
Unites and mingles with the mighty mass.
Hence men and beasts the breath of life obtain,

868 What a transition is here from hell to heaven! ... The whole des-
cription is so charming that it is almost Elysium to read it.
                                                           Trapp

And birds of air, and monsters of the main.
The ethereal vigour is in all the same;
And every soul is filled with equal flame:
As much as earthly limbs, and gross allay
Of mortal members, subject to decay,
Blunt not the beams of heaven and edge of day.
From this coarse mixture of terrestrial parts,
Desire and fear by turns possess their hearts,
And grief, and joy! nor can the grovelling mind,
In the dark dungeon of the limbs confined,
Assert the native skies, or own its heavenly kind:
Nor death itself can wholly wash their stains;
But long-contracted filth e'en in the soul remains.
The relics of inveterate vice they wear;
And spots of sin obscene in every face appear.
For this are various penances enjoined;
And some are hung to bleach upon the wind;
Some plunged in waters, others purged in fires,
Till all the dregs are drained, and all the rust expires.
All have their manes, and those manes bear:
The few, so cleansed, to these abodes repair,
And breathe, in ample fields, the soft Elysian air.
Then are they happy, when by length of time
The scurf is worn away, of each committed crime;
No speck is left of their habitual stains;
But the pure ether of the soul remains.
But, when a thousand rolling years are past
(So long their punishments and penance last),
Whole droves of minds, are by the driving god
Compelled to drink the deep Lethæan flood;
In large forgetful draughts to steep the cares
Of their past labours, and their irksome years;
That, unremembering of its former pain,
The soul may suffer mortal flesh again.'
  Thus having said, the father-spirit leads
The priestess and his son through swarms of shades,
And takes a rising ground, from thence to see
The long procession of his progeny.
'Survey (pursued the sire) this airy throng,
As, offered to the view, they pass along.
These are the Italian names, which Fate will join
With ours, and graff upon the Trojan line.
Observe, the youth who first appears in sight,
And holds the nearest station to the light,
Already seems to snuff the vital air,

And leans just forward on a shining spear:
Silvius is he, thy last-begotten race,
But first in order sent, to fill thy place—
An Alban name, but mixed with Dardan blood;
Born in the covert of a shady wood.
Him fair Lavinia, thy surviving wife,
Shall breed in groves, to lead a solitary life.
In Alba he shall fix his royal seat,
1040 And, born a king, a race of kings beget;
. . .

See Romulus the great! born to restore
The crown that once his injured grandsire wore.
This prince, a priestess of our blood shall bear;
And like his sire in arms he shall appear.
Two rising crests his royal head adorn:
1060 Born from a god, himself to godhead born;
His sire already signs him for the skies,
And marks his seat amidst the deities.
Auspicious chief! thy race, in times to come,
Shall spread the conquests of imperial Rome—
Rome, whose ascending towers shall heaven invade,
Involving earth and ocean in her shade;
High as the mother of the gods in place,
And proud, like her, of an immortal race.
Then, when in pomp she makes the Phrygian round,
1070 With golden turrets on her temples crowned:
A hundred gods her sweeping train supply,
Her offspring all; and all command the sky.

Now fix your sight, and stand intent, to see
Your Roman race, and Julian progeny!
There mighty Cæsar waits his vital hour,
Impatient for the world, and grasps his promised power.
But next behold the youth of form divine—
Cæsar himself, exalted in his line—
Augustus, promised oft, and long foretold,
1080 Sent to the realm that Saturn ruled of old;
Born to restore a better age of gold.
Afric and India shall his power obey;
He shall extend his propagated sway
Beyond the solar year; without the starry way,
Where Atlas turns the rolling heavens around,
And his broad shoulders with their lights are crowned.
At his foreseen approach, already quake
The Caspian kingdoms and Mæotian lake.

Their seers behold the tempest from afar ;
1090 And threatening oracles denounce the war.
Nile hears him knocking at his seven-fold gates,
And seeks his hidden spring, and fears his nephew's fates.
Nor Hercules more lands or labours knew,
Not though the brazen-footed hind he slew,
Freed Erymanthus from the foaming boar,
And dipped his arrows in Lernæan gore ;
Nor Bacchus, turning from his Indian war,
By tigers drawn triumphant in his car,
From Nysa's top descending on the plains,
1100 With curling vines around his purple reins.
And doubt we, yet through dangers to pursue
The paths of honour, and a crown in view?

. . .

Let others better mould the running mass
Of metals, and inform the breathing brass,
1170 And soften into flesh a marble face ;
Plead better at the bar ; describe the skies,
And when the stars descend, and when they rise.
But, Rome ! 'tis thine alone, with awful sway,
To rule mankind, and make the world obey :
Disposing peace and war thy own majestic way.
To tame the proud, the fettered slave to free,
These are imperial arts, and worthy thee.'
 He paused—and, while with wondering eyes they viewed
The passing spirits, thus his speech renewed :
1180 'See great Marcellus ! how, untired in toils,
He moves with manly grace, how rich with regal spoils !
He, when his country (threatened with alarms)
Requires his courage and his conquering arms,
Shall more than once the Punic bands affright ;
Shall kill the Gaulish king in single fight ;
Then to the Capitol in triumph move ;
And the third spoils shall grace Feretrian Jove.'
Æneas here beheld, of form divine,
A godlike youth in glittering armour shine ;
1190 With great Marcellus keeping equal pace ;
But gloomy were his eyes, dejected was his face.
He saw, and, wondering, asked his airy guide,
What, and of whence, was he who pressed the hero's side ?

'His son, or one of his illustrious name?
How like the former, and almost the same!
Observe the crowds that compass him around:
All gaze and all admire, and raise a shouting sound:
But hovering mists around his brows are spread;
And night, with sable shades, involves his head.'
1200 'Seek not to know (the ghost replied with tears)
The sorrows of thy sons in future years.
This youth, the blissful vision of a day,
Shall just be shewn on earth, and snatched away.
The gods, too high had raised the Roman state:
Were but their gifts as permanent as great!
What groans of men shall fill the Martian field!
How fierce a blaze his flaming pile shall yield!
What funeral pomp shall floating Tiber see,
When, rising from his bed, he views the sad solemnity!
1210 No youth shall equal hopes of glory give;
No youth afford so great a cause to grieve.
The Trojan honour, and the Roman boast;
Admired when living, and adored when lost!
Mirror of ancient faith in early youth!
Undaunted worth, inviolable truth!
No foe, unpunished, in the fighting field
Shall dare thee, foot to foot, with sword and shield;
Much less in arms oppose thy matchless force,
When thy sharp spurs shall urge thy foaming horse.
1220 Ah! couldst thou break through Fate's severe decree,
A new Marcellus shall arise in thee!
Full canisters of fragrant lilies bring,
Mixed with the purple roses of the spring:
Let me with funeral flowers his body strow;
This gift which parents to their children owe,
This unavailing gift, at least, I may bestow!'
  Thus having said, he led the hero round
The confines of the blest Elysian ground;
1230 Which when Anchises to his son had shown,
And fired his mind to mount the promised throne,
He tells the future wars, ordained by Fate;
The strength and customs of the Latian state;

1221 Here it was that Octavia fainted away, and well she might; the poet's suppressing the name to the last being most artful and judicious.

Trapp

The prince and people; and fore-arms his care
With rules, to push his fortune, or to bear.
  Two gates the silent house of Sleep adorn;
Of polished ivory this, that of transparent horn
True visions through transparent horn arise;
Through polished ivory pass deluding lies.
Of various things discoursing as he passed,
1240 Anchises hither bends his steps at last;
Then, through the gate of ivory, he dismissed
His valiant offspring, and divining guest.
. . .

1241 Virgil dismisses Aeneas through the gate of falsehood. Now what is this, but to inform us that all he relates is nothing but a dream, and that dream a falsehood? I submit it to the critics who are more disposed to find fault that I am to determine whether Virgil ought to be censured for such an acknowledgement or praised for his ingenuity?

Pope on *Odyssey* XI concluding remark

BOOK VII

THE ARGUMENT

King Latinus entertains Æneas, and promises him his only daughter Lavinia, the heiress of his crown. Turnus, being in love with her, favoured by her mother, and stirred up by Juno and Alecto, breaks the treaty which was made, and engages in his quarrel Mezentius, Camilla, Messapus, and many other of the neighbouring princes; whose forces, and the names of their commanders, are particularly related.

. . .

    Now, Erato! thy poet's mind inspire,
And fill his soul with thy celestial fire.
Relate what Latium was; her ancient kings:
Declare the past and present state of things;
When first the Trojan fleet Ausonia sought,
And how the rivals loved, and how they fought.
These are my theme; and how the war began,
And how concluded by the godlike man;
60 For I shall sing of battles, blood, and rage,
Which princes and their people did engage;
And haughty souls, that, moved with mutual hate,
In fighting fields pursued and found their fate;

In the first six books he has imitated the *Odyssey*; in the last six he proposes the *Iliad* for his pattern. He himself give us notice by the invocation toward the beginning of this seventh book that he took this part to be more important than the first.

Warton

Let the judicious reader weigh the following remark of M. Voltaire. 'It is a just criticism on Virgil, that the latter part of his poem is less animated than the first; not, that the last six books are entirely languishing but their milder light is overpowered by the lustre of the other. That great defect is owing to the disposition of the poem, and to the nature of the things. The design of a match between Aeneas and Lavinia, unknown and indifferent to each other, and a war raised about a stag wounded by a young boy could not indeed command our concern so much as the burning of Troy and the love of Dido. 'Tis a great mistake to believe that an author can soar when the subject sinks.'

(Voltaire's Essay on Epic Poetry p. 41)
Warton

That roused the Tyrrhene realm with loud alarms,
And peaceful Italy involved in arms.
A larger scene of action is displayed ;
And, rising hence, a greater work is weighed.
   Latinus, old and mild, had long possessed
The Latian sceptre, and his people blessed :
70 His father Faunus : a Laurentian dame
His mother ; fair Marica was her name.
But Faunus came from Picus : Picus drew
His birth from Saturn, if records be true.
Thus king Latinus, in the third degree,
Had Saturn author of his family.
But this old peaceful prince, as heaven decreed,
Was blessed with no male issue to succeed :
His sons in blooming youth were snatched by fate ;
One only daughter heired the royal state.
80 Fired with her love, and with ambition led,
The neighbouring princes court her nuptial bed.
Among the crowd, but far above the rest,
Young Turnus to the beauteous maid addressed.
Turnus, for high descent and graceful mien
Was first, and favoured by the Latian queen :
With him she strove to join Lavinia's hand ;
But dire portents the purposed match withstand.
   Deep in the palace, of long growth there stood
A laurel's trunk, a venerable wood ;
90 Where rites divine were paid ; whose holy hair
Was kept and cut with superstitious care.
This plant, Latinus, when his town he walled
Then found, and from the tree Laurentum called ;
And last, in honour of his new abode,
He vowed the laurel to the laurel's god.
It happened once (a boding prodigy !)
A swarm of bees, that cut the liquid sky
(Unknown from whence they took their airy flight),
Upon the topmost branch in clouds alight ;
100 There, with their clasping feet, together clung,
And a long cluster from the laurel hung.
An ancient augur prophesied from hence :
' Behold ! on Latian shores a foreign prince ;
From the same parts of heaven his navy stands,
To the same parts on earth : his army lands ;
The town he conquers, and the tower commands.'
   Yet more ; when fair Lavinia fed the fire
Before the gods, and stood beside her sire,

BOOK VII

110   (Strange to relate !) the flames, involved in smoke
      Of incense, from the sacred altar broke,
      Caught her dishevelled hair, and rich attire ;
      Her crown and jewels crackled in the fire :
      From thence the fuming trail began to spread,
      And lambent glories danced about her head.
      This new portent the seer with wonder views,
      Then pausing, thus his prophecy renews :
      ' The nymph who scatters flaming fires around,
      Shall shine with honour, shall herself be crowned ;
      But, caused by her irrevocable fate,
120   War shall the country waste, and change the state.
         Latinus, frightened with this dire ostent,
      For counsel to his father Faunus went ;
      And sought the shades renowned for prophecy,
      Which near Albunea's sulphurous fountain lie.
      To those, the Latian and the Sabine land
      Fly when distressed ; and thence relief demand.
      The priest on skins of offerings takes his ease,
      And nightly visions in his slumber sees ;
      A swarm of thin aërial shapes appears,
130   And, fluttering round his temples, deafs his ears.
      These he consults, the future fates to know,
      From powers above, and from the fiends below.
      Here, for the god's advice, Latinus flies,
      Offering a hundred sheep for sacrifice :
      Their woolly fleeces, as the rites required,
      He laid beneath him, and to rest retired.
      No sooner were his eyes in slumber bound,
      When, from above, a more than mortal sound
      Invades his ears ; and thus the vision spoke :
140   ' Seek not, my seed, in Latian bands to yoke
      Our fair Lavinia, nor the gods provoke.
      A foreign son upon the shore descends,
      Whose martial fame from pole to pole extends.
      His race, in arms and arts of peace renowned,
      Not Latium shall contain, nor Europe bound :
      'Tis theirs, whate'er the sun surveys around.'
      These answers, in the silent night received,
      The king himself divulged, the land believed :
      The fame through all the neighbouring nations flew,
150   When now the Trojan navy was in view.
         . . .

The pious chief, who sought by peaceful ways
To found his empire, and his town to raise,
A hundred youths from all his train selects,
And to the Latian court their course directs
(The spacious palace where their prince resides),
And all their heads with wreaths of olive hides.
They go, commissioned to require a peace;
210 And carry presents, to procure access.

. . .

The palace, built by Picus, vast and proud,
230 Supported by a hundred pillars stood,
And round encompassed with a rising wood.

. . .

In this high temple, on a chair of state,
The seat of audience, old Latinus sat;
Then gave admission to the Trojan train;
And thus with pleasing accents he began:
270 'Tell me, ye Trojans—for that name you own;
Nor is your course upon our coasts unknown—
Say what you seek, and whither were you bound;
Were you by stress of weather cast aground?
(Such dangers of the sea are often seen,
And oft befall to miserable men),
Or come your shipping in our ports to lay,
Spent and disabled in so long a way?
Say what you want? the Latians you shall find
Not forced to goodness, but by will inclined;
280 For, since the time of Saturn's holy reign,
His hospitable customs we retain.

. . .

290   He said.—Ilioneus made this reply:
'O king, of Faunus' royal family!
Nor wintry winds to Latium forced our way,
Nor did the stars our wandering course betray.
Willing we sought your shores; and, hither bound,
The port, so long desired, at length we found;
From our sweet homes and ancient realms expelled—
Great as the greatest that the sun beheld.

. . .

How dire a tempest, from Mycenæ poured,
Our plains, our temples, and our town, devoured;

What was the waste of war, what fierce alarms
Shook Asia's crown with European arms;
E'en such have heard, if any such there be,
Whose earth is bounded by the frozen sea;
And such as, born beneath the burning sky
And sultry sun, betwixt the tropics lie.
310 From that dire deluge, through the watery waste
(Such length of years, such various perils, past),
At last escaped, to Latium we repair,
To beg what you without your want may spare—
The common water, and the common air;
Sheds which ourselves will build, and mean abodes,
Fit to receive and serve our banished gods.
Nor our admission shall your realm disgrace,
Nor length of time our gratitude efface;
Besides what endless honour you shall gain,
320 To save and shelter Troy's unhappy train.
. . .

Fate and the gods, by their supreme command,
Have doomed our ships to seek the Latian land.
To these abodes our fleet Apollo sends;
330 Here Dardanus was born, and hither tends;
Where Tuscan Tiber rolls with rapid force,
And where Numicus opes his holy source.
Besides, our prince presents with his request,
Some small remains of what his sire possessed:
This golden charger, snatched from burning Troy,
Anchises did in sacrifice employ:
This royal robe and this tiara wore
Old Priam, and this golden sceptre bore
In full assemblies, and in solemn games:
340 These purple vests were weaved by Dardan dames.
    Thus while he spoke, Latinus rolled around
His eyes, and fixed awhile upon the ground:
Intent he seemed, and anxious in his breast;

Not by the sceptre moved, or kingly vest,
But pondering future things of wondrous weight—
Succession, empire, and his daughter's fate.
On these he mused within his thoughtful mind;
And then revolved what Faunus had divined.
This was the foreign prince, by fate decreed
350 To share his sceptre, and Lavinia's bed;
This was the race that sure portents foreshow
To sway the world, and land and sea subdue.

At length he raised his cheerful head, and spoke:
'The powers (said he) the powers we both invoke,
To you, and yours, and mine, propitious be,
And firm our purpose with their augury!
Have what you ask: your presents I receive:
Land, where and when you please, with ample leave:
Partake and use my kingdom as your own:
360 All shall be yours, while I command the crown.
And, if my wished alliance please your king,
Tell him he should not send the peace, but bring:
Then let him not a friend's embraces fear;
The peace is made when I behold him here.
Besides this answer, tell my royal guest
I add to his commands my own request:
Only one daughter heirs my crown and state,
Whom not our oracles, nor heaven, nor fate,
Nor frequent prodigies, permit to join
370 With any native of the Ausonian line.
A foreign son-in-law shall come from far
(Such is our doom), a chief renowned in war,
Whose race shall bear aloft the Latian name,
And through the conquered world diffuse our fame.
Himself to be the man the fates require,
I firmly judge, and what I judge, desire.'
He said; and then on each bestowed a steed.

. . .

Sublime on stately steeds the Trojans borne,
To their expecting lord with peace return.
    But jealous Juno, from Pachynus' height,
As she from Argos took her airy flight,
Beheld, with envious eyes this hateful sight.
She saw the Trojan and his joyful train
Descend upon the shore; desert the main;
400 Design a town; and, with unhoped success,
The ambassadors return with promised peace.
Then, pierced with pain, she shook her haughty head,
Sighed from her inward soul, and thus she said:
'O hated offspring of my Phrygian foes!
O fates of Troy, which Juno's fates oppose!
Could they not fall unpitied on the plain?
But, slain, revive, and, taken, 'scape again!
When execrable Troy in ashes lay,
Through fires and swords and seas they forced their way!

BOOK VII

410 Then vanquished Juno must in vain contend;
     Her rage disarmed, her empire at an end!
     Breathless and tired, is all my fury spent?
     Or does my glutted spleen at length relent?
     . . .

430 If native power prevail not, shall I doubt
     To seek for needful succour from without?
     If Jove and heaven my just desires deny,
     Hell shall the power of heaven and Jove supply!
     Grant that the Fates have firmed, by their decree,
     The Trojan race to reign in Italy:
     At least I can defer the nuptial day,
     And, with protracted wars, the peace delay:
     With blood the dear alliance shall be bought,
     And both the people near destruction brought.
440 So shall the son-in-law and father join,
     With ruin, war, and waste of either line.
     O fatal maid! thy marriage is endowed
     With Phrygian, Latian, and Rutulian blood.
     Bellona leads thee to thy lover's hand:
     Another queen brings forth another brand,
     To burn with foreign fires another land:
     A second Paris, differing but in name,
     Shall fire his country with a second flame.'
     Thus having said, she sinks beneath the ground
450 With furious haste, and shoots the Stygian sound,
     To rouse Alecto from the infernal seat
     Of her dire sisters, and their dark retreat.
     This Fury, fit for her intent, she chose;
     One who delights in wars, and human woes.
     E'en Pluto hates his own mis-shapen race;
     Her sister Furies fly her hideous face;
     So frightful are the forms the monster takes,
     So fierce the hissings of her speckled snakes.
     Her, Juno finds, and thus inflames her spite:
460 'O virgin daughter of eternal Night!
     Give me this once thy labour, to sustain
     My right, and execute my just disdain.

451 Juvenal never showed his judgement more than when he referred to this machine of Allecto as a most signal instance of poetical spirit and sublimity.

Trapp

Let not the Trojans with a feigned pretence
Of proffered peace, delude the Latian prince:
Expel from Italy that odious name,
And let not Juno suffer in her fame.
'Tis thine to ruin realms, o'erturn a state,
Betwixt the dearest friends to raise debate,
And kindle kindred blood to mutual hate.
470 Thy hand o'er towns the funeral torch displays,
And forms a thousand ills ten thousand ways.
Now, shake from out thy fruitful breast, the seeds
Of envy, discord, and of cruel deeds:
Confound the peace established, and prepare
Their souls to hatred, and their hands to war.'
    Smeared as she was with black Gorgonean blood,
The Fury sprang above the Stygian flood;
And on her wicker wings, sublime, through night,
She to the Latian palace took her flight;
480 There sought the queen's apartment, stood before
The peaceful threshold, and besieged the door.
Restless Amata lay, her swelling breast
Fired with disdain for Turnus dispossessed,
And the new nuptials of the Trojan guest.
From her black bloody locks, the Fury shakes
Her darling plague, the favourite of her snakes.
With her full force she threw the poisonous dart,
And fixed it deep within Amata's heart;
That, thus envenomed, she might kindle rage,
490 And sacrifice to strife her house and husband's age.
Unseen, unfelt, the fiery serpent skims
Betwixt her linen and her naked limbs;
His baneful breath inspiring as he glides:
Now like a chain around her neck he rides;
Now like a fillet to her head repairs,
And with his circling volumes folds her hairs.
At first the silent venom slid with ease,
And seized her cooler senses by degrees;
Then, ere the infected mass was fired too far,
500 In plaintive accents she began the war,
And thus bespoke her husband: 'Shall (she said)
A wandering prince enjoy Lavinia's bed?
If nature plead not in a parent's heart,
Pity my tears, and pity her desert.
I know, my dearest lord, the time will come,
You would, in vain, reverse your cruel doom:
The faithless pirate soon will set to sea,

BOOK VII

    And bear the royal virgin far away !
    A guest like him (a Trojan guest) before,
510 In show of friendship sought the Spartan shore,
    And ravished Helen from her husband bore.
    Think on a king's inviolable word ;
    And think on Turnus, her once plighted lord.
    To this false foreigner you give your throne,
    And wrong a friend, a kinsman, and a son.
    Resume your ancient care ; and, if the god
    Your sire, and you, resolve on foreign blood,
    Know all are foreign, in a larger sense,
    Not born your subjects, or derived from hence.
520 Then, if the line of Turnus you retrace,
    He springs from Inachus of Argive race.'
    But, when she saw her reasons idly spent,
    And could not move him from his fixed intent,
    She flew to rage ; for now the snake possessed
    Her vital parts, and poisoned all her breast.

. . .

    She flies the town, and, mixing with the throng
    Of madding matrons, bears the bride along ;
540 Wandering through woods and wilds, and **devious** ways,
    And with these arts the Trojan match delays.
    She feigned the rites of Bacchus, cried aloud,
    And to the buxom god the virgin vowed.

. . .

    Amata's breast the Fury thus invades,
    And fires with rage, amid the sylvan shades.
    Then, when she found her venom spread so far,
    The royal house embroiled in civil war,
    Raised on her dusky wings, she cleaves the skies,
570 And seeks the palace where young Turnus lies.

. . .

538 This incident of the queen's running into the woods and mountains with her felldow Bacchanals adds much to the heightening and swelling of the confusion and madness.

                                                            Trapp

Here, in his lofty palace, Turnus lay,
Betwixt the confines of the night and day,
580 Secure in sleep.—The Fury laid aside
Her looks and limbs, and with new methods tried
The foulness of the infernal form to hide.
Propped on a staff, she takes a trembling mien;
Her face is furrowed, and her front obscene;
Deep-dinted wrinkles on her cheek she draws;
Sunk are her eyes, and toothless are her jaws;
Her hoary hair with holy fillets bound;
Her temples with an olive wreath are crowned
Old Chalybe, who kept the secret fane
590 Of Juno, now she seemed, and thus began
(Appearing in a dream) to rouse the careless man:
'Shall Turnus then such endless toil sustain
In fighting-fields, and conquer towns in vain?
Win, for a Trojan head to wear the prize,
Usurp thy crown, enjoy thy victories?
The bride and sceptre, which thy blood has bought,
The king transfers; and foreign heirs are sought!
Go now, deluded man, and seek again
New toils, new dangers, on the dusty plain!
600 Repel the Tuscan foes, their city seize:
Protect the Latians in luxurious ease!
This dream all-powerful Juno sends: I bear
Her mighty mandates, and her words you hear.
Haste! arm your Ardeans; issue to the plain;
With faith to friend, assault the Trojan train:
Their thoughtless chiefs; their painted ships that lie
In Tiber's mouth, with fire and sword destroy.
The Latian king, unless he shall submit,
Own his old promise, and his new forget—
610 Let him, in arms the power of Turnus prove;
And learn to fear whom he disdains to love.
For such is heaven's command.' The youthful prince
With scorn replied, and made this bold defence:
'You tell me, mother, what I knew before,
The Phrygian fleet is landed on the shore.
I neither fear nor will provoke the war;
My fate is Juno's most peculiar care.
But time has made you dote, and vainly tell
Of arms imagined in your lonely cell.
620 Go! be the temple and the gods your care:
Permit to men the thought of peace and war.'

These haughty words Alecto's rage provoke,
And frightened Turnus trembled as she spoke.
Her eyes grow stiffened, and with sulphur burn;
Her hideous looks and hellish form return;
Her curling snakes with hissings fill the place,
And open all the furies of her face:
Then, darting fire from her malignant eyes,
She cast him backward as he strove to rise,
630 And lingering sought to frame some new replies.
High on her head she rears two twisted snakes;
Her chains she rattles, and her whip she shakes;
And churning bloody foam, thus loudly speaks:
' Behold whom time has made to dote and tell
Of arms imagined in her lonely cell!
Behold the Fates' infernal minister!
War, death, destruction, in my hand I bear.'
Thus having said, her smouldering torch, impressed
With her full force, she plunged into his breast.
640 Aghast he waked; and starting from his bed,
Cold sweat, in clammy drops, his limbs o'erspread.
' Arms! arms! (he cries): my sword and shield prepare!'
He breathes defiance, blood, and mortal war.
So, when with crackling flames a caldron fries,
The bubbling waters from the bottom rise;
Above the brims they force their fiery way;
Black vapours climb aloft, and cloud the day.
The peace polluted thus, a chosen band
He first commissions to the Latian land,
650 In threatening embassy; then raised the rest
To meet in arms the intruding Trojan guest;
To force the foes from the Lavinian shore,
And Italy's endangered peace restore.
Himself alone an equal match he boasts,
To fight the Phrygian and Ausonian hosts.
The gods invoked, the Rutuli prepare
Their arms, and warm each other to the war.
. . .

660 While Turnus urges thus his enterprise,
The Stygian Fury to the Trojans flies;
New frauds invents, and takes a steepy stand,
Which overlooks the vale with wide command;
Where fair Ascanius and his youthful train,
With horns and hounds a hunting match ordain,

And pitch their toils around the shady plain.
The Fury fires the pack; they snuff, they vent,
And feed their hungry nostrils with the scent.
'Twas of a well-grown stag, whose antlers rise
670 High o'er his front, his beams invade the skies.
From this light cause, the infernal maid prepares
The country churls to mischief, hate, and wars.
　The stately beast the two Tyrrhidæ bred,
Snatched from his dam, and the tame youngling fed.
Their father, Tyrrheus, did his fodder bring—
Tyrrheus chief ranger to the Latian king:
Their sister Silvia, cherished with her care
The little wanton, and did wreaths prepare
To hang his budding horns; with ribbons tied
680 His tender neck, and combed his silken hide,
And bathed his body.　Patient of command
In time he grew, and, growing used to hand,
He waited at his master's board for food;
Then sought his savage kindred in the wood,
Where grazing all the day; at night he came
To his known lodgings, and his country dame.
This household beast, that used the woodland grounds,
Was viewed at first by the young hero's hounds,
As down the stream he swam, to seek retreat
690 In the cool waters, and to quench his heat.
Ascanius, young and eager of his game,
Soon bent his bow, uncertain in his aim;
But the dire fiend the fatal arrow guides,
Which pierced his bowels through his panting sides.
The bleeding creature issues from the floods,
Possessed with fear, and seeks his known abodes,
His old familiar hearth, and household gods.
He falls; he fills the house with heavy groans;
Implores their pity, and his pain bemoans.
700 Young Silvia beats her breast, and cries aloud
For succour from the clownish neighbourhood.
The churls assemble; for the fiend who lay
In the close woody covert, urged their way.
One with a brand yet burning from the flame;
Armed with a knotty club another came:
Whate'er they catch or find, without their care,
Their fury makes an instrument of war.
Tyrrheus, the foster-father of the beast,
Then clenched a hatchet in his horny fist,
710 But held his hand from the descending stroke,

And left his wedge within the cloven oak,
To whet their courage, and their rage provoke.
And now the goddess, exercised in ill,
Who watched an hour to work her impious will,
Ascends the roof, and to her crooked horn,
Such as was then by Latian shepherds borne,
Adds all her breath. The rocks and woods around,
And mountains, tremble at the infernal sound.
. . .
    The clowns, a boisterous, rude, ungoverned crew,
With furious haste to the loud summons flew.
The powers of Troy, then issuing on the plain,
With fresh recruits their youthful chief sustain :
Nor theirs a raw and unexperienced train,
But a firm body of embattled men.
730 At first, while fortune favoured neither side,
The fight with clubs and burning brands was tried ;
But now, both parties reinforced, the fields
Are bright with flaming swords and brazen shields.
A shining harvest either host displays,
And shoots against the sun with equal rays.
    Thus, when a black-browed gust begins to rise,
White foam at first on the curled ocean fries ;
Then roars the main, the billows mount the skies ;
Till, by the fury of the storm full blown,
740 The muddy bottom o'er the clouds is thrown.
    First Almon falls, old Tyrrheus' eldest care,
Pierced with an arrow from the distant war ;
Fixed in his throat the flying weapon stood,
And stopped his breath, and drank his vital blood.
Huge heaps of slain around the body rise ;
Among the rest, the rich Galesus lies—
A good old man, while peace he preached in vain,

669 The killing of this favourite deer may to some critics who relish nothing but pompous circumstances in a poem appear to be but a trifling occasion for the raising of this terrible war. But surely nothing could be more natural; nay, its being a little circumstance renders its beauty still more pleasing to a lover of nature who knows how many important events have been occasioned by circumstances seemingly trifling in themselves.

                                                          Warton

Amidst the madness of the unruly train:
Five herds, five bleating flocks, his pastures filled;
750 His lands a hundred yoke of oxen tilled.
Thus, while in equal scales their fortune stood,
The Fury bathed them in each other's blood;
Then, having fixed the fight, exulting flies,
And bears fulfilled her promise to the skies.
. . .

    Saturnian Juno, now, with double care,
790 Attends the fatal process of the war.
The clowns, returned from battle, bear the slain;
Implore the gods, and to their king complain.
The corpse of Almon, and the rest, are shown:
Shrieks, clamours, murmurs, fill the frighted town.
Ambitious Turnus in the press appears,
And, aggravating crimes, augments their fears;
Proclaims his private injuries aloud—
A solemn promise made, and disavowed;
A foreign son is sought, and a mixed mongrel brood.
800 Then they, whose mothers, frantic with their fear,
In woods and wilds the flags of Bacchus bear,
And lead his dances with dishevelled hair,
Increase the clamour, and the war demand
(Such was Amata's interest in the land),
Against the public sanctions of the peace,
Against all omens of their ill success.
    With fates averse, the rout in arms resort
To force their monarch, and insult the court.
But, like a rock unmoved, a rock that braves
810 The raging tempest and the rising waves,
Propped on himself he stands: his solid sides
Wash off the sea-weeds, and the sounding tides—
So stood the pious prince unmoved; and long
Sustained the madness of the noisy throng.
But, when he found that Juno's power prevailed,
And all the methods of cool counsel failed,
He calls the gods to witness their offence;
Disclaims the war, asserts his innocence.
    'Hurried by fate (he cries), and borne before
820 A furious wind, we leave the faithful shore!
O more than madmen! you yourselves shall bear
The guilt of blood and sacrilegious war:
Thou, Turnus, shall atone it by thy fate,
And pray to Heaven for peace, but pray too late.

For me, my stormy voyage at an end,
I to the port of death securely tend.
The funeral pomp which to your kings you pay,
Is all I want, and all you take away.
He said no more, but, in his walls confined,
830 Shut out the woes which he too well divined ;
Nor with the rising storm would vainly strive,
But left the helm, and let the vessel drive.
    A solemn custom was observed of old,
Which Latium held, and now the Romans hold ;
. . .
840 Two gates of steel (the name of Mars they bear,
And still are worshipped with religious fear)
Before his temple stand : the dire abode,
And the feared issues of the furious god,
Are fenced with brazen bolts ; without the gates,
The wary guardian Janus doubly waits.
Then, when the sacred senate votes the wars,
The Roman consul their decree declares,
And in his robes the sounding gates unbars.
The youth in military shouts arise,
850 And the loud trumpets break the yielding skies.
These rites, of old by sovereign princes used,
Were the king's office : but the king refused,
Deaf to their cries ; nor would the gates unbar
Of sacred peace, or loose the imprisoned war ;
But hid his head, and, safe from loud alarms,
Abhorred the wicked ministry of arms.
Then, heaven's imperious queen shot down from high ;
At her approach the brazen hinges fly ;
The gates are forced, and every falling bar ;
860 And like a tempest, issues out the war.
    The peaceful cities of the Ausonian shore,
Lulled in their ease, and undisturbed before,
Are all on fire ; and some, with studious care,
Their restive steeds in sandy plains prepare ;
Some their soft limbs in painful marches try ;
And war is all their wish, and arms the general cry.
Part scour their rusty shields with seam ; and part
New-grind the blunted axe, and point the dart ;
With joy they view the waving ensigns fly,
870 And hear the trumpet's clangour pierce the sky.
. . .

Some hammer helmets for the fighting field;
Some twine young sallows to support the shield;
The corselet some, and some the cuishes mould,
With silver plated, and with ductile gold.
The rustic honours of the scythe and share,
880 Give place to swords and plumes, the pride of war.
Old falchions are new-tempered in the fires:
The sounding trumpet every soul inspires.
The word is given; with eager speed they lace
The shining head-piece, and the shield embrace.
The neighing steeds are to the chariots tied;
The trusty weapon sits on every side.

From the catalogue of forces

    Mezentius first appeared upon the plain:
Scorn sat upon his brows, and sour disdain,
Defying earth and heaven. Etruria lost,
He brings to Turnus' aid his baffled host.
The charming Lausus, full of youthful fire,
900 Rode in the rank, and next his sullen sire;
To Turnus only second in the grace
Of manly mien, and features of the face.
A skilful horseman, and a huntsman bred;
With fates averse, a thousand men he led:
His sire unworthy of so brave a son;
Himself well worthy of a happier throne.
  . . .

1071 Amid the troops, and like the leading god,
High o'er the rest in arms, the graceful Turnus **rode;**
A triple pile of plumes his crest adorned,
On which with belching flames Chimæra burned:
The more the kindled combat rises higher,
The more with fury burns the blazing fire.
  . . .

1083 A cloud of foot succeeds, and fills the fields
With swords, and pointed spears, and clattering shields;
  . . .

    Last, from the Volscians fair Camilla came,
And led her warlike troops—a warrior dame;
Unbred to spinning, in the loom unskilled;
She chose the nobler Pallas of the field.

Mixed with the first, the fierce virago fought;
Sustained the toils of arms, the danger sought;
1100 Outstripped the winds in speed upon the plain,
Flew o'er the field, nor hurt the bearded grain:
She swept the seas, and, as she skimmed along,
Her flying feet unbathed on billows hung.
Men, boys, and women, stupid with surprise,
Where'er she passes, fixed their wondering eyes:
Longing they look, and gaping at the sight,
Devour her o'er and o'er with vast delight.
Her purple habit sits with such a grace
On her smooth shoulders, and so suits her face;
1110 Her head with ringlets of her hair is crowned;
And in a golden caul the curls are bound.
She shakes her myrtle javelin; and, behind,
Her Lycian quiver dances in the wind.

1100 These lines in the original are often produced as a striking instance
–1103 of the sound's being and echo to the sense ... there is a celebrated
passage on the same subject in Mr. Pope's *Essay on Criticism*:

> Not so, when swift Camilla scours the plain,
> Flies o'er th'unbending corn, and skims along the main. (372–73)

Warton

The poet illustrates the swiftness of these horses by describing them as running over the standing corn, and surface of waters, without making any impression. Virgil has imitated these lines and adapts what Homer says of these horses to the swiftness of Camilla. ... The reader will easily perceive that Virgil's is almost a literal translation; he has imitated the very run of the verses, which flow nimbly away in dactyls, and as swift as the wind they describe.

Pope on *Iliad* XX, 270

Here is Pope's version of the lines in Homer:

> These lightly skimming, when they swept the plain,
> Nor ply'd the grass, nor bent the tender grain;
> And when along the level seas they flew,
> Scarce on the surface curl'd the briny dew.

BOOK VIII

THE ARGUMENT

The war being now begun, both the generals make all possible preparations. Turnus sends to Diomedes. Æneas goes in person to beg succours from Evander and the Tuscans. Evander receives him kindly, furnishes him with men, and sends his son Pallas with him. Vulcan, at the request of Venus, makes arms for her son Æneas, and draws on his shield the most memorable actions of his posterity.

. . .

    While Turnus and the allies thus urge the war,
The Trojan, floating in a flood of care,
Beholds the tempest which his foes prepare.
30 This way, and that, he turns his anxious mind;
Thinks, and rejects the counsels he designed;
Explores himself in vain in every part,
And gives no rest to his distracted heart.
So, when the sun by day, or moon by night,
Strike on the polished brass their trembling light,
The glittering species here and there divide,
And cast their dubious beams from side to side;
Now on the walls, now on the pavement play,
And to the ceiling flash the glaring day.
40 'Twas night; and weary nature lulled asleep
The birds of air, and fishes of the deep,
And beasts, and mortal men. The Trojan chief
Was laid on Tiber's banks, oppressed with grief,
And found in silent slumber, late relief.
Then, through the shadows of the poplar wood,
Arose the father of the Roman flood;
An azure robe was o'er his body spread,
A wreath of shady reeds adorned his head:
Thus, manifest to sight, the god appeared,
50 And with these pleasing words his sorrow cheered:
'Undoubted offspring of ethereal race,
O long expected in this promised place!
Who, through the foes, hast borne thy banished gods,
Restored them to their hearths, and old abodes;
This is thy happy home, the clime where fate
Ordains thee to restore the Trojan state.
Fear not! The war shall end in lasting peace,
And all the rage of haughty Juno cease.
And that this nightly vision may not seem
60 The effect of fancy, or an idle dream,

A sow beneath an oak shall lie along,
All white herself, and white her thirty young.
When thirty rolling years have run their race,
Thy son Ascanius, on this empty space,
Shall build a royal town, of lasting fame,
Which from this omen shall receive the name.
Time shall approve the truth.—For what remains,
And how with sure success to crown thy pains,
With patience next attend.   A banished band,
70   Driven with Evander from the Arcadian land,
Have planted here, and placed on high their walls :
Their town the founder, Pallanteum calls,
Derived from Pallas, his great grandsire's name :
But the fierce Latians old possession claim,
With war infesting the new colony :
These make thy friends, and on their aid rely.
To thy free passage I submit my streams.
Wake, son of Venus, from thy pleasing dreams !
And when the setting stars are lost in day,

When we are in the height of expectation and suspense for the event of a most important war just ready to begin, what an agreeable transition of thought is it to be for a while diverted from those military preparations by such narratives and facts of a quite different nature as to make us forget that about which we were before so curious and impatient. Not that these episodes are separated or disjointed from the main subject ... the venerable simplicity of manners in those ancient times, and the royal poverty of Evander and his court in a place which was afterwards to be the seat of Rome, the mistress of the universe, makes a most delightful contrast of ideas, and is to the last degree affecting.

Trapp

34   Commending a Homeric simile, Pope comments: It is more to be admired because it is very difficult to find sensible images proper to represent the motions of the mind; whereof we but rarely meet with such comparisons even in the best poets. There is one of great beauty in Virgil ... where he compares his hero's mind ... to a dancing light reflected from a vessel of water in motion.

Pope on *Iliad* XIV, 21

80 To Juno's power thy just devotion pay;
    With sacrifice the wrathful queen appease:
    Her pride at length shall fall, her fury cease.
    When thou return'st victorious from the war,
    Perform thy vows to me with grateful care.
    The god am I, whose yellow water flows
    Around these fields, and fattens as it goes:
    Tiber my name—among the rolling floods
    Renowned on earth, esteemed among the gods.
    This is my certain seat. In times to come,
90 My waves shall wash the walls of mighty Rome!
        He said; and plunged below. While yet he spoke,
    His dream Æneas and his sleep forsook.
    He rose, and looking up, beheld the skies
    With purple blushing, and the day arise.
    Then water in his hollow palm he took
    From Tiber's flood, and thus the powers bespoke:
    ' Laurentian nymphs, by whom the streams are fed,
    And father Tiber, in thy sacred bed
    Receive Æneas, and from danger keep!
100 Whatever fount, whatever holy deep,
    Conceals thy watery stores—where'er they rise,
    And, bubbling from below, salute the skies—
    Thou, king of horned floods, whose plenteous urn
    Suffices fatness to the fruitful corn,
    For this, thy kind compassion of our woes,
    Shalt share my morning song, and evening vows.
    But, oh! be present to thy people's aid,
    And firm the gracious promise thou hast made.'
        Thus having said, two galleys from his stores
110 With care he chooses, mans, and fits with oars.
    Now on the shore the fatal swine is found—
    Wondrous to tell!—She lay along the ground:
    Her well-fed offspring at her udders hung;
    She white herself, and white her thirty young.
    Æneas takes the mother and her brood,
    And all on Juno's altar are bestowed.
    The following night, and the succeeding day,
    Propitious Tiber smoothed his watery way;
    He rolled his river back, and poised he stood,
120 A gentle swelling, and a peaceful flood.
    The Trojans mount their ships; they put from shore,
    Borne on the waves, and scarcely dip an oar.
    Shouts from the land give omen to their course;
    And the pitched vessels glide with easy force.

The woods and waters wonder at the gleam
Of shields, and painted ships that stem the stream.
One summer's night and one whole day they pass
Betwixt the green-wood shades, and cut the liquid glass.
The fiery sun had finished half his race,
130 Looked back and doubted in the middle space,
When they from far beheld the rising towers,
The tops of sheds, and shepherds' lowly bowers,
Thin as they stood, which then of homely clay,
Now rise in marble, from the Roman sway.
These cots (Evander's kingdom, mean and poor)
The Trojan saw, and turned his ships to shore.
'Twas on a solemn day: the Arcadian states,
The king and prince, without the city gates,
Then paid their offerings in a sacred grove
140 To Hercules, the warrior son of Jove.
. . .

The rites performed, the cheerful train retire.
Betwixt young Pallas and his aged sire,
410 The Trojan passed, the city to survey;
And pleasing talk beguiled the tedious way.
The stranger cast around his curious eyes,
New objects viewing still with new surprise;
With greedy joy inquires of various things,
And acts and monuments of ancient kings.
Then thus the founder of the Roman towers:
'These woods were first the seat of sylvan powers,
Of nymphs and fauns, and savage men who took
Their birth from trunks of trees and stubborn oak.
420 Nor laws they knew, nor manners, nor the care
Of labouring oxen, nor the shining share,
Nor arts of gain, nor what they gained to spare.
Their exercise the chase: the running flood
Supplied their thirst; the trees supplied their food.
Then Saturn came, who fled the power of Jove,
Robbed of his realms, and banished from above.
The men dispersed on hills, to towns he brought;
And laws ordained, and civil customs taught;
And Latium called the land where safe he lay
430 From his unduteous son, and his usurping sway.
With his mild empire, peace and plenty came;
And hence the golden times derived their name.
A more degenerate and discoloured age
Succeeded this, with avarice and rage.

The Ausonians then, and bold Sicanians, came;
And Saturn's empire often changed the name.
Then kings (gigantic Tibris, and the rest)
With arbitrary sway the land oppressed:
For Tiber's flood was Albula before,
440 Till, from the tyrant's fate, his name it bore.
I last arrived, driven, from my native home
By fortune's power, and fate's resistless doom.
Long tossed on seas, I sought this happy land,
Warned by my mother-nymph, and called by heaven's
    command.'
    Thus, walking on, he spoke, and showed the gate,
Since called Carmental by the Roman state;
Where stood an altar, sacred to the name
Of old Carmenta; the prophetic dame
Who to her son foretold the Ænean race,
450 Sublime in fame, and Rome's imperial place.
. . .
Thence, to the steep Tarpeian rock he leads—
Now roofed with gold, then thatched with homely
    reeds.
A reverent fear (such superstition reigns
460 Among the rude) e'en then possessed the swains:
Some god, they knew (what god, they could not tell)
Did there amidst the sacred horror dwell.
The Arcadians thought him Jove; and said they saw
The mighty Thunderer with majestic awe;
Who shook his shield, and dealt his bolts around,
And scattered tempests on the teeming ground.
. . .
    Discoursing thus together, they resort
Where poor Evander kept his country court.
They viewed the ground of Rome's litigious hall:
(Once oxen lowed, where now the lawyers bawl),
Then, stooping, through the narrow gate they pressed,
When thus the king bespoke his Trojan guest:
' Mean as it is, this palace, and this door,
Received Alcides, then a conqueror.
Dare to be poor: accept our homely food,
480 Which feasted him; and emulate a god.'
Then underneath a lowly roof he led
The weary prince, and laid him on a bed;
The stuffing leaves with hides of bears o'erspread.

Now night had shed her silver dews around,
And with her sable wings embraced the ground,
When love's fair goddess, anxious for her son
(New tumults rising, and new wars begun),
Couched with her husband in his golden bed,
With these alluring words invokes his aid—
490 And, that her pleasing speech his mind may move,
Inspires each accent with the charms of love :
'While cruel fate conspired with Grecian powers,

457 ... there is something marvellously grand and awful in the image, both as it is in itself, a hill covered with a wood supposed to be at some times the peculiar residence of the supreme deity, and also its connection with what is to follow; the Capitol is to be built upon it.
Trapp

471– There is at once much majesty and elegancy in this prolepsis which
476 the poet makes use of by joining together the contrary images of the supposed present and the future, what the thing is and what it is to be. Such confounding of ideas such as this (it were well if there were no other) is not only allowable but an excellence. It tends to delight but not to error; it pleases all but deceives none.
Trapp

479 What modern language, or what poet, can express the majestic beauty of this one verse, amongst a thousand others?

> Aude, hospes, contemnere opes, et te quoque dignum
> Finge deo ...

For my part, I am lost in the admiration of it: I contemn the world when I think on it, and myself when I translate it.
Dryden 'Dedication'

Who that reads this does not envy the old Arcadians, and pity the old Romans, wish for the virtuous poverty of the one, and fear the luxurious greatness of the other?
Trapp

492 And was ever anything so sweetly soft as Venus's speech? ... And how strongly expressive is that which describes the effect of her caresses!
Trapp

To level with the ground the Trojan towers,
I asked not aid the unhappy to restore;
Nor did the succour of thy skill implore;
Nor urged the labours of my lord in vain,
A sinking empire longer to sustain:
Though much I owed to Priam's house, and more
The danger of Æneas did deplore.
500 But now by Jove's command, and fate's decree,
His race is doomed to reign in Italy;
With humble suit I beg thy needful art,
O still propitious power, that rul'st my heart!
A mother kneels a suppliant for her son.
By Thetis and Aurora thou wert won
To forge impenetrable shields, and grace
With fated arms a less illustrious race.
Behold, what haughty nations are combined
Against the relics of the Phrygian kind!
510 With fire and sword my people to destroy,
And conquer Venus twice, in conquering Troy.'
    She said; and straight, her arms of snowy hue
About her unresolving husband threw.
Her soft embraces soon infuse desire;
His bones and marrow sudden warmth inspire;
And all the godhead feels the wonted fire.
Not half so swift the rattling thunder flies,
Or forky lightnings flash along the skies.
The goddess, proud of her successful wiles,
520 And conscious of her form, in secret smiles.
Then thus the power, obnoxious to her charms,
Panting, and half dissolving in her arms:
'Why seek you reasons for a cause so just;
Or your own beauties or my love distrust?
Long since, had you required my helpful hand,
The artificer, and art, you might command,
To labour arms for Troy: nor Jove, nor Fate,
Confined their empire to so short a date.
And, if you now desire new wars to wage,
530 My skill I promise, and my pains engage:
Whatever melting metals can conspire,
Or breathing bellows, or the forming fire,
Is freely yours: your anxious fears remove,
And think no task is difficult to love.'
Trembling he spoke; and, eager of her charms,
He snatched the willing goddess to his arms;
Till, in her lap infused, he lay possessed

Of full desire, and sunk to pleasing rest.
Now when the night her middle race had rode,
540 And his first slumber had refreshed the god—
The time when early housewives leave the bed;
When living embers on the hearth they spread:
Supply the lamp, and call the maids to rise;
With yawning mouths, and with half-opened eyes,
They ply the distaff by the winking light,
And to their daily labour add the night:
Thus frugally they earn their children's bread,
And uncorrupted keep their nuptial bed:
Not less concerned, nor at a later hour,
550 Rose from his downy couch the forging Power.
Sacred to Vulcan's name, an isle there lay,
Betwixt Sicilia's coasts and Lipare,
Raised high on smoking rocks; and, deep below,
In hollow caves the fires of Ætna glow.
The Cyclops here their heavy hammers deal:
Loud strokes, and hissing of tormented steel,
Are heard around: the boiling waters roar;
And smoky flames through fuming tunnels soar.
Hither the father of the fire, by night,
560 Through the brown air precipitates his flight.
On their eternal anvils here he found
The brethren beating, and the blows go round;
A load of pointless thunder now there lies
Before their hands, to ripen for the skies:
These darts, for angry Jove, they daily cast—
Consumed on mortals with prodigious waste.
Three rays of writhen rain, of fire three more;
Of wingèd southern winds and cloudy store
As many parts, the dreadful mixture frame;
570 And fears are added, and avenging flame.
Inferior ministers, for Mars, repair
His broken axle-trees, and blunted war;
And send him forth again with furbished arms,
To wake the lazy war, with trumpet's loud alarms.
The rest refresh the scaly snakes that fold
The shield of Pallas, and renew their gold:
Full on the crest the Gorgon's head they place,
With eyes that roll in death, and with distorted face.
'My sons! (said Vulcan), set your tasks aside;
580 Your strength and master-skill must now be tried.
Arms for a hero forge—arms that require
Your force, your speed, and all your forming fire.'

He said. They set their former work aside,
And their new toils with eager haste divide.
A flood of molten silver, brass, and gold,
And deadly steel, in the large furnace rolled:
Of this, their artful hands a shield prepare,
Alone sufficient to sustain the war.
Seven orbs within a spacious round they close.
590 One stirs the fire, and one the bellows blows.
The hissing steel is in the smithy drowned;
The grot with beaten anvils groans around.
By turns, their arms advance in equal time;
By turns, their hands descend, and hammers chime.
They turn the glowing mass with crooked tongs;
The fiery work proceeds with rustic songs.

    While, at the Lemnian god's command they urge
Their labours thus, and ply the Æolian forge,
The cheerful morn salutes Evander's eyes;
600 And songs of chirping birds invite to rise.
He leaves his lowly bed: his buskins meet
Above his ankles; sandals sheath his feet:
He sets his trusty sword upon his side,
And o'er his shoulder throws a panther's hide.
Two menial dogs before their master pressed.
Thus clad, and guarded thus, he seeks his kingly guest.
Mindful of promised aid, he mends his pace,
But meets Æneas in the middle space.
Young Pallas did his father's steps attend;
610 And true Achates waited on his friend.
They join their hands: a secret seat they choose;
The Arcadian first their former talk renews:

    'Undaunted prince! I never can believe
The Trojan empire lost, while you survive.
Command the assistance of a faithful friend:
But feeble are the succours I can send.
Our narrow kingdom here the Tiber bounds:
That other side the Latian state surrounds,
Insults our walls, and wastes our fruitful grounds.
620 But mighty nations I prepare, to join
Their arms with yours, and aid your just design.
You come, as by your better genius sent;
And Fortune seems to favour your intent.
Not far from hence there stands a hilly town,
Of ancient building, and of high renown,
Torn from the Tuscans by the Lydian race,
Who gave the name of Cære to the place—

Once Agyllina called. It flourished long,
　　　In pride of wealth and warlike people strong;
630　Till cursed Mezentius, in a fatal hour
　　　Assumed the crown, with arbitrary power.
　　　What words can paint those execrable times,
　　　The subjects' sufferings, and the tyrant's crimes?
　　　That blood, those murders, O ye gods! replace
　　　On his own head, and on his impious race!
　　　The living and the dead, at his command
　　　Were coupled face to face, and hand to hand;
　　　Till, choked with stench, in loathed embraces tied,
　　　The lingering wretches pined away and died.
640　Thus plunged in ills, and meditating more—
　　　The people's patience, tried, no longer bore
　　　The raging monster; but with arms beset
　　　His house, and vengeance and destruction threat.
　　　They fire his palace: while the flame ascends,
　　　They force his guards and execute his friends.
　　　He cleaves the crowd, and, favoured by the night,
　　　To Turnus' friendly court directs his flight.
　　　By just revenge the Tuscans set on fire,
　　　With arms, their king to punishment require:
650　Their numerous troops, now mustered on the strand,
　　　My counsel shall submit to your command.
　　　Their navy swarms upon the coasts; they cry
　　　To hoist their anchors; but the gods deny.
　　　An ancient augur, skilled in future fate,
　　　With these foreboding words restrains their hate:
　　　"Ye brave in arms, ye Lydian blood, the flower
　　　Of Tuscan youth, and choice of all their power,
　　　Whom just revenge against Mezentius arms,
　　　To seek your tyrant's death by lawful arms!
660　Know this: no native of our land may lead
　　　This powerful people: seek a foreign head."
　　　Awed with these words, in camps they still abide;
　　　And wait with longing looks their promised guide.
　　　Tarchon, the Tuscan chief, to me has sent
　　　Their crown, and every regal ornament:
　　　The people join their own with his desire;
　　　And all, my conduct as their king, require.

597　The transition is most agreeably made from the smoke fire and noise
　　　of Vulcan's cave to the sweet morning air and the chirping of birds.
　　　　　　　　　　　　　　　　　　　　　　　　　　　　　　Trapp

But the chill blood that creeps within my veins,
And age, and listless limbs unfit for pains;
670 And a soul conscious of its own decay,
Have forced me to refuse imperial sway.
My Pallas were more fit to mount the throne
And should; but he's a Sabine mother's son,
And half a native: but, in you combine
A manly vigour, and a foreign line.
Where Fate and smiling Fortune show the way,
Pursue the ready path to sovereign sway.
The staff of my declining days, my son,
Shall make your good or ill success his own;
680 In fighting-fields, from you shall learn to dare,
And serve the hard apprenticeship of war;
Your matchless courage and your conduct view;
And early shall begin t' admire and copy you.
Besides, two hundred horse he shall command—
Though few, a warlike and well-chosen band.
These in my name are listed; and my son
As many more has added in his own.'

. . .

The horsemen march; the gates are opened wide;
Æneas at their head, Achates by his side.
Next these the Trojan leaders rode along:
Last, follows in the rear the Arcadian throng.
Young Pallas shone conspicuous o'er the rest:
Gilded his arms, embroidered was his vest.
So, from the seas, exerts his radiant head
The star by whom the lights of heaven are led;
780 Shakes from his rosy locks the pearly dews;
Dispels the darkness, and the day renews.
The trembling wives, the walls and turrets crowd,
And follow with their eyes the dusty cloud,
Which winds disperse by fits, and shew from far
The blaze of arms, and shields, and shining war.
The troops, drawn up in beautiful array,
O'er heathy plains pursue the ready way.
Repeated peals of shouts are heard around;
The neighing coursers answer to the sound;
790 And shake with horny hoofs the solid ground.

. . .

Meantime the mother-goddess, crowned with charms,
Breaks through the clouds, and brings the fated arms.

Within a winding vale she finds her son,
810 On the cool river's banks retired, alone.
She shews her heavenly form without disguise,
And gives herself to his desiring eyes.
'Behold! (she said) performed in every part,
My promise made, and Vulcan's laboured art.
Now seek, secure, the Latian enemy;
And haughty Turnus to the field defy.'
She said: and, having first her son embraced,
The radiant arms beneath an oak she placed.
Proud of the gift, he rolled his greedy sight
820 Around the work, and gazed with vast delight.
He lifts, he turns, he poises, and admires
The crested helm, that vomits radiant fires:
His hands the fatal sword and corslet hold—
One keen with tempered steel, one stiff with gold—
Both ample, flaming both, and beamy bright:
So shines a cloud, when edged with adverse light.
He shakes the pointed spear; and longs to try
The plaited cuishes on his manly thigh;
But most admires the shield's mysterious mould,
830 And Roman triumphs rising on the gold:
For there, embossed, the heavenly smith had wrought
(Not in the rolls of future fate untaught)
The wars in order; and the race divine
Of warriors issuing from the Julian line.
The cave of Mars was dressed with mossy greens:
There, by the wolf, were laid the martial twins.
Intrepid on her swelling dugs they hung:
The foster dam lolled out her fawning tongue:
They sucked secure, while, bending back her head,
840 She licked their tender limbs, and formed them as they fed.
Not far from thence new Rome appears; with games
Projected for the rape of Sabine dames.

829 To describe the engravings of a shield is Homer's invention [The shield of Achilles in *Iliad* XVIII], but to give us by way of prophecy a most important piece of history in those engravings and by that means to make them one of the most important parts of the whole poem, thus by an unexampled art to make the very ornaments and decorations one of the strongest and most necessary parts of the building, is entirely new and entirely Virgil's.

Trapp

...
    High on a rock, heroic Manlius stood
To guard the temple, and the temple's god.
Then Rome was poor ; and there you might behold
870 The palace thatched with straw, now roofed with gold.
The silver goose before the shining gate
There flew, and by her cackle saved the state.
She told the Gaul's approach : the approaching Gauls,
Obscure in night, ascend and seize the walls.
The gold dissembled well their yellow hair ;
And golden chains on their white necks they wear.
Gold are their vests ; long Alpine spears they wield ;
And their left arm sustains a length of shield.

...
    Betwixt the quarters, flows a golden sea ;
But foaming surges there in silver play.
The dancing dolphins with their tails divide
The glittering waves, and cut the precious tide.
Amid the main, two mighty fleets engage :
Their brazen beaks opposed with equal rage.
Actium surveys the well-disputed prize :
Leucate's watery plain with foamy billows fries.
Young Cæsar, on the stern in armour bright,
900 Here leads the Romans and their gods to fight :
His beamy temples shoot their flames afar ;
And o'er his head is hung the Julian star.
Agrippa seconds him, with prosperous gales,
And, with propitious gods, his foes assails.
A naval crown, that binds his manly brows,
The happy fortune of the fight foreshows.
    Ranged on the line opposed, Antonius brings
Barbarian aids, and troops of eastern kings,
The Arabians near, and Bactrians from afar,
910 Of tongues discordant, and a mingled war :
And, rich in gaudy robes, amidst the strife,
His ill fate follows him—the Egyptian wife.
Moving they fight : with oars and forky prows
The froth is gathered and the water glows.
It seems as if the Cyclades again
Were rooted up, and justled in the main ;
Or floating mountains floating mountains meet ;
Such is the fierce encounter of the fleet.
Fire-balls are thrown, and pointed javelins fly ;
920 The fields of Neptune take a purple dye.

BOOK VIII

The queen herself, amidst the loud alarms,
With cymbal tossed, her fainting soldiers warms—
Fool as she was! who had not yet divined
Her cruel fate ; nor saw the snakes behind.
Her country gods, the monsters of the sky,
Great Neptune, Pallas, and love's queen, defy.
The dog Anubis barks, but barks in vain,
Nor longer dares oppose the ethereal train.
Mars, in the middle of the shining shield
930 Is graved, and strides along the liquid field.
The Diræ souse from heaven with swift descent ;
And Discord, dyed in blood, with garments rent,
Divides the press : her steps Bellona treads,
And shakes her iron rod above their heads.
    This seen, Apollo, from his Actian height
Pours down his arrows ; at whose winged flight
The trembling Indians and Egyptians yield,
And soft Sabæans quit the watery field.
The fatal mistress hoists her silken sails,
940 And shrinking from the fight, invokes the gales.
Aghast she looks, and heaves her breast for breath,
Panting, and pale with fear of future death.
The god had figured her, as driven along
By winds and waves, and scudding through the throng.
Just opposite, sad Nilus opens wide
His arms and ample bosom to the tide,
And spreads his mantle o'er the winding coast ;
In which, he wraps his queen and hides the flying host.
    The victor to the gods his thanks expressed ;
950 And Rome triumphant with his presence blessed.
Three hundred temples in the town he placed ;
With spoils and altars every temple graced.
Three shining nights, and three succeeding days,
The fields resound with shouts, the streets with praise,
The domes with songs, the theatres with plays.
All altars flame : before each altar lies,
Drenched in his gore, the destined sacrifice.
Great Cæsar sits sublime upon his throne,
Before Apollo's porch of Parian stone ;
960 Accepts the presents vowed for victory ;
And hangs the monumental crowns on high.
Vast crowds of vanquished nations march along,
Various in arms, in habit, and in tongue.
. . .

973   These figures, on the shield divinely wrought,
By Vulcan laboured, and by Venus brought,
With joy and wonder fill the hero's thought.
Unknown the names, he yet admires the grace;
And bears aloft the fame and fortune of his race.

BOOK IX

THE ARGUMENT

Turnus takes advantage of Æneas' absence, fires some of his ships (which are transformed into sea-nymphs), and assaults his camp. The Trojans, reduced to the last extremities, send Nisus and Euryalus to recall Æneas; which furnishes the poet with that admirable episode of their friendship, generosity, and the conclusion of their adventures.

. . .

    Now march the bold confederates through the plain,
30 Well horsed, well clad, a rich and shining train.
Messapus leads the van; and, in the rear,
The sons of Tyrrheus in bright arms appear.
In the main battle, with his flaming crest,
The mighty Turnus towers above the rest.
Silent they move, majestically slow,
Like ebbing Nile, or Ganges in his flow.
The Trojans view the dusty cloud from far,
And the dark menace of the distant war.
Caïcus from the rampire saw it rise,
40 Black'ning the fields, and thick'ning through the skies:
Then to his fellows thus aloud he calls:
'What rolling clouds, my friends, approach the walls?
Arm! arm! and man the works! prepare your spears,
And pointed darts! the Latian host appears.'
    Thus warned, they shut their gates; with shouts ascend
The bulwarks, and, secure, their foes attend:
For their wise general, with foreseeing care,
Had charged them not to tempt the doubtful war,
Nor, though provoked, in open fields advance,
50 But close within their lines attend their chance.

    What most particularly distinguishes this book from the rest is the famous episode of Nisus and Euryalus so often mentioned, which is beautiful almost to a proverb, and is one of the most celebrated pieces of antiquity.
    The poet had in the fourth book exhausted the subject of love and now he gives us a specimen of his skill upon the power of friendship. Never was anything more artfully disposed, more fiery and noble, more moving and pathetical, than this consummate piece.

                                                   Trapp

. . .
200 To keep the nightly guard, to watch the walls,
To pitch the fires at distances around,
And close the Trojans in their scanty ground.
Twice seven Rutulian captains ready stand;
And twice seven hundred horse these chiefs command
All clad in shining arms the works invest,
Each with a radiant helm, and waving crest.
Stretched at their length, they press the grassy
  ground;
They laugh; they sing (the jolly bowls go round);
With lights and cheerful fires renew the day;
210 And pass the wakeful night in feasts and play.
  The Trojans, from above, their foes beheld,
And with armed legions all the rampires filled.
Seized with affright, their gates they first explore;
Join works to works with bridges, tower to tower:
Thus all things needful for defence abound:
Mnestheus and brave Serestus walk the round,
Commissioned by their absent prince to share
The common danger, and divide the care.
The soldiers draw their lots, and, as they fall,
220 By turns relieve each other on the wall.
  Nigh where the foes their utmost guards advance,
To watch the gate was warlike Nisus' chance.
His father Hyrtacus, of noble blood;
His mother was a huntress of the wood,
And sent him to the wars. Well could he bear
His lance in fight, and dart the flying spear;
But better skilled unerring shafts to send.
Beside him stood Euryalus, his friend—
Euryalus, than whom, the Trojan host
230 No fairer face, or sweeter air, could boast:
Scarce had the down to shade his cheeks begun.
One was their care, and their delight was one:
One common hazard in the war they shared;
And now were both by choice upon the guard.
  Then Nisus thus: 'Or do the gods inspire
This warmth, or make we gods of our desire?
A generous ardour boils within my breast,
Eager of action, enemy to rest:
This urges me to fight, and fires my mind
240 To leave a memorable name behind.
Thou seest the foe secure: how faintly shine
Their scattered fires: the most, in sleep supine

BOOK IX

Along the ground, an easy conquest lie:
The wakeful few the fuming flagon ply:
All hushed around. Now hear what I revolve—
A thought unripe—and scarcely yet resolve.
Our absent prince both camp and council mourn;
By message both would hasten his return:
If they confer what I demand, on thee
250 (For fame is recompense enough for me),
Methinks, beneath yon hill, I have espied
A way that safely will my passage guide.'
Euryalus stood listening while he spoke;
With love of praise and noble envy struck;
Then to his ardent friend exposed his mind:
' All this, alone, and leaving me behind!
Am I unworthy, Nisus, to be joined?
Think'st thou I can my share of glory yield,
Or send thee, unassisted, to the field?
260 Not so my father taught my childhood arms—
Born in a siege, and bred among alarms.
Nor is my youth unworthy of my friend,
Nor of the heaven-born hero I attend.
The thing called life with ease I can disclaim,
And think it over-sold to purchase fame.'
    Then Nisus thus: ' Alas! thy tender years
Would minister new matter to my fears.
So may the gods who view this friendly strife,
Restore me to thy loved embrace with life,
270 Condemned to pay my vows (as sure I trust),
This thy request is cruel and unjust.
But if some chance—as many chances are,
And doubtful hazards, in the deeds of war—
If one should reach my head, there let it fall,
And spare thy life: I would not perish all.
Thy blooming youth deserves a longer date:
Live thou to mourn thy love's unhappy fate,
To bear my mangled body from the foe,
Or buy it back, and funeral rites bestow.
280 Or, if hard fortune shall those dues deny,
Thou canst at least an empty tomb supply.
O! let not me the widow's tears renew;
Nor let a mother's curse my name pursue—
Thy pious parent, who, for love of thee,
Forsook the coasts of friendly Sicily;
Her age committing to the seas and wind,
When every weary matron stayed behind.'

To this, Euryalus : ' You plead in vain,
And but protract the cause you cannot gain.
290 No more delays ! but haste !' With that, he wakes
The nodding watch : each to his office takes.
    The guard relieved, the generous couple went
To find the council at the royal tent.
All creatures else forgot their daily care,
And sleep, the common gift of nature, share ;
Except the Trojan peers, who wakeful sat
In nightly council for the endangered state.
They vote a message to their absent chief,
Shew their distress, and beg a swift relief.
300 Amid the camp a silent seat they chose,
Remote from clamour, and secure from foes.
On their left arms their ample shields they bear,
Their right reclined upon the bending spear.
    Now Nisus and his friend approach the guard,
And beg admission, eager to be heard—
The affair important, not to be deferred.
Ascanius bids them be conducted in,
Ordering the more experienced to begin.
Then Nisus thus : ' Ye fathers, lend your ears ;
310 Nor judge our bold attempt beyond our years.
The foe, securely drenched in sleep and wine,
Neglect their watch ; the fires but thinly shine ;
And where the smoke in cloudy vapours flies,
Covering the plain, and curling to the skies,
Betwixt two paths which at the gate divide,
Close by the sea, a passage we have spied,
Which will our way to great Æneas guide.
Expect each hour to see him safe again,
Loaded with spoils of foes in battle slain.
320 Snatch we the lucky minute while we may ;
Nor can we be mistaken in the way ;
For, hunting in the vales, we both have seen
The rising turrets, and the stream between ;
And know the winding course, with every ford.'
He ceased ; and old Aletes took the word :
' Our country gods, in whom our trust we place,
Will yet from ruin save the Trojan race,
While we behold such dauntless worth appear
In dawning youth, and souls so void of fear.'
330 Then into tears of joy the father broke :
Each in his longing arms by turns he took ;
Panted and paused ; and thus again he spoke :

'Ye brave young men, what equal gifts can we,
In recompense of such desert, decree?
The greatest, sure, and best you can receive,
The gods and your own conscious worth will give.
The rest our grateful general will bestow,
And young Ascanius, till his manhood, owe.'
'And I, whose welfare in my father lies,
340 (Ascanius adds) by the great deities,
By my dear country, by my household gods,
By hoary Vesta's rites and dark abodes,
Adjure you both (on you my fortune stands:
That and my faith I plight into your hands):
Make me but happy in his safe return,
Whose wanted presence I can only mourn;
Your common gift shall two large goblets be
Of silver, wrought with curious imagery,
And high embossed, which, when old Priam reigned,
350 My conquering sire at sacked Arisba gained;
And, more, two tripods cast in antique mould,
With two great talents of the finest gold;
Beside a costly bowl, engraved with art,
Which Dido gave, when first she gave her heart.
But, if in conquered Italy we reign,
When spoils by lot the victor shall obtain—
Thou saw'st the courser by proud Turnus pressed,
That, Nisus! and his arms, and nodding crest,
And shield, from chance exempt, shall be thy share;
360 Twelve labouring slaves, twelve handmaids young and fair,
All clad in rich attire, and trained with care;
And, last, a Latian field with fruitful plains,
And a large portion of the king's domains.
But thou, whose years are more to mine allied,
No fate my vowed affection shall divide
From thee, heroic youth! Be wholly mine:
Take full possession: all my soul is thine.
One faith, one fame, one fate, shall both attend:
My life's companion, and my bosom friend—
370 My peace shall be committed to thy care;
And, to thy conduct, my concerns in war.'
  Then thus the young Euryalus replied:
'Whatever fortune, good or bad, betide,
The same shall be my age, as now my youth;
No time shall find me wanting to my truth,
This only from your goodness let me gain

(And, this ungranted, all rewards are vain):
Of Priam's royal race my mother came—
And sure the best that ever bore the name—
380 Whom neither Troy nor Sicily could hold
From me departing, but, o'erspent and old,
My fate she followed. Ignorant of this
(Whatever) danger, neither parting kiss
Nor pious blessing taken, her I leave,
And in this only act of all my life deceive.
By this right hand, and conscious night, I swear,
My soul so sad a farewell could not bear.
Be you her comfort; fill my vacant place
(Permit me to presume so great a grace);
390 Support her age, forsaken and distressed.
That hope alone will fortify my breast
Against the worst of fortunes and of fears.'
He said. The moved assistants melt in tears.
Then thus Ascanius, wonder-struck to see
That image of his filial piety:
'So great beginnings, in so green an age,
Exact the faith which I again engage.
Thy mother all the dues shall justly claim,
Creüsa had, and only want the name.
400 Whate'er event thy bold attempt shall have,
'Tis merit to have borne a son so brave.
Now by my head, a sacred oath, I swear
(My father used it), what, returning here
Crowned with success, I for thyself prepare;
That, if thou fail, shall thy loved mother share.'
    He said, and, weeping while he spoke the word,
From his broad belt he drew a shining sword,
Magnificent with gold. Lycaon made,
And in an ivory scabbard sheathed the blade.
410 This was his gift. Great Mnestheus gave his friend
A lion's hide, his body to defend;
And good Aletes furnished him, beside,
With his own trusty helm, of temper tried.
    Thus armed they went. The noble Trojans wait
Their issuing forth, and follow to the gate
With prayers and vows. Above the rest appears
Ascanius, manly far beyond his years,
And messages committed to their care,
Which all in winds were lost, and flitting air.
420 The trenches first they passed; then took their way

Where their proud foes in pitched pavilions lay:
To many fatal, ere themselves were slain.
They found the careless host dispersed upon the plain,
Who, gorged, and drunk with wine, supinely snore.
Unharnessed chariots stand along the shore:
Amidst the wheels and reins, the goblet by,
A medley of debauch and war, they lie.
Observing Nisus shewed his friend the sight:
' Behold a conquest gained without a fight.
430 Occasion offers; and I stand prepared :
There lies our way: be thou upon the guard,
And look around, while I securely go,
And hew a passage through the sleeping foe.'
Softly he spoke; then, striding took his way,
With his drawn sword, where haughty Rhamnes lay;
His head raised high on tapestry beneath,
And heaving from his breast, he drew his breath—
A king and prophet, by king Turnus loved ;
But fate by prescience cannot be removed.
440 Him and his sleeping slaves he slew ; then spies
Where Remus, with his rich retinue, lies.
His armour-bearer first, and next he kills
His charioteer, intrenched betwixt the wheels
And his loved horses : last invades their lord ;
Full on his neck he drives the fatal sword ;
The gasping head flies off; a purple flood
Flows from the trunk, that welters in the blood,
Which, by the spurning heels dispersed around,
The bed besprinkles, and bedews the ground.
450 Lamus the bold and Lamyrus the strong,
He slew, and then Sarranus fair and young.
From dice and wine the youth retired to rest,
And puffed the fumy god from out his breast :
E'en then he dreamt of drink and lucky play—
More lucky, had it lasted till the day.
  The famished lion thus, with hunger bold,
O'erleaps the fences of the nightly fold,
And tears the peaceful flocks : with silent awe
Trembling they lie, and pant beneath his paw.
460 Nor with less rage Euryalus employs
The wrathful sword, or fewer foes destroys :
But on the ignoble crowd his fury flew :
He Fadus, Hebesus, and Rhœtus, slew.
Oppressed with heavy sleep the former fall,
But Rhœtus wakeful, and observing all :

Behind a spacious jar he slinked for fear:
The fatal iron found and reached him there;
For, as he rose, it pierced his naked side,
And, reeking, thence returned in crimson dyed.
470 The wound pours out a stream of wine and blood;
The purple soul comes floating in the flood.
　Now, where Messapus quartered, they arrive.
The fires were fainting there, and just alive;
The warrior-horses, tied in order, fed:
Nisus observed the discipline, and said:
' Our eager thirst of blood may both betray:
And see, the scattered streaks of dawning day,
Foe to nocturnal thefts! No more, my friend:
Here let our glutted execution end.
480 A lane through slaughtered bodies we have made.'
The bold Euryalus, though loth, obeyed.
Of arms, and arras, and of plate, they find
A precious load; but these they leave behind.
Yet, fond of gaudy spoils, the boy would stay
To make the rich caparison his prey,
Which on the steed of conquered Rhamnes lay.
Nor did his eyes less longingly behold
The girdle-belt, with nails of burnished gold.
This present Cædicus the rich bestowed
490 On Remulus, when friendship first they vowed,
And, absent, joined in hospitable ties;
He, dying, to his heir bequeathed the prize;
Till, by the conquering Ardean troops oppressed,
He fell; and they the glorious gift possessed.
These glittering spoils (now made the victor's gain)
He to his body suits, but suits in vain.
Messapus' helm he finds among the rest,
And laces on, and wears the waving crest.
Proud of their conquest, prouder of their prey,
500 They leave the camp, and take the ready way.
　But far they had not passed, before they spied
Three hundred horse, with Volscens for their guide.
The queen a legion to king Turnus sent;
But the swift horse the slower foot prevent,
And now, advancing, sought the leader's tent.
They saw the pair; for, through the doubtful shade,
His shining helm Euryalus betrayed,
On which the moon with full reflection played.
' 'Tis not for nought (cried Volscens from the crowd),
510 These men go there (then raised his voice aloud):

Stand! stand! why thus in arms? and whither bent
From whence, to whom, and on what errand sent?'
Silent they scud away, and haste their flight
To neighbouring woods, and trust themselves to night.
The speedy horse all passages belay,
And spur their smoking steeds to cross their way,
And watch each entrance of the winding wood.
Black was the forest: thick with beech it stood,
Horrid with fern, and intricate with thorn:
520 Few paths of human feet, or tracks of beasts, were worn.
The darkness of the shades, his heavy prey,
And fear, misled the younger from his way.
But Nisus hit the turns with happier haste,
And thoughtless of his friend, the forest passed,
And Alban plains (from Alba's name so called)
Where king Latinus then his oxen stalled;
Till, turning at the length, he stood his ground,
And missed his friend, and cast his eyes around.
'Ah wretch! (he cried) where have I left behind
530 The unhappy youth? where shall I hope to find?
Or what way take?' Again he ventures back,
And treads the mazes of his former track.
He winds the wood, and, listening, hears the noise
Of trampling coursers, and the riders' voice.
The sound approached; and suddenly he viewed
The foes inclosing, and his friend pursued,
Forelaid and taken, while he strove in vain
The shelter of the friendly shades to gain.
What should he next attempt? what arms employ,
540 What fruitless force, to free the captive boy?
Or desperate should he rush and lose his life,
With odds oppressed, in such unequal strife?
Resolved at length, his pointed spear he shook;
And, casting on the moon a mournful look:

507 The discovery of our adventurers is finely conducted. They are detected merely by so slight a circumstance as that of an helmet reflecting the moonbeams. What can be more natural than this! The beauty of this discovery consists in the slightness of the circumstance which occasioned it. We are to remember too that they are betrayed by the part of the spoil they had just been taking, Messapus's helmet.

Warton

'Guardian of groves, and goddess of the night!
Fair queen! (he said) direct my dart aright.
If e'er my pious father, for my sake,
Did grateful off'rings on thy altars make,
Or I increased them with my sylvan toils,
550 And hung thy holy roofs with savage spoils,
Give me to scatter these.' Then from his ear
He poised, and aimed, and launched the trembling spear.
The deadly weapon, hissing from the grove,
Impetuous on the back of Sulmo drove;
Pierced his thin armour, drank his vital blood,
And in his body left the broken wood.
He staggers round; his eyeballs roll in death;
And with short sobs he gasps away his breath.
All stand amazed:—a second javelin flies
560 With equal strength, and quivers through the skies.
This through thy temples, Tagus, forced the way,
And in the brain-pan warmly buried lay.
Fierce Volscens foams with rage, and gazing round,
Descried not him who gave the deadly wound,
Nor knew to fix revenge: 'But thou (he cries),
Shalt pay for both,' and at the prisoner flies
With his drawn sword. Then, struck with deep despair,
That cruel sight the lover could not bear;
But from his covert rushed in open view.
570 And sent his voice before him as he flew:
Me! me! (he cried) turn all your swords alone
On me—the fact confessed, the fault my own.
He neither could nor durst, the guiltless youth—
Ye moon and stars, bear witness to the truth!
His only crime (if friendship can offend)
Is too much love to his unhappy friend.'
Too late he speaks: the sword, which fury guides,
Driven with full force, had pierced his tender sides.
Down fell the beauteous youth: the yawning wound
580 Gushed out a purple stream, and stained the ground.
His snowy neck reclines upon his breast,
Like a fair flower by the keen share oppressed—
Like a white poppy sinking on the plain,
Whose heavy head is overcharged with rain.
    Despair, and rage, and vengeance justly vowed,
Drove Nisus headlong on the hostile crowd.
Volscens he seeks; on him alone he bends:
Borne back and bored by his surrounding friends,
Onward he pressed, and kept him still in sight,

590 Then whirled aloft his sword with all his might:
The unerring steel descended while he spoke,
Pierced his wide mouth, and through his weazon
    broke.
Dying, he slew; and staggering on the plain,
With swimming eyes he sought his lover slain;
Then quiet on his bleeding bosom fell,
Content, in death, to be revenged so well.
   O happy friends! for, if my verse can give
Immortal life, your fame shall ever live,
Fixed as the Capitol's foundation lies,
600 And spread, where'er the Roman eagle flies!
   The conquering party first divide the prey,
Then their slain leader to the camp convey.
With wonder, as they went, the troops were filled,
To see such numbers whom so few had killed.
Sarranus, Rhamnes, and the rest, they found:
Vast crowds the dying and the dead surround;
And the yet reeking blood overflows the ground.
All knew the helmet which Messapus lost,
But mourned a purchase that so dear had cost.
610   Now rose the ruddy morn from Tithon's bed,
And with the dawn of day the skies o'erspread;
Nor long the sun his daily course withheld,
But added colours to the world revealed;
When, early, Turnus, wakening with the light,
All clad in armour, calls his troops to fight.
His martial men with fierce harangues he fired,
And his own ardour in their souls inspired.
This done—to give new terror to his foes,
The heads of Nisus and his friend he shows,
620 Raised high on pointed spears—a ghastly sight!
Loud peals of shouts ensue, and barbarous delight.
   Meantime the Trojans run where danger calls;
They line their trenches, and they man their walls.
In front extended to the left they stood:
Safe was the right, surrounded by the flood.
But, casting from their towers a frightful view,
They saw the faces, which too well they knew,
Though then disguised in death, and smeared all
    o'er

571 That *Me me* is the most elegant abruptness, the very perfection of an imperfect sentence.

Trapp

With filth obscene, and dropping putrid gore.
630 Soon, hasty fame through the sad city bears
The mournful message to the mother's ears.
An icy cold benumbs her limbs; she shakes;
Her cheeks the blood, her hand the web, forsakes.
She runs the rampires round, amidst the war,
Nor fears the flying darts: she rends her hair,
And fills with loud laments the liquid air.
'Thus, then, my loved Euryalus appears!
Thus looks the prop of my declining years!
Was't on this face my famished eyes I fed?
640 Ah! how unlike the living is the dead!
And couldst thou leave me, cruel, thus alone!
Not one kind kiss from a departing son!
No look, no last adieu, before he went,
In an ill-boding hour to slaughter sent!
Cold on the ground, and pressing foreign clay,
To Latian dogs and fowls he lies a prey!
Nor was I near to close his dying eyes,
To wash his wounds, to weep his obsequies,
To call about his corpse his crying friends,
650 Or spread the mantle (made for other ends)
On his dear body, which I wove with care,
Nor did my daily pains or nightly labour spare.
Where shall I find his corpse? what earth sustains
His trunk dismembered, and his cold remains?
For this, alas! I left my needful ease,
Exposed my life to winds, and winter seas!
If any pity touch Rutulian hearts,
Here empty all your quivers, all your darts:
Or, if they fail, thou, Jove, conclude my woe,
660 And send me thunder-struck to shades below!'
Her shrieks and clamours pierce the Trojans' ears,
Unman their courage, and augment their fears:
Nor young Ascanius could the sight sustain,
Nor old Ilioneus his tears restrain,
But Actor and Idæus jointly sent,
To bear the madding mother to her tent.
And now the trumpets terribly, from far,
With rattling clangour, rouse the sleepy war.
The soldiers' shouts succeed the brazen sounds;
670 And heaven, from pole to pole, the noise rebounds.
. . .

BOOK X

THE ARGUMENT

Jupiter, calling a council of the gods, forbids them to engage in either party. At Æneas' return there is a bloody battle; Turnus killing Pallas; Æneas, Lausus and Mezentius. Mezentius is described as an atheist; Lausus as a pious and virtuous youth. The different actions and death of these two are the subject of a noble episode.

THE gates of heaven unfold : Jove summons all
The gods to council in the common hall.
Sublimely seated, he surveys from far
The fields, the camp, the fortune of the war,
And all the inferior world. From first to last,
The sovereign senate in degrees are placed.
   Then thus the almighty sire began : ' Ye gods,
Natives or denizens of blest abodes !
From whence these murmurs, and this change of mind,
10 This backward fate from what was first designed ?
Why this protracted war, when my commands
Pronounced a peace, and gave the Latian lands?
What fear or hope on either part divides
Our heavens, and arms our powers on different sides ?
. . .

   ' Celestials ! your attentive ears incline !
160 Since (said the god) the Trojans must not join
In wished alliance with the Latian line—
Since endless jarrings, and immortal hate,
Tend but to discompose our happy state—
The war henceforward be resigned to fate :
Each to his proper fortune stand or fall ;
Equal and unconcerned I look on all.
Rutulians, Trojans, are the same to me ;
And both shall draw the lots their fates decree.
Let these assault, if Fortune be their friend ;
170 And, if she favours those, let those defend :
The fates will find their way.' The Thunderer said ;
And shook the sacred honours of his head,
Attesting Styx, the inviolable flood,
And the black regions of his brother-god.
Trembled the poles of heaven ; and earth confessed the
   nod.
This end the sessions had : the senate rise,
And to his palace wait their sovereign through the skies.

. . .
      To the rude shock of war both armies came;
610 Their leaders equal, and their strength the same.
The rear so pressed the front, they could not wield
Their angry weapons, to dispute the field.
Here Pallas urges on, and Lausus there:
Of equal youth and beauty both appear,
But both by fate forbid to breathe their native air.
Their congress in the field great Jove withstands—
Both doomed to fall, but fall by greater hands.
      Meantime Juturna warns the Daunian chief
Of Lausus' danger, urging swift relief.
620 With his driven chariot he divides the crowd,
And, making to his friends, thus calls aloud:
'Let none presume his needless aid to join:
Retire, and clear the field; the fight is mine:
To this right hand is Pallas only due:
Oh! were his father here, my just revenge to view!'
From the forbidden space his men retired.
Pallas their awe, and his stern words, admired;
Surveyed him o'er and o'er with wondering sight,
Struck with his haughty mien and towering height.
630 Then to the king: 'Your empty vaunts forbear:
Success I hope and fate I cannot fear.
Alive, or dead, I shall deserve a name:
Jove is impartial, and to both the same.'
He said, and to the void advanced his pace:
Pale horror sat on each Arcadian face.
Then Turnus, from his chariot leaping light,
Addressed himself on foot to single fight.
And, as a lion—when he spies from far
A bull that seems to meditate the war,
640 Bending his neck, and spurning back the sand—
Runs roaring downward from his hilly stand:
Imagine eager Turnus not more slow
To rush from high on his unequal foe.
      Young Pallas, when he saw the chief advance
Within due distance of his flying lance,
Prepares to charge him first—resolved to try
If Fortune would his want of force supply;
And thus to heaven and Hercules addressed:
'Alcides, once on earth Evander's guest!
650 His son adjures thee by those holy rights,
That hospitable board, those genial nights;
Assist my great attempt to gain this prize,

And let proud Turnus view, with dying eyes,
His ravished spoils.' 'Twas heard, the vain request;
Alcides mourned, and stifled sighs within his breast.
Then Jove, to soothe his sorrow, thus began:
'Short bounds of life are set to mortal man:
'Tis virtue's work alone to stretch the narrow span.
So many sons of gods, in bloody fight
660 Around the walls of Troy, have lost the light:
My own Sarpedon fell beneath his foe;
Nor I, his mighty sire, could ward the blow.
E'en Turnus shortly shall resign his breath,
And stands already on the verge of death.'
This said, the god permits the fatal fight,
But from the Latian fields averts his sight.
Now with full force his spear young Pallas threw;
And, having thrown, his shining falchion drew.
The steel just grazed along the shoulder-joint,
670 And marked it slightly with the glancing point.
Fierce Turnus first to nearer distance drew,
And poised his pointed spear, before he threw:
Then, as the wingèd weapon whizzed along,
'See now (said he), whose arm is better strung.'
The spear kept on the fatal course unstayed
By plates of iron, which o'er the shield were laid:

618 It was natural for the reader to think that these two young princes being so equally matched and now so near together must meet and fight. The poet shows us that he was not unmindful of this and so starts this idea, but passes from it to a quite different one, and gives us a hint of what would be the fate of them both. This is extremely ingenious and judicious, first causing in the mind that which never fails to please it, vicissitude and surprise, secondly showing the art of the poet in telling us what he could have done though he does it not. It may be observed too that it was more glory to these two youthful heroes to be slain, as they were, by enemies so far superior to themselves than for either of them to have killed the other, or for both to have been killed by each other, not to mention the beautiful use which the poet afterwards makes of their deaths.

Trapp

657 The sententious sayings in Virgil are always most majestically moral, and none of his smallest beauties.

Trapp

Through folded brass, and tough bull-hides, it passed,
His corselet pierced, and reached his heart at last.
In vain the youth tugs at the broken wood;
680 The soul comes issuing with the vital blood:
He falls; his arms upon his body sound;
And with his bloody teeth he bites the ground.
   Turnus bestrode the corpse: 'Arcadians, hear
(Said he), my message to your master bear:
Such as the sire deserved, the son I send;
It costs him dear to be the Phrygian's friend.
The lifeless body, tell him, I bestow
Unasked, to rest his wandering ghost below.'
He said, and trampled down, with all the force
690 Of his left foot, and spurned the wretched corpse;
Then snatched the shining belt, with gold inlaid—
The belt Eurytion's artful hands had made,
Where fifty fatal brides, expressed to sight,
All, in the compass of one mournful night,
Deprived their bridegrooms of returning light.
   In an ill hour insulting Turnus tore
Those golden spoils, and in a worse he wore.
O mortals! blind in fate, who never know
To bear high fortune, or endure the low!
700 The time shall come, when Turnus, but in vain,
Shall wish untouched the trophies of the slain
Shall wish the fatal belt were far away,
And curse the dire remembrance of the day.
   The sad Arcadians, from the unhappy field,
Bear back the breathless body on a shield.
O grace and grief of war! at once restored,
With praises, to thy sire, at once deplored.
One day first sent thee to the fighting-field,
Beheld whole heaps of foes in battle killed;
710 One day behold thee dead, and borne upon thy shield.
This dismal news, not from uncertain fame,
But sad spectators, to the hero came:
His friends upon the brink of ruin stand,
Unless relieved by his victorious hand.
He whirls his sword around, without delay,
And hews through adverse foes an ample way,
To find fierce Turnus, of his conquest proud.
Evander, Pallas, all that friendship owed
To large deserts, are present to his eyes—
720 His plighted hand, and hospitable ties.
   Four sons of Sulmo, four whom Ufens bred,

He took in fight, and living victims led,
To please the ghost of Pallas, and expire,
In sacrifice, before his funeral fire.
At Magus next he threw: he stooped below
The flying spear, and shunned the promised blow,
Then, creeping, clasped the hero's knees, and prayed:
' By young Iulus, by thy father's shade,
O ! spare my life, and send me back to see
730 My longing sire, and tender progeny,
A lofty house I have, and wealth untold,
In silver ingots, and in bars of gold :
All these, and sums besides, which see no day,
The ransom of this one poor life shall pay.
If I survive, will Troy the less prevail ?
A single soul's too light to turn the scale.'
He said. The hero sternly thus replied :
' Thy bars and ingots, and the sums beside,
Leave for thy children's lot. Thy Turnus broke
740 All rules of war by one relentless stroke,
When Pallas fell : so deems, nor deems alone,
My father's shadow, but my living son.'
Thus having said, of kind remorse bereft,
He seized his helm, and dragged him with his left ;
Then with his right hand, while his neck he wreathed,
Up to the hilts his shining falchion sheathed.

. . .

698 These beautiful anticipations are frequent in the poets who affect to speak in the character of prophets and men inspired with knowledge of futurity. Thus Virgil to Turnus,

Nescia mens hominum (501)

Pope on *Iliad* XVII, 564

725 Virgil had this part of Homer in his view [*Iliad* VI, 46–60] when he described the death of Magus. . . . Those lines . . . also receive a great addition of beauty and propriety from the occasion on which he inserts them. . . . Nothing can be a more artful piece of address than the first lines of that supplication, if we consider the character of Aeneas to whom it is made. . . . And what can exceed the closeness and fulness of that reply to it? . . . This removes the imputation of cruelty from Aeneas.

Pope on *Iliad* VI, 57

Then Tarquitus the field in triumph trod;
A nymph his mother, and his sire a god.
Exulting in bright arms, he braves the prince:
770 With his protended lance he makes defence;
Bears back his feeble foe; then, pressing on,
Arrests his better hand, and drags him down;
Stands o'er the prostrate wretch, and (as he lay,
Vain tales inventing, and prepared to pray)
Mows off his head: the trunk a moment stood,
Then sunk, and rolled along the sand in blood.
  The vengeful victor thus upbraids the slain:
'Lie there, proud man, unpitied on the plain:
Lie there, inglorious, and without a tomb,
780 Far from thy mother and thy native home;
Exposed to savage beasts, and birds of prey,
Or thrown for food to monsters of the sea.'
  On Lucas and Antæus next he ran,
Two chiefs of Turnus, and who led his van.
They fled for fear; with these, he chased along
Camers the yellow-locked, and Numa strong;
Both great in arms, and both were fair and young.

Jupiter allows Juno to prolong the life of Turnus

  Then shortly thus the sovereign god replied:
'Since in my power and goodness you confide,
880 If, for a little space, a lengthened span,
You beg reprieve for this expiring man,
I grant you leave to take your Turnus hence
From instant fate, and can so far dispense.
But, if some secret meaning lies beneath,
To save the short-lived youth from destined death;
Or, if a farther thought you entertain,
To change the fates; you feed your hopes in vain.'
  To whom the goddess thus, with weeping eyes:
'And what if that request your tongue denies,
890 Your heart should grant—and not a short reprieve.
But length of certain life, to Turnus give?
Now speedy death attends the guiltless youth,
If my presaging soul divines with truth;
Which, O! I wish might err, through causeless fears,
And you (for you have power) prolong his years!'
  Thus having said, involved in clouds, she flies,
And drives a storm before her through the skies.
Swift she descends, alighting on the plain,

Where the fierce foes a dubious fight maintain.
900 Of air condensed, a spectre soon she made ;
And, what Æneas was, such seemed the shade.
Adorned with Dardan arms, the phantom bore
His head aloft ; a plumy crest he wore :
This hand appeared a shining sword to wield,
And that sustained an imitated shield.
With manly mien he stalked along the ground,
Nor wanted voice belied, nor vaunting sound.
(Thus haunting ghosts appear to waking sight,
Or dreadful visions in our dreams by night.)
910 The spectre seems the Daunian chief to dare,
And flourishes his empty sword in air.
At this, advancing, Turnus hurled his spear :
The phantom wheeled, and seemed to fly for fear.
Deluded Turnus thought the Trojan fled,
And with vain hopes his haughty fancy fed.
' Whither, O coward ? (thus he calls aloud,
Nor found he spoke to wind, and chased a cloud),
Why thus forsake your bride ! Receive from me
The fated land you sought so long by sea.'
920 He said, and, brandishing at once his blade,
With eager pace pursued the flying shade.
By chance a ship was fastened to the shore,
Which from old Clusium king Osinius bore :
The plank was ready laid for safe ascent ;
For shelter there the trembling shadow bent,
And skipped and skulked, and under hatches went.
Exulting Turnus, with regardless haste,
Ascends the plank, and to the galley passed.
Scarce had he reached the prow ; Saturnia's hand
930 The halsers cuts, and shoots the ship from land.
With wind in poop, the vessel ploughs the sea,

901 The fiction of a god's placing a phantom instead of the hero to delude the enemy and continue the engagement means no more than that the enemy thought he was in the battle. This is the language of poetry which prefers a marvellous fiction to a plain and simple truth the recital whereof would be cold and unaffecting. . . . Whoever will compare the two authors on this subject [Homer *Iliad* V, 449ff.] will observe with what admirable art and with what exquisite ornaments the latter [Virgil] has improved and beautified his original.

Pope on *Iliad* V, 546

And measures back with speed her former way.
Meantime Æneas seeks his absent foe,
And sends his slaughtered troops to shades below.
The guileful phantom now forsook the shroud,
And flew sublime, and vanished in a cloud.
Too late young Turnus the delusion found,
Far on the sea, still making from the ground.
Then, thankless for a life redeemed by shame,
940 With sense of honour stung, and forfeit fame,
Fearful besides of what in fight had passed,
His hands and haggard eyes to heaven he cast:
'O Jove! (he cried) for what offence have I
Deserved to bear this endless infamy?
Whence am I forced, and whither am I borne?
How, and with what reproach, shall I return?
Shall ever I behold the Latian plain,
Or see Laurentum's lofty towers again?
What will they say of their deserting chief?
950 The war was mine: I fly from their relief!
I led to slaughter, and in slaughter leave;
And e'en from hence their dying groans receive.
Here, over-matched in fight, in heaps they lie;
There, scattered o'er the fields, ignobly fly.
Gape wide, O earth, and draw me down alive!
Or, oh! ye pitying winds, a wretch relieve!
On sands or shelves the splitting vessel drive;
Or set me shipwrecked on some desert shore,
Where no Rutulian eyes may see me more—
960 Unknown to friends, or foes, or conscious fame,
Lest she should follow, and my flight proclaim.'
Thus Turnus raved, and various fates revolved:
The choice was doubtful, but the death resolved.
And now the sword, and now the sea, took place—
That to revenge, and this to purge disgrace.
Sometimes he thought to swim the stormy main,
By stretch of arms the distant shore to gain.
Thrice he the sword essayed, and thrice the flood;
But Juno, moved with pity, both withstood,
970 And thrice repressed his rage; strong gales supplied,
And pushed the vessel o'er the swelling tide.
At length she lands him on his native shores,
And to his father's longing arms restores.

The fighting continues in the absence of Turnus

Thus equal deaths are dealt with equal chance:
By turns they quit their ground, by turns advance,
Victors and vanquished in the various field,
Nor wholly overcome, nor wholly yield.
The gods from heaven survey the fatal strife,
And mourn the miseries of human life.
Above the rest, two goddesses appear
Concerned for each : here Venus, Juno there.
Amidst the crowd, infernal Atè shakes
1080 Her scourge aloft, and crest of hissing snakes.
Once more the proud Mezentius, with disdain,
Brandished his spear, and rushed into the plain,
Where towering in the midmost ranks he stood,
Like tall Orion stalking o'er the flood ;
(When with his brawny breast he cuts the waves,
His shoulders scarce the topmost billow laves),
Or like a mountain-ash, whose roots are spread,
Deep fixed in earth—in clouds he hides his head.
The Trojan prince beheld him from afar,
1090 And dauntless undertook the doubtful war.
Collected in his strength, and like a rock
Poised on his base, Mezentius stood the shock.
He stood, and, measuring first with careful eyes

1071 The death of Lausus is one of the finest pieces in the *Aeneis* to raise pity and admiration, as the death of his father to raise terror and admiration and (though he is so wicked a prince) even some pity.

Every thing is excellent in this incident of Lausus's death, especially the contrast of ideas between so wicked a father and so pious a son, between the rash valour of the youth and the generous care and concern and friendly dissuasions of his heroic enemy, as also the obstinate provocations of the first overpowering the patience of the last. ... The sword is figured to us to be almost as big as the body it pierces, and seems to devour and exhaust it. The image of his mother's needlework upon his vest adds extremely to the softness and pathos of the idea. Nothing can be more tender and affecting, unless the compassion and even yearnings of his generous enemy are not yet more pathetical.

Trapp

1085 The mixture of martial and pastoral circumstances is highly beautiful.

Warton

The space his spear could reach, aloud he cries:
' My strong right hand, and sword, assist my stroke!
(Those only gods Mezentius will invoke),
His armour from the Trojan pirate torn,
By my triumphant Lausus shall be worn.'
He said ; and with his utmost force he threw
1100 The massy spear, which, hissing as it flew,
Reached the celestial shield : that stopped the course ;
But, glancing thence, the yet unbroken force
Took a new bent obliquely, and, betwixt
The side and bowels, famed Antores fixed.
Antores had from Argos travelled far,
Alcides' friend, and brother of the war ;
Till, tired with toils, fair Italy he chose,
And in Evander's palace sought repose.
Now falling by another's wound, his eyes
1110 He casts to heaven, on Argos thinks, and dies.
 The pious Trojan then his javelin sent :
The shield gave way : through triple plates it went
Of solid brass, of linen triply rolled,
And three bull hides which round the buckler rolled.
All these it passed, resistless in the course,
Transpierced his thigh, and spent its dying force.
The gaping wound gushed out a crimson flood.
The Trojan, glad with sight of hostile blood,
His falchion drew, to closer fight addressed,
1120 And with new force his fainting foe oppressed.
 His father's peril Lausus viewed with grief ;
He sighed, he wept, he ran to his relief.
And here, heroic youth, 'tis here I must
To thy immortal memory be just,
And sing an act so noble and so new,
Posterity will scarce believe 'tis true.
Pained with his wound, and useless for the fight,
The father sought to save himself by flight :
Encumbered, slow he dragged the spear along,
1130 Which pierced his thigh, and in his buckler hung.
The pious youth, resolved on death, below
The lifted sword, springs forth to face the foe ;
Protects his parent, and prevents the blow.
Shouts of applause ran ringing through the field,
To see the son the vanquished father shield.
All, fired with generous indignation, strive,
And, with a storm of darts, to distance drive
The Trojan chief, who, held at bay from far,

On his Vulcanian orb sustained the war.
1140   As, when thick hail comes rattling in the wind,
The ploughman, passenger, and labouring hind,
For shelter to the neighbouring covert fly,
Or housed, or safe in hollow caverns, lie;
But that o'erblown, when heaven above them smiles,
Return to travail, and renew their toils:
Æneas thus, o'erwhelmed on every side,
The storm of darts, undaunted, did abide;
And thus to Lausus, loud, with friendly threatening cried:
'Why wilt thou rush to certain death, and rage
1150 In rash attempts, beyond thy tender age,
Betrayed by pious love?'—Nor, thus forborne,
The youth desists, but with insulting scorn
Provokes the lingering prince, whose patience, tired,
Gave place; and all his breast with fury fired.
For now the Fates prepared their sharpened shears;
And lifted high the flaming sword appears,
Which, full descending with a frightful sway,
Through shield and corselet forced the impetuous way,
And buried deep in his fair bosom lay.
1160 The purple streams through the thin armour strove,
And drenched the embroidered coat his mother wove;
And life at length forsook his heaving heart,
Loth from so sweet a mansion to depart.
   But when, with blood and paleness all o'erspread,
The pious prince beheld young Lausus dead,
He grieved; he wept (the sight an image brought
Of his own filial love—a sadly-pleasing thought),
Then stretched his hand to hold him up, and said:
'Poor hapless youth! what praises can be paid
1170 To love so great, to such transcendent store
Of early worth, and sure presage of more?
Accept whate'er Æneas can afford:
Untouched thy arms, untaken be thy sword;
And all that pleased thee living, still remain
Inviolate, and sacred to the slain.
Thy body on thy parents I bestow,
To rest thy soul, at least, if shadows know,
Or have a sense of human things below.
There to thy fellow-ghosts with glory tell,
1180 'Twas by the great Æneas' hand I fell.'
   With this, his distant friends he beckons near,
Provokes their duty, and prevents their fear:
Himself assists to lift him from the ground,

With clotted locks, and blood that welled from out the
   wound.
Meantime, his father (now no father) stood,
And washed his wounds, by Tiber's yellow flood:
Oppressed with anguish, panting, and o'erspent,
His fainting limbs against an oak he leant.
A bough his brazen helmet did sustain;
1190 His heavier arms lay scattered on the plain:
A chosen train of youth around him stand;
His drooping head was rested on his hand;
His grisly beard his pensive bosom sought;
And all on Lausus ran his restless thought.
Careful, concerned his danger to prevent,
He much inquired, and many a message sent
To warn him from the field—alas! in vain!
Behold! his mournful followers bear him slain:
O'er his broad shield still gushed the yawning wound,
1200 And drew a bloody trail along the ground.
Far off he heard their cries, far off divined
The dire event with a foreboding mind.
With dust he sprinkled first his hoary head;
Then both his lifted hands to heaven he spread;
Last, the dear corpse embracing, thus he said:
' What joys, alas! could this frail being give,
That I have been so covetous to live?
To see my son, and such a son, resign
His life a ransom for preserving mine?
1210 And am I then preserved, and art thou lost?
How much too dear has that redemption cost!
'Tis now my bitter banishment I feel:
This is a wound too deep for time to heal.
My guilt thy growing virtues did defame:
My blackness blotted thy unblemished name.
Chased from a throne, abandoned, and exiled
For foul misdeeds, were punishments too mild.
I owed my people these, and, from their hate,
With less resentment could have borne my fate.
1220 And yet I live, and yet sustain the sight
Of hated men, and of more hated light—
But will not long.' With that he raised from ground
His fainting limbs that staggered with his wound;
Yet, with a mind resolved, and unappalled
With pains or perils, for his courser called—
Well-mouthed, well-managed, whom himself did dress
With daily care, and mounted with success—

His aid in arms, his ornament in peace.
Soothing his courage with a gentle stroke,
1230 The steed seemed sensible, while thus he spoke:
' O Rhœbus ! we have lived too long for me—
If life and long were terms that could agree.
This day thou either shalt bring back the head
And bloody trophies of the Trojan dead—
This day thou either shalt revenge my woe,
For murdered Lausus, on his cruel foe ;
Or, if inexorable Fate deny
Our conquest, with thy conquered master die :
For, after such a lord, I rest secure,
1240 Thou wilt no foreign reins, or Trojan load, endure.'
He said ; and straight the officious courser kneels,
To take his wonted weight. His hands he fills
With pointed javelins ; on his head he laced
His glittering helm, which terribly was graced
With waving horse-hair, nodding from afar ;
Then spurred his thundering steed amidst the war.
Love, anguish, wrath, and grief, to madness wrought,
Despair, and secret shame, and conscious thought
Of inborn worth, his labouring soul oppressed,
1250 Rolled in his eyes, and raged within his breast.
Then loud he called Æneas thrice by name :

1206 This speech of Mezentius over his son's dead body is perhaps as fine a piece of pathos as any in our poet. It is highly aggravated by the confession of his guilt. The pangs of the exile, and of the childless father at once rush upon him. The one is awakened and augmented by the other. However revenge soon reasserts its station in his violent temper, and notwithstanding his wound he resolutely marches out to meet Aeneas.

Warton

1231 However a mere modern may be facetious upon the absurdity of a man's making a speech to his horse, Virgil very judiciously imitates Homer in this particular [Achilles addresses his horse in *Iliad* XIX]. And to justify it we need not recur (as some do) to the ancient opinion of metempsychosis, since the thing is not only beautiful in poetry but agreeable to fact. Many a man has made a short speech to his horse, nay to his sword, or the like, as Turnus in the twelfth book does to his spear.

Trapp

>The loud repeated voice to glad Æneas came.
>'Great Jove (he said), and the far-shooting god,
>Inspire thy mind to make thy challenge good!'
>He spoke no more, but hastened, void of fear,
>And threatened with his long protended spear.
>
>>To whom Mezentius thus: 'Thy vaunts are vain.
>My Lausus lies extended on the plain :
>He's lost! thy conquest is already won;
1260
>The wretched sire is murdered in the son.
>Nor fate I fear, but all the gods defy.
>Forbear thy threats: my business is to die;
>But first receive this parting legacy.'
>He said; and straight a whirling dart he sent;
>Another after, and another, went.
>Round in a spacious ring he rides the field,
>And vainly plies the impenetrable shield.
>Thrice rode he round; and thrice Æneas wheeled,
>Turned as he turned: the golden orb withstood
1270
>The strokes, and bore about an iron wood.
>Impatient of delay, and weary grown,
>Still to defend, and to defend alone,
>To wrench the darts which in his buckler light,
>Urged and o'erlaboured in unequal fight—
>At length resolved, he throws, with all his force,
>Full at the temples of the warrior-horse.
>Just where the stroke was aimed, the unerring spear
>Made way, and stood transfixed through either ear.
>Seized with unwonted pain, surprised with fright,
1280
>The wounded steed curvets, and raised upright,
>Lights on his feet before; his hoofs behind
>Spring up in air aloft, and lash the wind.
>Down comes the rider headlong from his height;
>His horse came after with unwieldy weight,
>And, floundering forward, pitching on his head,
>His lord's encumbered shoulder overlaid.
>
>>From either host, the mingled shouts and cries
>Of Trojans and Rutulians rend the skies:
>Æneas, hastening, waved his fatal sword
1290
>High o'er his head, with this reproachful word:
>'Now! where are now thy vaunts, the fierce disdain
>Of proud Mezentius, and the lofty strain?'
>
>>Struggling, and wildly staring on the skies
>With scarce recovered sight, he thus replies:
>'Why these insulting words, this waste of breath,
>To souls undaunted, and secure of death?

'Tis no dishonour for the brave to die!
Nor came I here with hopes of victory;
Nor ask I life, nor fought with that design:
1300 As I had used my fortune, use thou thine.
My dying son contracted no such band;
The gift is hateful from his murderer's hand.
For this, this only favour, let me sue;
If pity can to conquered foes be due,
Refuse it not; but let my body have
The last retreat of human-kind, a grave.
Too well I know the insulting people's hate:
Protect me from their vengeance after fate:
This refuge for my poor remains provide;
1310 And lay my much-loved Lausus by my side.'
He said, and to the sword his throat applied:
The crimson stream distained his arms around,
And the disdainful soul came rushing through the
    wound.

BOOK XI

THE ARGUMENT

Æneas erects a trophy of the spoils of Mezentius, grants a truce for burying the dead, and sends home the body of Pallas with great solemnity. Latinus calls a council, to propose offers of peace to Æneas; which occasions great animosity betwixt Turnus and Drances. In the meantime there is a sharp engagement of the horse, wherein Camilla signalizes herself, is killed, and the Latin troops are entirely defeated.

SCARCE had the rosy morning raised her head
Above the waves, and left her watery bed:
The pious chief, whom double cares attend
For his unburied soldiers and his friend,
Yet first to heaven performed a victor's vows:
He bared an ancient oak of all her boughs;
Then on a rising ground the trunk he placed,
Which with the spoils of his dead foe he graced.
The coat of arms by proud Mezentius worn,
10 Now on a naked snag in triumph borne,
Was hung on high, and glittered from afar,
A trophy sacred to the god of war.
Above his arms, fixed on the leafless wood,
Appeared his plumy crest, besmeared with blood.
His brazen buckler on the left was seen:
Truncheons of shivered lances hung between;
And on the right was placed his corselet, bored;
And to the neck was tied his unavailing sword.
A crowd of chiefs inclose the godlike man,
20 Who thus, conspicuous in the midst, began:
'Our toils, my friends, are crowned with sure success:
The greater part performed, achieve the less.
Now follow cheerful to the trembling town:
Press but an entrance, and presume it won.
Fear is no more: for fierce Mezentius lies,
As the firstfruits of war, a sacrifice.
Turnus shall fall extended on the plain,
And, in this omen, is already slain.
Prepared in arms, pursue your happy chance;
30 That none unwarned may plead his ignorance;
And I, at heaven's appointed hour, may find
Your warlike ensigns waving in the wind.
Meantime the rites and funeral pomps prepare,
Due to your dead companions of the war—
The last respect the living can bestow,

To shield their shadows from contempt below.
That conquered earth be theirs, for which they fought,
And which for us with their own blood they bought.
But first the corpse of our unhappy friend,
40 To the sad city of Evander send,
Who, not inglorious, in his age's bloom
Was hurried hence by too severe a doom.'
　　Thus, weeping while he spoke, he took his way,
Where, new in death, lamented Pallas lay.
Acœtes watched the corpse; whose youth deserved
The father's trust; and now the son he served
With equal faith, but less auspicious care.
The attendants of the slain his sorrow share.
A troop of Trojans mixed with these appear,
50 And mourning matrons with dishevelled hair.
Soon as the prince appears, they raise a cry;
All beat their breasts, and echoes rend the sky.
They rear his drooping forehead from the ground:
But, when Æneas viewed the grisly wound
Which Pallas in his manly bosom bore,
And the fair flesh distained with purple gore,
First, melting into tears, the pious man
Deplored so sad a sight, then thus began:
'Unhappy youth! when Fortune gave the rest
60 Of my full wishes, she refused the best!
She came; but brought not thee along, to bless
My longing eyes, and share in my success:
She grudged thy safe return, the triumphs due
To prosperous valour, in the public view.
Not thus I promised, when thy father lent
Thy needless succour with a sad consent;
Embraced me, parting for the Etrurian land,
And sent me to possess a large command.
He warned, and from his own experience told,
70 Our foes were warlike, disciplined, and bold.
And now, perhaps, in hopes of thy return,
Rich odours on his loaded altars burn,
While we, with vain officious pomp, prepare
To send him back his portion of the war,
A bloody breathless body, which can owe
No farther debt, but to the powers below.
The wretched father, ere his race is run,
Shall view the funeral honours of his son!
These are my triumphs of the Latian war,
80 Fruits of my plighted faith and boasted care!

And yet, unhappy sire, thou shalt not see
A son, whose death disgraced his ancestry :
Thou shalt not blush, old man, however grieved :
Thy Pallas no dishonest wound received.
He died no death to make thee wish, too late,
Thou hadst not lived to see his shameful fate.
But what a champion has the Ausonian coast,
And what a friend hast thou, Ascanius, lost !'
    Thus having mourned, he gave the word around,
90 To raise the breathless body from the ground ;
And chose a thousand horse, the flower of all
His warlike troops, to wait the funeral,
To bear him back, and share Evander's grief—
A well-becoming, but a weak relief.
Of oaken twigs they twist an easy bier,
Then on their shoulders the sad burden rear.
The body on this rural hearse is borne :
Strewed leaves and funeral greens the bier adorn.
All pale he lies, and looks a lovely flower,
100 New cropt by virgin hands, to dress the bower :
Unfaded yet, but yet, unfed below,
No more to mother earth or the green stem shall owe.
Then two fair vests, of wondrous work and cost,
Of purple woven, and with gold embossed,
For ornament the Trojan hero brought,
Which with her hands Sidonian Dido wrought.
One vest arrayed the corpse ; and one they spread
O'er his closed eyes, and wrapped around his head,
That, when the yellow hair in flame should fall,
110 The catching fire might burn the golden caul.
Besides, the spoils of foes in battle slain,
When he descended on the Latian plain—
Arms, trappings, horses, by the hearse are led
In long array—the achievements of the dead.
Then, pinioned with their hands behind, appear
The unhappy captives, marching in the rear,
Appointed offerings in the victor's name,
To sprinkle with their blood the funeral flame.
Inferior trophies by the chiefs are borne :
120 Gauntlets and helms their loaded hands adorn ;
And fair inscriptions fixed, and titles read
Of Latian leaders conquered by the dead.

. . .

140 Thus while the Trojan and Arcadian horse
To Palantean towers direct their course,
In long procession ranked; the pious chief
Stopped in the rear, and gave a vent to grief.
'The public care (he said) which war attends,
Diverts our present woes, at least suspends.
Peace with the manes of great Pallas dwell!
Hail, holy relics! and a last farewell!'
. . .

And now the fatal news by Fame is blown
210 Through the short circuit of the Arcadian town,
Of Pallas slain—by Fame, which just before
His triumph on distended pinions bore.
Rushing from out the gate, the people stand,
Each with a funeral flambeau in his hand.
Wildly they stare, distracted with amaze:
The fields are lightened with a fiery blaze,
That casts a sullen splendour on their friends—
The marching troop which their dead prince attends.
Both parties meet: they raise a doleful cry:
220 The matrons from the walls with shrieks reply;
And their mixed mourning rends the vaulted sky.
The town is filled with tumult and with tears,
Till the loud clamours reach Evander's ears:
Forgetful of his state, he runs along,
With a disordered pace, and cleaves the throng;
Falls on the corpse; and groaning there he lies,
With silent grief, that speaks but at his eyes.
Short sighs and sobs succeed; till sorrow breaks
A passage, and at once he weeps and speaks:
230 'O Pallas! thou hast failed thy plighted word!
To fight with caution, not to tempt the sword,
I warned thee, but in vain; for well I knew
What perils youthful ardour would pursue—
That boiling blood would carry thee too far,
Young as thou wert in dangers, raw to war!
O curst essay of arms! disastrous doom!
Prelude of bloody fields, and fights to come!
Hard elements of inauspicious war!
Vain vows to heaven, and unavailing care!
. . .

250 Yet will I not my Trojan friend upbraid,
Nor grudge the alliance I so gladly made.

'Twas not his fault, my Pallas fell so young,
But my own crime for having lived too long.
Yet, since the gods had destined him to die,
At least, he led the way to victory:
First for his friends he won the fatal shore,
And sent whole herds of slaughtered foes before—
A death too great, too glorious to deplore.
Nor will I add new honours to thy grave,
260 Content with those the Trojan hero gave—
. . .
But why, unhappy man! dost thou detain
270 These troops, to view the tears thou shedd'st in vain?
Go, friends! this message to your lord relate:
Tell him, that, if I bear my bitter fate,
And, after Pallas' death, live lingering on,
'Tis to behold his vengeance for my son.
I stay for Turnus, whose devoted head
Is owing to the living and the dead.
My son and I expect it from his hand;
'Tis all that he can give, or we demand.
Joy is no more: but I would gladly go,
280 To greet my Pallas with such news below.'

After the council Turnus and Camilla renew the fight

Now Turnus arms for fight. His back and breast
Well-tempered steel and scaly brass invest:
The cuishes, which his brawny thighs infold,
Are mingled metal damasked o'er with gold.
His faithful falchion sits upon his side;
Nor casque, nor crest, his manly features hide
But, bare to view, amid surrounding friends,
740 With godlike grace, he from the tower descends.
Exulting in his strength, he seems to dare
His absent rival, and to promise war.
    Freed from his keepers, thus, with broken reins,
The wanton courser prances o'er the plains,
Or in the pride of youth o'erleaps the mounds,
And snuffs the females in forbidden grounds;
Or seeks his watering in the well-known flood,
To quench his thirst, and cool his fiery blood:
He swims luxuriant in the liquid plain,
750 And o'er his shoulder flows his waving mane:
He neighs, he snorts, he bears his head on high;
Before his ample chest the frothy waters fly.

Soon as the prince appears without the gate,
The Volscians, and their virgin leader, wait
His last commands. Then, with a graceful mien,
Lights from her lofty steed the warrior-queen:
Her squadron imitates, and each descends;
Whose common suit Camilla thus commends:
'If sense of honour, if a soul secure
760 Of inborn worth, that can all tests endure,
Can promise aught, or on itself rely,
Greatly to dare to conquer or to die;
Then, I alone, sustained by these, will meet
The Tyrrhene troops, and promise their defeat.
Ours be the danger, ours the sole renown:
You, general, stay behind, and guard the town.'
Turnus awhile stood mute with glad surprise,
And on the fierce virago fixed his eyes,
Then thus returned: 'O grace of Italy!
770 With what becoming thanks can I reply?
Not only words lie labouring in my breast,
But thought itself is by thy praise oppressed.
Yet rob me not of all; but let me join
My toils, my hazard, and my fame, with thine.
The Trojan, not in stratagem unskilled,
Sends his light horse before to scour the field:
Himself, through steep ascents and thorny brakes,
A larger compass to the city takes.
This news my scouts confirm: and I prepare
780 To foil his cunning, and his force to dare;
With chosen foot his passage to forelay,
And place an ambush in the winding way.
Thou, with thy Volscians, face the Tuscan horse:
The brave Messapus shall my troops inforce
With those of Tibur, and the Latian band,
Subjected all to thy supreme command.'
    This said, he warns Messapus to the war,
Then every chief exhorts with equal care.
All thus encouraged, his own troop he joins,
790 And hastes to prosecute his deep designs.
    Inclosed with hills, a winding valley lies,
By nature formed for fraud, and fitted for surprise.
A narrow track, by human steps untrode,
Leads, through perplexing thorns, to this obscure abode.
High o'er the vale a steepy mountain stands,
Whence the surveying sight the nether ground commands.

  The top is level—an offensive seat
Of war ; and from the war a safe retreat :
For, on the right and left, is room to press
800 The foes at hand, or from afar distress ;
To drive them headlong downward ; and to pour,
On their descending backs, a stony shower.
Thither young Turnus took the well-known way,
Possessed the pass, and in blind ambush lay.
  Meantime, Latonian Phœbe, from the skies,
Beheld the approaching war with hateful eyes,
And called the light-foot Opis to her aid,
Her most beloved and ever-trusty maid ;
Then with a sigh began : 'Camilla goes
810 To meet her death amidst her fatal foes—
The nymph I loved of all my mortal train,
Invested with Diana's arms, in vain.
Nor is my kindness for the virgin new :
'Twas born with her ; and with her years it grew.

. . .

  And, oh ! I wish, contented with my cares
Of savage spoils, she had not sought the wars :
Then had she been of my celestial train,
And shunned the fate that dooms her to be slain.
But since, opposing heaven's decree, she goes
880 To find her death among forbidden foes,
Haste with these arms, and take thy steepy flight,
Where, with the gods averse, the Latins fight.
This bow to thee, this quiver, I bequeath,
This chosen arrow, to revenge her death :
By whate'er hand Camilla shall be slain,
Or of the Trojan or Italian train,
Let him not pass unpunished from the plain.
Then, in a hollow cloud, myself will aid
To bear the breathless body of my maid :
890 Unspoiled shall be her arms, and unprofaned
Her holy limbs with any human hand,
And in a marble tomb laid in her native land.'
  She said. The faithful nymph descends from high
With rapid flight, and cuts the sounding sky :
Black clouds and stormy winds around her body fly.

. . .

  Resistless, through the war Camilla rode,
In danger unappalled, and pleased with blood.

One side was bare for her exerted breast;
One shoulder with her painted quiver pressed.
Now from afar her fatal javelins play;
Now with her axe's edge, she hews her way:
Diana's arms upon her shoulder sound;
And when, too closely pressed, she quits the ground,
970 From her bent bow she sends a backward wound.
Her maids, in martial pomp, on either side,
Larina, Tulla, fierce Tarpeia, ride—
Italians all—in peace their queen's delight;
In war, the bold companions of the fight.
 So marched the Thracian Amazons of old,
When Thermodon with bloody billows rolled:
Such troops as these in shining arms were seen,
When Theseus met in fight their maiden queen:
Such to the field Penthesilea led,
980 From the fierce virgin when the Grecians fled;
With such returned triumphant from the war.
Her maids with cries attend the lofty car;
They clash with manly force their moony shields;
With female shouts resound the Phrygian fields.
 Who foremost, and who last, heroic maid,
On the cold earth were by thy courage laid?
Thy spear, of mountain-ash, Eunæus first,
With fury driven, from side to side transpierced:
A purple stream came spouting from the wound;
990 Bathed in his blood he lies, and bites the ground.
Liris and Pegasus at once she slew:
The former, as the slackened reins he drew,
Of his faint steed—the latter, as he stretched
His arm to prop his friend—the javelin reached.
By the same weapon, sent from the same hand,
Both fall together, and both spurn the sand.
. . .

985   This manner of breaking out into an interrogation amidst the description of a battle is what serves very much to awaken the reader [at *Iliad* V 703–4] . . . Virgil, I think, has improved the strength of this figure by addressing the apostrophe to the person whose exploits he is celebrating.

              Pope on *Iliad* V, 864

Young Ornytus bestrode a hunter steed,
Swift for the chase, and of Apulian breed.
Him, from afar, she spied in arms unknown :
O'er his broad back an ox's hide was thrown ;
His helm a wolf, whose gaping jaws were spread
A covering for his cheeks, and grinned around his head.
He clenched within his hand an iron prong,
1010 And towered above the rest, conspicuous in the throng.
Him soon she singled from the flying train,
And slew with ease ; then thus insults the slain :
'Vain hunter ! didst thou think through woods to chase
The savage herd, a vile and trembling race?
Here cease thy vaunts, and own my victory :
A woman warrior was too strong for thee.
Yet, if the ghosts demand the conqueror's name,
Confessing great Camilla, save thy shame.'
. . .

Astonished Aunus just arrives by chance,
To see his fall, nor farther dares advance ;
But, fixing on the horrid maid his eye,
He stares, and shakes, and finds it vain to fly ;
Yet, like a true Ligurian, born to cheat,
(At least while Fortune favoured his deceit),
1040 Cries out aloud : 'What courage have you shewn,
Who trust your courser's strength, and not your own?
Forego the 'vantage of your horse, alight,
And then on equal terms begin the fight :
It shall be seen, weak woman, what you can,
When foot to foot, you combat with a man.'
He said. She glows with anger and disdain,
Dismounts with speed to dare him on the plain,
And leaves her horse at large among her train ;
With her drawn sword defies him to the field,
1050 And, marching, lifts aloft her maiden shield.
The youth, who thought his cunning did succeed,
Reins round his horse, and urges all his speed :
Adds the remembrance of the spur, and hides
The goring rowels in his bleeding sides.
'Vain fool, and coward ! (said the lofty maid),
Caught in the train which thou thyself hast laid !
On others practise thy Ligurian arts :
Thin stratagems, and tricks of little hearts,
Are lost on me ; nor shalt thou safe retire,
1060 With vaunting lies, to thy fallacious sire.'

At this, so fast her flying feet she sped,
That soon she strained beyond his horse's head:
Then turning short, at once she seized the rein,
And laid the boaster grovelling on the plain.
Not with more ease the falcon, from above,
Trusses, in middle air, the trembling dove,
Then plumes the prey, in her strong pounces bound:
The feathers, foul with blood, come tumbling to the
    ground.
  Now mighty Jove, from his superior height,
1070 With his broad eye surveys the unequal fight.
He fires the breast of Tarchon with disdain,
And sends him to redeem the abandoned plain.
Between the broken ranks the Tuscan rides,
And these encourages, and those he chides;
Recalls each leader, by his name, from flight;
Renews their ardour, and restores the fight.
' What panic fear has seized your souls? O shame,
O brand perpetual of the Etrurian name!
Cowards incurable! a woman's hand
1080. Drives, breaks, and scatters, your ignoble band!
Now cast away the sword, and quit the shield!
What use of weapons which you dare not wield?
Not thus you fly your female foes by night,
Nor shun the feast, when the full bowls invite;
When to fat offerings the glad augur calls,
And the shrill horn-pipe sounds to bacchanals.
These are your studied cares, your lewd delight—
Swift to debauch, but slow to manly fight.'
Thus having said, he spurs amidst the foes,
1090 Not managing the life he meant to lose.
The first he found he seized, with headlong haste,
In his strong gripe, and clasped around the waist:
'Twas Venulus, whom from his horse he tore,
And (laid athwart his own) in triumph bore.
Loud shouts ensue; the Latins turn their eyes,
And view the unusual sight with vast surprise.
The fiery Tarchon, flying o'er the plains,
Pressed in his arms the ponderous prey sustains,
Then, with his shortened spear, explores around
1100 His jointed arms, to fix a deadly wound.
Nor less the captive struggles for his life:
He writhes his body to prolong the strife,
And, fencing for his naked throat, exerts
His utmost vigour, and the point averts.

So stoops the yellow eagle from on high,
And bears a speckled serpent through the sky,
Fastening his crooked talons on the prey :
The prisoner hisses through the liquid way ;
Resists the royal hawk ; and, though oppressed,
She fights in volumes, and erects her crest :
Turned to her foe, she stiffens every scale,
And shoots her forky tongue, and whisks her threaten-
   ing tail.
Against the victor, all defence is weak :
The imperial bird still plies her with his beak ;
He tears her bowels, and her breast he gores,
Then claps his pinions, and securely soars.
   Thus, through the midst of circling enemies,
Strong Tarchon snatched and bore away his prize.
The Tyrrhene troops, that shrunk before, now press
The Latins, and presume the like success.
   Then Arruns, doomed to death, his arts essayed
To murder, unespied, the Volscian maid :
This way and that his winding course he bends,
And wheresoe'er she turns, her steps attends.
When she retires victorious from the chase,
He wheels about with care, and shifts his place :
When, rushing on, she seeks her foes in fight,
He keeps aloof, but keeps her still in sight ;
He threats, and trembles, trying every way,
Unseen to kill, and safely to betray.
   Chloreus, the priest of Cybele, from far,
Glittering in Phrygian arms amidst the war,
Was by the virgin viewed.   The steed he pressed
Was proud with trappings ; and his brawny chest
With scales of gilded brass was covered o'er :
A robe of Tyrian dye the rider wore.
With deadly wounds he galled the distant foe ;
Gnossian his shafts, and Lycian was his bow :
A golden helm his front and head surrounds ;
A gilded quiver from his shoulder sounds.
Gold, weaved with linen, on his thighs he wore,
With flowers of needle-work distinguished o'er,
With golden buckles bound, and gathered up before.
Him the fierce maid beheld with ardent eyes,
Fond and ambitious of so rich a prize,
Or that the temple might his trophies hold,
Or else to shine herself in Trojan gold.
Blind in her haste, she chases him alone,

And seeks his life, regardless of her own.
1150 This lucky moment the sly traitor chose;
Then, starting from his ambush, up he rose,
And threw, but first to heaven addressed his vows
'O patron of Soracte's high abodes!
Phœbus, the ruling power among the gods!
Whom first we serve; whole woods of unctuous pine
Are felled for thee, and to thy glory shine;
By thee protected, with our naked soles,
Through flames unsinged we march, and tread the
   kindled coals.
Give me, propitious power, to wash away
1160 The stains of this dishonourable day:
Nor spoils, nor triumph, from the fact I claim,
But with my future actions trust my fame.
Let me, by stealth, this female plague o'ercome,
And from the field return inglorious home.'
Apollo heard, and, granting half his prayer,
Shuffled in winds the rest, and tossed in empty air.
He gives the death desired: his safe return
By southern tempests to the seas is borne.
Now, when the javelin whizzed along the skies,

1131 The beauty of this exquisite description is here most properly and judiciously introduced to account for Camilla's eager and incautious pursuit of this Chloreus, and to make Aruns's design upon her more practicable.

Trapp

1145 Mr Addison observes [*Spectator* 15] that Virgil has very finely touched upon the female passion for dress and shew in the character of Camilla, who, though she seems to have shaken off all the other weaknesses of her sex, is still described as a woman in this particular. ... This heedless pursuit after these glittering trifles, the poet, by a nice concealed moral, represents to have been the destruction of his female hero.

Warton

1149 As Camilla is a person altogether particular, her death is described with a greater variety of particular circumstances than any in the whole poem.

Trapp

1170 Both armies on Camilla turned their eyes,
Directed by the sound. Of either host,
The unhappy virgin, though concerned the most,
Was only deaf; so greedy was she bent
On golden spoils, and on her prey intent;
Till in her pap the wingèd weapon stood
Infixed, and deeply drunk the purple blood.
Her sad attendants hasten to sustain
Their dying lady drooping on the plain.
Far from their sight the trembling Arruns flies,
1180 With beating heart, and fear confused with joys;
Nor dares he farther to pursue his blow,
Or e'en to bear the sight of his expiring foe.
 As, when the wolf has torn a bullock's hide
At unawares, or ranched a shepherd's side,
Conscious of his audacious deed, he flies,
And claps his quivering tail between his thighs:
So, speeding once, the wretch no more attends,
But, spurring forward, herds among his friends.
She wrenched the javelin with her dying hands,
1190 But wedged within her breast the weapon stands;
The wood she draws, the steely point remains:
She staggers in her seat with agonizing pains
(A gathering mist o'erclouds her cheerful eyes;
And from her cheeks the rosy colour flies):
Then turns to her, whom, of her female train
She trusted most, and thus she speaks with pain:
'Acca, 'tis past! he swims before my sight,
Inexorable Death; and claims his right.
Bear my last words to Turnus: fly with speed,
1200 And bid him timely to my charge succeed,
Repel the Trojans, and the town relieve:
Farewell! and in this kiss my parting breath receive.'
She said, and, sliding, sunk upon the plain:
Dying, her opened hand forsakes the rein:
Short, and more short, she pants: by slow degrees
Her mind the passage from her body frees.
She drops her sword; she nods her plumy crest,
Her drooping head declining on her breast;
In the last sigh her struggling soul expires,
1210 And, murmuring with disdain, to Stygian sounds retires.
 A shout, that struck the golden stars ensued;
Despair and rage, and languished fight renewed.
The Trojan troops and Tuscans, in a line,
Advance to charge; the mixed Arcadians join.

But Cynthia's maid, high seated, from afar
Surveys the field, and fortune of the war,
Unmoved awhile, till, prostrate on the plain,
Weltering in blood, she sees Camilla slain,
And, round her corpse, of friends and foes a fighting train.
1220 Then, from the bottom of her breast, she drew
A mournful sigh, and these sad words ensue :
'Too dear a fine, ah, much lamented maid !
For warring with the Trojans thou hast paid :
Nor aught availed, in this unhappy strife,
Diana's sacred arms, to save thy life.
Yet unrevenged thy goddess will not leave
Her votary's death, nor with vain sorrow grieve.
Branded the wretch, and be his name abhorred ;
But, after ages shall thy praise record.
1230 The inglorious coward soon shall press the plain :
Thus vows thy queen, and thus the Fates ordain.'
   High o'er the field, there stood a hilly mound—
Sacred the place, and spread with oaks around—
Where, in a marble tomb, Dercennus lay,
A king that once in Latium bore the sway.
The beauteous Opis thither bent her flight,
To mark the traitor Arruns from the height.
Him in refulgent arms she soon espied,
Swoln with success ; and loudly thus she cried.
1240 'Thy backward steps, vain boaster, are too late ;
Turn, like a man, at length, and meet thy fate.
Charged with my message, to Camilla go,
And say I sent thee to the shades below—
An honour undeserved from Cynthia's bow.'
   She said, and from her quiver chose with speed
The wingèd shaft, predestined for the deed ;
Then to the stubborn yew her strength applied,

1197 Wonderful is the magnamimity of this short speech. She makes no womanish complaints, but employs her last breath in giving orders for the battle.

                                                                                            Warton

1245 But why should the drawing a bow to kill Aruns, an incident of little consequence, be described with so much circumstantial exactness? All that can be answered is that though the death of Aruns be of

Till the far-distant horns approached on either side.
The bow-string touched her breast, so strong she drew;
1250 Whizzing in air the fatal arrow flew.
At once the twanging bow and sounding dart
The traitor heard, and felt the point within his heart.
Him, beating with his heels in pangs of death,
His flying friends to foreign fields bequeath.
The conquering damsel, with expanded wings,
The welcome message to her mistress brings.
 Their leader lost, the Volscians quit the field;
And, unsustained, the chiefs of Turnus yield.
The frighted soldiers, when their captains fly,
1260 More on their speed than on their strength rely.
Confused in flight, they bear each other down,
And spur their horses headlong to the town.
. . .

Meantime to Turnus, ambushed in the shade,
With heavy tidings came the unhappy maid:
'The Volscians overthrown—Camilla killed—
The foes entirely masters of the field,
Like a resistless flood, come rolling on:
The cry goes off the plain, and thickens to the town.'
 Inflamed with rage (for so the Furies fire
1300 The Daunian's breast, and so the Fates require),
He leaves the hilly pass, the woods in vain
Possessed, and downward issues on the plain.
Scarce was he gone, when to the straits, now freed
From secret foes, the Trojan troops succeed.
Through the black forest and the ferny brake,
Unknowingly secure, their way they take;
From the rough mountains to the plain descend,
And there, in order drawn, their line extend.
Both armies now in open fields are seen;
1310 Not far the distance of the space between.
Both to the city bend. Æneas sees,
Through smoking fields, his hastening enemies;
And Turnus views the Trojans in array,
And hears the approaching horses proudly neigh.
Soon had their hosts in bloody battle joined;
But westward to the sea the sun declined.
Intrenched before the town, both armies lie,
While night with sable wings involves the sky.

BOOK XII

THE ARGUMENT

Turnus challenges Æneas to a single combat : articles are agreed on, but broken by the Rutuli, who wound Æneas. He is miraculously cured by Venus, forces Turnus to a duel, and concludes the poem with his death.

After the broken truce, Turnus pursues the Trojans in the plain while Aeneas storms the city

    But Fate and envious Fortune now prepare
To plunge the Latins in the last despair.
The queen, who saw the foes invade the town,
870 And brands on tops of burning houses thrown,
Cast round her eyes, distracted with her fear :—
No troops of Turnus in the field appear.
Once more she stares abroad, but still in vain,
And then concludes the royal youth is slain.
Mad with her anguish, impotent to bear
The mighty grief, she loathes the vital air.
She calls herself the cause of all this ill,
And owns the dire effects of her ungoverned will :
She raves against the gods ; she beats her breast ;
880 She tears with both her hands her purple vest :
Then round a beam a running noose she tied,
And, fastened by the neck, obscenely died.
    Soon as the fatal news by fame was blown,
And to her dames and to her daughter known,
The sad Lavinia rends her yellow hair,
And rosy cheeks : the rest her sorrow share :
With shrieks the palace rings, and madness of despair.
The spreading rumour fills the public place :
Confusion, fear, distraction, and disgrace,
890 And silent shame, are seen in every face.
Latinus tears his garments as he goes,
Both for his public and his private woes ;

little consequence yet in itself it is a grand incident, as it is a revenge for the death of a heroine who has performed so many remarkable exploits. In short this minute description renders the death of Camilla more significant.

                                                  Warton

With filth his venerable beard besmears,
And sordid dust deforms his silver hairs.
And much he blames the softness of his mind,
Obnoxious to the charms of woman-kind,
And soon reduced to change what he so well designed—
To break the solemn league so long desired,
Nor finish what his fates, and those of Troy, required.
900   Now Turnus rolls aloof, o'er empty plains,
And here and there some straggling foes he gleans.
His flying coursers please him less and less,
Ashamed of easy fight, and cheap success.
Thus half contented, anxious in his mind,
The distant cries come driving in the wind—
Shouts from the walls, but shouts in murmurs drowned;
A jarring mixture, and a boding sound.
'Alas! (said he) what mean these dismal cries?
What doleful clamours from the town arise?'
910 Confused, he stops, and backward pulls the reins.
She, who the driver's office now sustains,
Replies, 'Neglect, my lord, these new alarms:
Here fight, and urge the fortune of your arms:
There want not others to defend the wall.
If by your rival's hand the Italians fall,
So shall your fatal sword his friends oppress,
In honour equal, equal in success.'
    To this, the prince: 'O sister!—for I knew,
The peace infringed proceeded first from you:
920 I knew you, when you mingled first in fight:
And now in vain you would deceive my sight—
Why, goddess, this unprofitable care?
Who sent you down from heaven, involved in air,
Your share of mortal sorrows to sustain,
And see your brother bleeding on the plain?
For to what power can Turnus have recourse,
Or how resist his fate's prevailing force?
These eyes beheld Murrhanus bite the ground—
Mighty the man, and mighty was the wound.
930 I heard my dearest friend, with dying breath,
My name invoking to revenge his death.
Brave Ufens fell with honour on the place,
To shun the shameful sight of my disgrace.
On earth supine, a manly corpse he lies;
His vest and armour are the victor's prize.
Then, shall I see Laurentum in a flame,
Which only wanted, to complete my shame?

How will the Latins hoot their champion's flight!
How Drances will insult, and point them to the sight!
940　Is death so hard to bear?—Ye gods below!
(Since those above so small compassion show),
Receive a soul unsullied yet with shame,
Which not belies my great forefathers' name.'
　　He said: and while he spoke, with flying speed
Came Saces urging on his foamy steed:
Fixed on his wounded face a shaft he bore,
And, seeking Turnus, sent his voice before:
'Turnus! on you, on you alone, depends
Our last relief;—compassionate your friends!
950　Like lightning, fierce Æneas, rolling on,
With arms invests, with flames invades, the town;
The brands are tossed on high; the winds conspire
To drive along the deluge of the fire.
All eyes are fixed on you: your foes rejoice;
E'en the king staggers, and suspends his choice—
Doubts to deliver or defend the town,
Whom to reject, or whom to call his son.
The queen, on whom your utmost hopes were placed,
Herself suborning death, has breathed her last.
960　'Tis true, Messapus, fearless of his fate,
With fierce Atinas' aid, defends the gate:
On every side surrounded by the foe,
The more they kill, the greater numbers grow;
An iron harvest mounts, and still remains to mow.
You, far aloof from your forsaken bands,
Your rolling chariot drive o'er empty sands.'
　　Stupid he sat, his eyes on earth declined,
And various cares revolving in his mind:
Rage, boiling from the bottom of his breast,
970　And sorrow mixed with shame, his soul oppressed;
And conscious worth lay labouring in his thought,
And love by jealousy to madness wrought.
By slow degrees his reason drove away
The mists of passion, and resumed her sway.
Then, rising on his car, he turned his look,
And saw the town involved in fire and smoke.
A wooden tower with flames already blazed,
Which his own hands on beams and rafters raised,
And bridges laid above to join the space,
980　And wheels below to roll from place to place.
'Sister! the Fates have vanquished: let us go
The way which heaven and my hard fortune show.

The fight is fixed ; nor shall the branded name
Of a base coward blot your brother's fame.
Death is my choice : but suffer me to try
My force, and vent my rage before I die.'
He said : and leaping down without delay,
Through crowds of scattered foes he freed his way.
Striding he passed, impetuous as the wind,
990 And left the grieving goddess far behind.
  As, when a fragment, from a mountain torn
By raging tempests, or by torrents borne,
Or sapped by time, or loosened from the roots—
Prone through the void the rocky ruin shoots,
Rolling from crag to crag, from steep to steep ;
Down sink, at once, the shepherds and their sheep,
Involved alike, they rush to nether ground ;
Stunned with the shock they fall, and stunned from
    earth rebound :
So Turnus, hasting headlong to the town,
1000 Shouldering and shoving, bore the squadrons down.
Still pressing onward, to the walls he drew,
Where shafts and spears and darts promiscuous flew,
And sanguine streams the slippery ground embrue.
First stretching out his arm, in sign of peace,
He cries aloud, to make the combat cease :
' Rutulians, hold ! and, Latin troops, retire !
The fight is mine ; and me the gods require.
'Tis just that I should vindicate alone
The broken truce, or for the breach atone.
1010 This day shall free from war the Ausonian state,
Or finish my misfortunes in my fate.'
  Both armies from their bloody work desist,
And, bearing backward, form a spacious list,
The Trojan hero, who received from fame
The welcome sound, and heard the champion's name,
Soon leaves the taken works and mounted walls :
Greedy of war where greater glory calls,
He springs to fight, exulting in his force ;
His jointed armour rattles in the course.
1020 Like Eryx, or like Athos, great he shows,
Or father Apennine, when, white with snows,
His head divine obscure in clouds he hides,
And shakes the sounding forests on his sides.
  The nations, overawed, surcease the fight ;
Immoveable their bodies, fixed their sight ;
E'en death stands still ; nor from above they throw

Their darts, nor drive their battering-rams below.
In silent order either army stands,
And drop their swords, unknowing, from their hands.
1030 The Ausonian king beholds, with wondering sight,
Two mighty champions matched in single fight,
Born under climes remote, and brought by fate,
With swords to try their titles to the state.
  Now, in closed field, each other from afar
They view ; and, rushing on, begin the war.
They launch their spears; then hand to hand they meet:
The trembling soil resounds beneath their feet ;
Their bucklers clash ; thick blows descend from high,
And flakes of fire from their hard helmets fly.
1040 Courage conspires with chance ; and both engage
With equal fortune yet, and mutual rage.
  As, when two bulls for their fair female fight
In Sila's shades, or on Taburnus' height,
With horns adverse they meet ; the keeper flies ;

1020 But is it not absurd to compare an active hero in the very height of his courage and sprightliness to so lumpish a thing as a mountain? I answer first, the transfering of ideas from one adjunct to another by the fiction just now mentioned gives a poetical i.e. an imaginary activity to the mountains themselves. ... But secondly, we have often observed that comparisons are not obliged to answer in all circumstances. The thing to be resembled here is height of stature. That of Aeneas was always great, but as he is now in the full sublimity and exaltation of his courage and all our ideas of him swell and are enlarged, he seems to grow bigger and taller than before and would actually appear so to the eye or at least to the fancy, could we see the figure he is supposed to make. For the rest therefore it is nothing but a poetical and heroical hyperbole which is not only to be permitted but to be admired as one of the greatest beauties in poetry. Thus Milton in *Paradise Lost*

> On th'other side Satan alarm'd
> Collecting all his might, dilated stood;
> Like Teneriff or Atlas unremov'd:
> His stature reach'd the sky, and on his crest
> Sat horror plum'd.

(Book IV, 985–89)

Trapp

Mute stands the herd ; the heifers roll their eyes,
And wait the event—which victor they shall bear,
And who shall be the lord, to rule the lusty year :
With rage of love the jealous rivals burn,
And push for push, and wound for wound, return ;
1050 Their dewlaps gored, their sides are laved in blood ;
Loud cries and roaring sounds rebellow through the wood :
Such was the combat in the listed ground ;
So clash their swords, and so their shields resound,
Jove sets the beam : in either scale he lays
The champion's fate, and each exactly weighs.
On this side, life, and lucky chance, ascends ;
Loaded with death, that other scale descends.
Raised on the stretch, young Turnus aims a blow
Full on the helm of his unguarded foe :
1060 Shrill shouts and clamours ring on either side,
As hopes and fears their panting hearts divide.
But all in pieces flies the traitor sword,
And, in the middle stroke, deserts his lord.
Now 'tis but death or flight : disarmed he flies,
When in his hand an unknown hilt he spies.
Fame says that Turnus, when his steeds he joined,
Hurrying to war, disordered in his mind,
Snatched the first weapon which his haste could find.
'Twas not the fated sword his father bore,
1070 But that his charioteer Metiscus wore.
This, while the Trojans fled, the toughness held ;
But, vain against the great Vulcanian shield,
The mortal-tempered steel deceived his hand :
The shivered fragments shone amid the sand.
Surprised with fear, he fled along the field,
And now forthright, and now in orbits wheeled :
For here the Trojan troops the list surround,
And there the pass is closed with pools and marshy ground.
Æneas hastens, though with heavier pace—
1080 His wound, so newly knit, retards the chase,
And oft his trembling knees their aid refuse—
Yet, pressing foot by foot, his foe pursues.
Thus, when a fearful stag is closed around
With crimson toils, or in a river found,
High on the bank the deep-mouthed hound appears,
Still opening, following still, where'er he steers :
The persecuted creature, to and fro,

Turns here and there, to escape his Umbrian foe:
Steep is the ascent, and, if he gains the land,
1090 The purple death is pitched along the strand :
His eager foe, determined to the chase,
Stretched at his length, gains ground at every pace :
Now to his beamy head he makes his way,
And now he holds, or thinks he holds, his prey ;
Just at the pinch, the stag springs out with fear,
He bites the wind, and fills his sounding jaws with air:
The rocks, the lakes, the meadows, ring with cries ;
The mortal tumult mounts, and thunders in the skies.
    Thus flies the Daunian prince, and, flying, blames
1100 His tardy troops, and, calling by their names,
Demands his trusty sword.   The Trojan threats
The realm with ruin, and their ancient seats
To lay in ashes, if they dare supply,
With arms or aid, his vanquished enemy :
Thus menacing, he still pursues the course
With vigour, though diminished of his force.
Ten times already, round the listed place,
One chief had fled, and t'other given the chase :
No trivial prize is played ; for, on the life
1110 Or death of Turnus, now depends the strife.
    Within the space, an olive tree had stood,
A sacred shade, a venerable wood,
For vows to Faunus paid, the Latins' guardian god.
Here hung the vests, and tablets were engraved,
Of sinking mariners from shipwreck saved.
With heedless hands the Trojans felled the tree,
To make the ground inclosed for combat, free.
Deep in the root, whether by fate, or chance,
Or erring haste, the Trojan drove his lance ;
1120 Then stooped, and tugged with force immense, to free
The encumbered spear from the tenacious tree ;
That, whom his fainting limbs pursued in vain,
His flying weapon might from far attain.
    Confused with fear, bereft of human aid,
Then Turnus to the gods, and first to Faunus, prayed :
'O Faunus ! pity ! and thou, mother Earth,
Where I thy foster-son received my birth,
Hold fast the steel !   If my religious hand
Your plant has honoured, which your foes profaned,
1130 Propitious hear my pious prayer !'   He said,
Nor with successless vows invoked their aid.
The incumbent hero wrenched and pulled and strained:

But still the stubborn earth the steel detained.
Juturna took her time ; and, while in vain
He strove, assumed Metiscus' form again,
And, in that imitated shape, restored
To the despairing prince his Daunian sword.
The queen of love—who, with disdain and grief,
Saw the bold nymph afford this prompt relief—
1140 To assert her offspring with a greater deed,
From the tough root the lingering weapon freed.
  Once more erect, the rival chiefs advance :
One trusts the sword, and one the pointed lance ;
And both resolved alike, to try their fatal chance.
  Meantime imperial Jove to Juno spoke,
Who from a shining cloud beheld the shock :
'What new arrest, O queen of heaven ! is sent
To stop the Fates now labouring in the event?
What further hopes are left thee to pursue?
1150 Divine Æneas (and thou know'st it too),
Foredoomed, to these celestial seats is due.
What more attempts for Turnus can be made,
That thus thou lingerest in this lonely shade?
Is it becoming of the due respect
And awful honour of a god elect,
A wound unworthy of our state to feel,
Patient of human hands, and earthly steel?
Or seems it just, the sister should restore
A second sword, when one was lost before,
1160 And arm a conquered wretch against his conqueror?
For what, without thy knowledge and avow,
Nay more, thy dictate, durst Juturna do?
At last, in deference to my love, forbear
To lodge within thy soul this anxious care :
Reclined upon my breast, thy grief unload :
Who should relieve the goddess, but the god?
Now all things to their utmost issue tend,
Pushed by the Fates to their appointed end.
While leave was given thee, and a lawful hour
1170 For vengeance, wrath, and unresisted power,
Tossed on the seas thou could'st thy foes distress,
And, driven ashore, with hostile arms oppress ;
Deform the royal house ; and, from the side
Of the just bridegroom, tear the plighted bride :—
Now cease at my command.' The thunderer said ;
And, with dejected eyes, this answer Juno made :
'Because your dread decree too well I knew,

From Turnus and from earth unwilling I withdrew.
Else should you not behold me here, alone,
1180 Involved in empty clouds, my friends bemoan,
But, girt with vengeful flames, in open sight,
Engaged against my foes in mortal fight.
'Tis true, Juturna mingled in the strife
By my command, to save her brother's life,
At least to try ; but (by the Stygian lake—
The most religious oath the gods can take)
With this restriction, not to bend the bow,
Or toss the spear, or trembling dart to throw.
And now, resigned to your superior might,
1190 And tired with fruitless toils, I loathe the fight.
This let me beg (and this no fates withstand)
Both for myself and for your father's land,
That, when the nuptial bed shall bind the peace
(Which I, since you ordain, consent to bless),
The laws of either nation be the same ;
But let the Latins still retain their name,
Speak the same language which they spoke before,
Wear the same habits which their grandsires wore.
Call them not Trojans : perish the renown
1200 And name of Troy, with that detested town.
Latium be Latium still ; let Alba reign,
And Rome's immortal majesty remain.'
Then thus the founder of mankind replies
(Unruffled was his front, serene his eyes) :
' Can Saturn's issue, and heaven's other heir,
Such endless anger in her bosom bear ?
Be mistress, and your full desires obtain ;
But quench the choler you foment in vain.
From ancient blood, the Ausonian people sprung,
1210 Shall keep their name, their habit, and their tongue :
The Trojans to their customs shall be tied :
I will, myself, their common rites provide :
The natives shall command, the foreigners subside.
All shall be Latium ; Troy without a name ;

1145 Just as we expected the heroes would engage in a decisive combat,
the poet stops short and introduces a dialogue betwixt Jupiter and
Juno on this important action. Such unexpected pauses are highly
judicious, awaken and raise the reader's attention, and make him
impatient for the event.

                                                            Warton

And her lost sons forget from whence they came.
From blood so mixed, a pious race shall flow,
Equal to gods, excelling all below.
No nation more respect to you shall pay,
Or greater offerings on your altars lay.'
1220 Juno consents, well pleased that her desires
Had found success, and from the cloud retires.
 The peace thus made, the thunderer next prepares
To force the watery goddess from the wars.
Deep in the dismal regions void of light,
Three daughters, at a birth, were born to Night:
These their brown mother, brooding on her care,
Indued with windy wings, to flit in air,
With serpents girt alike, and crowned with hissing hair.
In heaven the Diræ called, and still at hand,
1230 Before the throne of angry Jove they stand,
His ministers of wrath, and ready still
The minds of mortal men with fears to fill,
Whene'er the moody sire, to wreak his hate
On realms or towns deserving of their fate,
Hurls down diseases, death, and deadly care,
And terrifies the guilty world with war.
One sister plague of these, from heaven he sent,
To fright Juturna with a dire portent.
The pest comes whirling down: by far more slow
1240 Springs the swift arrow from the Parthian bow,
Or Cydon yew, when, traversing the skies,
And drenched in poisonous juice, the sure destruction
  flies.
With such a sudden, and unseen a flight,
Shot through the clouds the daughter of the Night.
Soon as the field inclosed she had in view,
And from afar her destined quarry knew—
Contracted, to the boding bird she turns,
Which haunts the ruined piles and hallowed urns,
And beats about the tombs with nightly wings,
1250 Where songs obscene on sepulchres she sings.
Thus lessened in her form, with frightful cries
The Fury round unhappy Turnus flies,
Flaps on his shield, and flutters o'er his eyes.
 A lazy chillness crept along his blood;
Choked was his voice; his hair with horror stood.
Juturna from afar beheld her fly,
And knew the ill omen, by her screaming cry,
And stridor of her wings. Amazed with fear,

>   Her beauteous breast she beat, and rent her flowing
>   hair.
> 1260 'Ah me! (she cries) in this unequal strife,
>   What can thy sister more, to save thy life?
>   Weak as I am, can I, alas! contend
>   In arms with that inexorable fiend?
>   Now, now, I quit the field! forbear to fright
>   My tender soul, ye baleful birds of night!
>   The lashing of your wings I know too well,
>   The sounding flight, and funeral screams of hell!
>   These are the gifts you bring from haughty Jove,
>   The worthy recompense of ravished love!
> 1270 Did he for this, exempt my life from fate?
>   O hard conditions of immortal state!
>   Though born to death, not privileged to die,
>   But forced to bear imposed eternity!
>   Take back your envious bribes, and let me go
>   Companion to my brother's ghost below!
>   The joys are vanished: nothing now remains
>   Of life immortal, but immortal pains.
>   What earth will open her devouring womb,
>   To rest a weary goddess in the tomb?'
> 1280 She drew a length of sighs; nor more she said,
>   But in her azure mantle wrapped her head,
>   Then plunged into her stream, with deep despair,
>   And her last sobs came bubbling up in air.
>   Now stern Æneas waves his weighty spear
>   Against his foe, and thus upbraids his fear:
>   'What farther subterfuge can Turnus find?
>   What empty hopes are harboured in his mind?
>   'Tis not thy swiftness can secure thy flight;
>   Not with their feet, but hands, the valiant fight.
> 1290 Vary thy shape in thousand forms, and dare
>   What skill and courage can attempt in war:
>   Wish for the wings of winds, to mount the sky;
>   Or hid within the hollow earth to lie!'
>   The champion shook his head, and made this short
>   reply:
>   'No threats of thine my manly mind can move;
>   'Tis hostile heaven I dread, and partial Jove.'
>   He said no more, but, with a sigh, repressed

1295 The brevity of that answer is most emphatical.

Trapp

The mighty sorrow in his swelling breast.
Then, as he rolled his troubled eyes around,
1300 An antique stone he saw, the common bound
Of neighbouring fields, and barrier of the ground—
So vast, that twelve strong men of modern days
The enormous weight from earth could hardly raise.
He heaved it at a lift, and, poised on high,
Ran staggering on against his enemy;
But so disordered, that he scarcely knew
His way, or what unwieldy weight he threw.
His knocking knees are bent beneath the load;
And shivering cold congeals his vital blood.
1310 The stone drops from his arms, and, falling short
For want of vigour, mocks his vain effort.
And as, when heavy sleep has closed the sight,
The sickly fancy labours in the night;
We seem to run; and, destitute of force,
Our sinking limbs forsake us in the course:
In vain we heave for breath; in vain we cry:
The nerves, unbraced, their usual strength deny;
And on the tongue the faltering accents die:
So Turnus fared: whatever means he tried,
1320 All force of arms, and points of art employed,
The Fury flew athwart, and made the endeavour void.

   A thousand various thoughts his soul confound:
He stared about, nor aid nor issue found:
His own men stop the pass, and his own walls surround.
Once more he pauses, and looks out again,
And seeks the goddess charioteer in vain.
Trembling he views the thundering chief advance,
And brandishing aloft the deadly lance:
Amazed he cowers beneath his conquering foe,
1330 Forgets to ward, and waits the coming blow.
Astonished while he stands, and fixed with fear,
Aimed at his shield he sees the impending spear.

   The hero measured first, with narrow view,
The destined mark; and, rising as he threw,
With its full swing the fatal weapon flew.
Not with less rage the rattling thunder falls,
Or stones from battering engines break the walls:
Swift as a whirlwind, from an arm so strong,
The lance drove on, and bore the death along.
1340 Nought could his sevenfold shield the prince avail,
Nor aught, beneath his arms, the coat of mail;

It pierced through all, and with a grisly wound
Transfixed his thigh, and doubled him to ground.
With groans the Latins rend the vaulted sky:
Woods, hills, and valleys, to the voice reply.
    Now low on earth the lofty chief is laid,
With eyes cast upwards, and with arms displayed,
And, recreant, thus to the proud victor prayed:
'I know my death deserved, nor hope to live:
1350 Use what the gods and thy good fortune give.
Yet think, oh think! if mercy may be shown,
(Thou hadst a father once, and hast a son),
Pity my sire, now sinking to the grave;
And, for Anchises' sake, old Daunus save!
Or, if thy vowed revenge pursue my death,
Give to my friends my body void of breath!
The Latian chiefs have seen me beg my life:
Thine is the conquest, thine the royal wife:
Against a yielded man, 'tis mean ignoble strife.'
1360   In deep suspense the Trojan seemed to stand,
And, just prepared to strike, repressed his hand.
He rolled his eyes, and every moment felt
His manly soul with more compassion melt;
When, casting down a casual glance, he spied
The golden belt that glittered on his side,
The fatal spoil which haughty Turnus tore
From dying Pallas, and in triumph wore.
Then, roused anew to wrath, he loudly cries
(Flames, while he spoke, came flashing from his eyes),
1370 'Traitor! dost thou, dost thou to grace pretend,
Clad, as thou art, in trophies of my friend?
To his sad soul a grateful offering go!
'Tis Pallas, Pallas gives this deadly blow.'
He raised his arm aloft, and, at the word,
Deep in his bosom drove the shining sword.
The streaming blood distained his arms around;
And the disdainful soul came rushing through the wound.

1321 The fury flapping upon the shield of Turnus is no objection to the courage of Aeneas, since (as Mr. Dryden again very well observes) it sufficiently appears from many other passages that Aeneas could have killed Turnus without this machine, which is therefore added purely as a dismal decoration to heighten the honour and solemnity of that hero's death.

                                                                               Trapp

THE END OF THE AENEID

But is it ended? Is it not an incomplete work? ... the objection is that the settlement of the Trojans in Italy, not the death of Turnus, is the action of the poem. Nay the very proposition, or exordium, of it sets forth the hero's building of his city — 'dum conderet urbem' [5]. But neither is his city built, nor himself and his Trojans settled. To this I answer, first, that even in the direct action the event is determined though not fully executed. We plainly see how it must be, and that it cannot be otherwise. And to conclude here is elegant and judicious; if the poet could have entertained us a little farther, it was however artful and ingenious to make us rise with an appetite from such a feast, and to make us wish he had not yet concluded. But secondly and chiefly, the poem is entire and complete, even as to those particulars upon which the objection is grounded. The marriage of Aeneas with Lavinia, the building of the city, his deification or his being made a god, the full and entire incorporation of the Trojans with the Italians ... are all included in this work, not as parts of the action indeed, but (which is far better) by way of prophesy interspersed up and down and delivered upon several occasions. ... As a heroic poem opens in the middle of affairs so it terminates before the conclusion of them. Both the beginning and the end are involved and wrapped up in other parts, that the reader may have the pleasing task of unravelling and adjusting them. This is the delightful method of epic poetry, and this is the great circumstance by which it is distinguished from history. A delightful method it is because it seems to be no method at all.

Trapp